BODYLEARNING

BODYLEARNING™

HOW THE MIND LEARNS FROM THE BODY:
A PRACTICAL APPROACH

Ginny Whitelaw, Ph.D.

Illustrated by Julianne Hawkins

A Perigee Book

A Perigee Book
Published by The Berkley Publishing Group
A member of Penguin Putnam Inc.
200 Madison Avenue
New York, NY 10016

First edition: May 1998

Published simultaneously in Canada.

The Penguin Putnam Inc. World Wide Web site address is
http://www.penguinputnam.com

Library of Congress Cataloging-in-Publication Data
Whitelaw, Ginny.
Bodylearning : how the mind learns from the body : a practical
approach / Ginny Whitelaw.—1st ed.
p.   cm.
"A Perigee book."
Includes bibliographical references and index.
ISBN 0-399-52406-1
1. Meditation.   2. Mind and body.   3. Stress management.
4. Respiration.   5. Exercise.   I. Title.
BL627.W485   1998
158.1—dc21   97-38352
CIP

PRINTED IN THE UNITED STATES OF AMERICA

10   9   8   7   6   5   4   3   2   1

To my grandmother, Mary Whitelaw,
who showed me the beauty of words,
and to my teachers—
Fumio Toyoda,
Dogen Hosokawa,
and Tenshin Tanouye—
who gave me words worth writing

Contents

STEP 2: BUILDING A PRACTICE

STEP 3: GROWING THE PRACTICE

A Zen Master's Foreword to BodyLearning

How are you going to resolve the mind-body dilemma, that feeling that your thoughts and your actions are two very different things and your wish that they weren't? In this book, Ginny Whitelaw writes, "Raw tomatoes give me indigestion . . . being told I'm worthless makes me feel inadequate." It is easy to classify those two statements into a physical awareness and a mental awareness, but Ginny doesn't buy that. Those are simply two things she notices about herself, each of them a collection of sensations that are visceral, emotional and thought generating. And in that noticing, she becomes free of the mind-body split.

With those few words, it sounds simple to live a whole life, to treat the mind and body as one thing. As a teacher of Zen students, medical students and physicians, I've learned that none of us finds this simple. Maybe that is why it is useful to have someone like Ginny—a NASA scientist, management consultant, martial artist and Zen priest—as a guide. We all stood out in the night air at one point in our childhood and wished we could fly to a radiant full moon. Ginny is one of the few people who actually knows how to manage such a voyage. She has the training and experience to form the team that would launch us into space, navigate us to the moon, react to emergencies along the way, and land us safely upon our return. Similarly, when it comes to the challenge of integrating our lives in this fractured world of the late twentieth century, few authors or seminar leaders are as capable of spelling out, with all the detail of a NASA flight manual, how to get us, and not just our imaginations, there and back.

This book starts with two very solid principles of BodyLearning: Use your breath to connect the mind and body, and train the whole by building awareness through all your senses. But the real richness is the detail with which Ginny helps you do those two things. She will tell a story to introduce a point she wants to make, and she will have you do an exercise to experience what she is talking about. She will have you reflect upon that experience, and she will have you develop a way to reinforce the experience. And she knows that you may need a backup approach because the first one isn't working, and maybe another backup just in case.

It hurts when your thoughts and actions are not coherent, are not one thing. But even though we know at some deep level that talking about a "mind" and a "body" is a false dichotomy, there is little in our language or institutions to help heal that division. From the point of view of traditional Japanese "Ways"—the "Do" in Kendo, Aikido, Judo—a life filled by practice is the healing. In her book as in her life, Ginny gives you clear instructions about how to find your way of practice. Go ahead and take the next step.

Hakuun Greene, Ph.D.
Daihonzan Chozen-ji
Honolulu, Hawaii

Acknowledgments

❧

Writing is a community effort. I offer my deepest gratitude and thanks to the community that has made this effort possible:

—To my parents, John and Betty Whitelaw, for somehow making me believe I could do anything. Your certainty has carried me through the uncertainties of this project—and so much more. Thank you, Jean and Mike Lane, Larry Whitelaw and Diane Chencharick, for endless encouragement. Diane, your help in designing the BodyLearning proposal and seminar materials helped this project take form from the start. What a joy it has been to step onto the artist's path with you.

—To my partner, Mark Kiefaber: This would never have happened without you. From your earliest advice on how to find an agent, to hours of discussion on designing a practice, to paving the way for new directions in my work, your insight and efforts have made an enormous difference.

—To John Botens, my grammatically correct wizard of words: Your patient corrections and suggestions over three (or was it four?) versions of this manuscript made the final version much more polished. There are not enough words to express my gratitude for all the useless "there are"s you pulled out of my writing.

—To my teachers, Fumio Toyoda Rokoji, Dogen Hosokawa Roshi and Tenshin Tanouye Rotaishi: Thank you for showing the way. I also thank Dogen Hosokawa Roshi for sharing your beautiful art of calligraphy in this book. And a special thanks to Gordon Greene Roshi for writing the foreword. My thanks to the Daihonzan Chozen-ji, the International Zen Dojo Sogenkai, the Institute of Zen Studies, the Aikido Association of America and all of the people whose tireless practice powers these organizations. Thank you for what you've brought to this book, and what you're bringing to this world.

—To Elizabeth Harper Neeld—writer extraordinaire—for inviting me to join the writers' group gathered around your dining-room table and teaching me that writing is about listening. Thank you, Carol Kaplan, for teaching me to loosen up, and David Kaplan, for pushing me to deepen. Thank you, Letitia Sweitzer, and the Cafe Writers' Group, for suffering through so many rounds of my book proposal and manuscript. And a special thanks to Spencer Dreischarf, whose comments so greatly improved the exercises.

—To Julie Hawkins, for beautifully illustrating the exercises. And to my friends—Scott Hawkins, Janet Treuhaft, Mary Gulash and Holly Kerby—thank you for your wonderful support of this project. I thank my students for helping to refine the exercises, whether you knew it or not.

—To my agents, Michael and Pat Snell, the masters of refining, who took this project from very rough clay to a very clear form. And finally, my deepest thanks to my editor, Sheila Curry, and Putnam/Perigee for believing in this project, and bringing it home.

BODYLEARNING

Introduction

It took me nineteen years to catch my breath. Between allergies and asthma, I wheezed through most of my childhood. Then, in the infinite wisdom of my teenage years, I started smoking. And coughing. Eventually I learned the first compelling lesson from my body: "You're destroying me."

That's when I started working out and cleaning out—first doing calisthenics, then swimming and martial arts. I started going to the gym every day, feeling stronger than I ever had before. But my life hardly centered on exercise. I was an ambitious college student, filling my head with physics and philosophy. It was only a matter of time before I had a heavy course load and decided I had no time to work out. Two-thirds of the way through the semester, I was in absolute despair. I hated myself, my courses, my roommates, my whole pathos-filled life. That was when I learned the second lesson from my body: "Don't ignore me; you need me for balance."

I returned to exercise with new conviction. Many activities opened up—weight lifting, jogging, skiing, Karate, Aikido and Zen. They delivered not only breath and balance but increased energy. I became fascinated with energy, pursuing it in my studies and work. I took a job in a high-energy physics lab. "High energy"—

I just liked the sound of it. But I also was drawn to it as the discipline penetrating the nature of reality. I learned that energy is matter and matter is energy. I learned that individual particles are also interwoven waves. Western science was pointing to the same truth as the spiritual traditions of the East: All is One.

Wanting to learn more about energy in living systems, I delved into biophysics in graduate school. I learned that every thought or emotion is a form of energy and that our body is rife with systems to translate energy into physical form. I learned about the workings of our brain, how it transforms wave patterns into our impressions of distinct memories and solid objects. "What must the world really look like entering the brain?" scientists began to ask as they learned how radically the brain was filtering the messages from our senses. They found that what enters our senses are interwoven waves, and that our brain processes those signals into apparently separate objects. In other words, our perception of separateness among tables and chairs and everything else in our world is an artifact of perception itself. The neuroscientists painted much the same picture of an interconnected reality as did the high-energy physicists.

My deepest learning about energy came from Aikido and Zen. Aikido is a Japanese martial art, literally translated as the "Way of Harmonizing Energy." It is an art of blending with an attack, turning it into a throw or pin. Zen is a branch of Buddhism that invites us to the direct experience of reality—being one with the present moment—harvested through the patient practice of sitting meditation or *Zazen*. Zen uses the body as a vessel for focusing and amplifying the energy of life and thereby unifying body, mind and spirit.

I wasn't thinking much about energy or unifying body, mind and spirit when I got into Aikido and Zen. I started Aikido for self-defense, and I started Zen because my Aikido teacher insisted upon it. For years I didn't pay much attention to what I was learning through these activities tucked, as they were, into the margins of a life focused on science and management. Working first at Bell Laboratories and then at the National Aeronautics and Space Administration (NASA), I was preoccupied with neural networks, computer networks, switching systems and the huge effort to build a space station.

As a manager in these organizations facing turbulent times, I learned that change is hard on people. It's often difficult to change as fast as the world changes around us. Yet I saw that the most successful people and organizations aligned their goals with reality and their day-to-day actions with their goals. I also learned that alignment with a moving target, in Zen what we call "according the myriad changes," is much easier said than done.

For years at NASA I managed parts of the constantly changing space station program, aligning the many organizations working on the project. Yet I was feeling a growing lack of alignment in my own life. NASA selected me for an executive development program that, perhaps because I got so much out of it, only worsened my discontent. In one particularly telling executive development session, the course facilitator was reviewing our personality profiles and, pointing to mine, commented, "Only one person in this room has this profile, and fewer than 2 percent of the people at NASA are of this type. This person probably feels like a fish out of water much of the time." I couldn't have said it better. The only reason I was still at NASA was my own reluctance to change.

Under other circumstances I might have been able to go on living this half-a-life. But by this time, too much was waking up. Over the years, I had started teaching Aikido and Zen, building a school in Houston, where I then lived. Somehow these activities from the margins of my life had been creeping more and more into the center. And now they were demanding fuller attention.

I started writing. And this book, in embryonic form, started emerging. The more I wrote the more I saw ways to integrate my work at NASA with the growing wisdom that had come through my Aikido and Zen practice. I wanted to take my work into a broader arena, helping individuals and organizations become better aligned. From Aikido and Zen I saw that the key to alignment was a physical practice, providing a way for the mind, body and spirit to come together.

I quit my job at NASA and began consulting with organizations on ways they could become better aligned with their goals. I also started teaching personal development seminars on ways to become more effective at reaching personal goals by learning through the body. The very transformation I was writing about and starting to teach was happening in my own life: an energy and wisdom coming through the body, far smarter than the "I" of my thoughts, was shaping my life in every enriching way.

I'm now in my third life, professionally speaking. And it combines the best of the first two—all that I learned as a scientist and as a manager—with all that has come through twenty-some years of my own learning through the body. Understanding and communicating what's at the heart of this remarkable process has become the core of my work. This is what I call BodyLearning: unlocking the wisdom of our body to energize and transform our life. Uniting the body and mind, we move toward wholeness.

1

❧

Joining Forces: Three Steps to a Whole Life

"The evolution of fitness is consciousness."
—Jonas Salk

What Is BodyLearning?

"Mind over matter," I was taught as a child; "If you put your mind to it, you can do it." I liked that message. It made me feel powerful, as if I could somehow defy natural laws. So I tried thinking my way out of allergies and skin rashes—to no avail. I tried to will myself over the hurdles in gym class, but the hurdle bars still clattered to the floor. When I decided I was too fat, I tried to think my way thin. It didn't work.

Much as we may like the idea of "mind over matter," we've all encountered matters we couldn't put our mind over. Illnesses we couldn't think our way out of. Goals we couldn't put our mind to. New Year's resolves that dissolved by spring. If the mind is so powerful, what seems to be the matter?

My Zen teacher, Hosokawa Roshi,[1] put it best. "The body and mind are one," he said. "But we are not of one body-mind." Yes, the body and mind are one: our body is a physical record of the thoughts, emotions, and behaviors that have shaped our life. The confidence in our posture, the tension in our muscles, the pressure of our blood—all reflect the same character and chemistry that inform our conscious thoughts.

> "This being of mine, whatever it really is, consists of a little flesh, a little breath and the part which governs."
> —Marcus Aurelius Antoninus, circa A.D. 150

But we are not always of one mind—much less one body-mind. Bill wants the big promotion at work, but he resents the longer hours. On the one hand, he wants the power and the perks that come with the larger job. On the other hand, he wants to spend evenings and weekends with his family, something the promotion will make impossible. Unable to balance their competing claims, Bill starts to resent both his job and his family. Whenever he's at home, part of him worries that he should be at work. When he works late, part of him worries that he should be at home. The result is that he's never anywhere very fully.

Susan wants to lose weight but can't resist feasting after a fast. "I only have so much willpower," she says. "I can only be good for so long, and then I completely blow it. I can't stuff food into my mouth fast enough." Part of Susan does want to lose weight. But part of her seeks the comfort that eating brings. Unable to reconcile the depth of her hunger, Susan fights her on-again, off-again battle of wills.

Adding to our internal discord, our thoughts are able to change much faster than our body. Bill thinks he can juggle the promotion and the family, but his blood pressure is climbing. Susan thinks she wants to lose weight, but the comfort of eating is the only way her body knows to manage stress. If we could look deeply, we'd see that the latest scheme of the conscious mind may be at odds with the embedded patterns of our body. The result is mixed signals. In ways mostly deeper than conscious, we partly defeat ourselves in all that we sort-of-halfway do.

Fortunately we can unscramble the mixed signals. We can become of one body-mind, clear in our intents and aligned from brain to bone in our actions. But we don't develop this depth of alignment through thoughts alone. We can gain this wholeness only through the body. I call the way toward wholeness *BodyLearning: the powerful process by which we get body and mind working together to energize and unify our life.* As we move toward whole-ness, we will become more aware, focused and aligned in our being and doing. We'll learn how to develop more inner strength and outward power, more resilience and less stress. In BodyLearning we use a physical practice, which may be a form of exercise or meditation, or any number of physical activities, to align body, mind and spirit. In this way we carve a path toward our fullest development.

"Mind over matter" is not enough. Or at least it's not enough to force a fractured mind to take on unrealistic goals and expect them to happen. But when our mind is fully aligned with the matter of our body, something magical does happen: once we quit de-feating ourselves, a whole world of victories opens up.

The Path of BodyLearning

BodyLearning is a journey of three steps: (1) developing breath and center, (2) building a practice, and (3) growing the practice. Developing our breath and center improves not only our physical condition, but our emotional condition as well. In a physical sense, our center is our center of gravity, located in our lower abdomen, a couple inches below our navel. Physically, it is the center of our most stable and powerful motion. Psychologically, we also have a sense of centeredness when we feel stable and collected.

Breath is the link between body and mind, between our conscious thoughts and deeper-than-conscious patterns within us. Even as you read these words, see if you can become

> "The physical center of the body is the part of us that remembers we belong to the universe."
> —George Leonard

aware of your breath moving through your body. Feel the inhale as your muscles stretch to accommodate the new air. Feel the ex-hale as oxygen flushes through every passage and the old air is released.

Paying attention to our breath opens a channel, so to speak, through which alignment of body, mind and spirit can proceed. Something changes in our perspective, as well. As we become aware of our breath, we connect to the present moment. It is as if our eyes suddenly see, and we no longer have to react blindly to whatever is going on around us. From this perspective we don't give way to knee-jerk reactions that fuel daily conflicts. We can be present in awareness and give the moment what it needs from the best within us. Breath awareness leads to all aspects of awareness; with awareness we are able to mine the present moment for greater insight and energy.

We begin our journey in BodyLearning by focusing on breath and center, as you'll have a chance to do in the early exercises in this book. However, the thought to follow our breath, like all thoughts, will not last very long if we don't support it. (You might count how many—or how few—paragraphs you can read before the thought to follow your breath is forgotten.) Therein lies the value of building a practice: the second step of BodyLearning. *A practice is a dedicated time and activity in our day in which we develop breath, center and being in the present moment.* It is a time—perhaps twenty minutes a day—to further our development and alignment. It is time when we fully enter the present moment, aware of our breath and body and being here now.

But what do we practice? Meditation—whether lying down, sitting or walking—is excellent for some people. If we are able to meditate, there's nothing better for developing breath and center. Along our journey, we'll learn a number of breathing exercises and meditation forms, along with ways to combine them into a daily practice.

Still, meditation is not for everyone. "I've tried meditation before," Bob said in one of my BodyLearning seminars. "But I just can't sit still and there's no way I'll stick with it." If we're like Bob, we do well to find a more active practice. Part of our journey in BodyLearning will be discovering what turns an ordinary physical activity into a powerful practice. We'll find that any number of physical activities from exercise and sports, arts and crafts, to everyday activities like walking or driving can be excellent sources of BodyLearning. Using a personal inventory and step-by-step process, we'll design an individualized practice that meets our own needs and interests. In addition to the basic gifts of BodyLearning— greater energy, awareness and wholeness—we'll find in this process that we can also *shape the impact of body on mind*, strengthening or coping with specific qualities we want to work on.

Jim, for example, wanted to manage his anger better. Based on his interests, he identified an aerobic activity (jogging) as a good way to blow off steam, as well as quieter activity (woodwork-

> "Integral practices orient us so that the full spectrum of grace can operate in us. . . . They place us on a path toward extraordinary life."
>
> —Michael Murphy

ing) for building patience and confidence. Sarah, who often felt "a day late and a dollar short," wanted to work on her sense of timing and awareness. She chose tennis as an aerobic practice to help her develop dynamic timing, along with the quieter activity of outdoor photography to develop her sense of nature's timing.

While it's true that we can learn from many activities, it is also true that we can do many things and learn very little from them. The difference is *awareness*: fully being in the present moment. From Zen training we distill the quality of awareness that transforms ordinary activities into extraordinary paths for growth. Then we apply it to whatever activities we have selected for our practice. Focusing on our breath, paying attention to all that our senses present, we fully enter the present moment. We learn to integrate our breathing into the motions of our practice; for example, matching a smooth exhale to the swing of a golf club or release of a bowling ball. When our mind wanders (as it will!), we simply bring it back. This is our practice.

At some point we'll experience a nudge, perhaps a push. The energy, awareness and alignment of our practice will demand more expression in our life, propelling us toward the third step of Body-Learning: growing the practice. Growing our practice is allowing it to transform our life. There are three ways a practice grows, and these happen in any order, any number of times. We can *intensify* our practice, stretching ourselves further. Janet, for example, intensified her running practice from three miles a day to entering 10K races to running a marathon. We can *diversify* our practice, finding new activities to build new strengths or work around barriers. For example, I found yoga and dance made it possible to intensify my Zen training. The third way to grow our practice is to *apply* it in daily life. For example, when tempers start to flare, immediately we can find our breath, find our center and be at our best. By applying the quality of awareness to other moments in our day, moment by moment we wake up.

The payoff is enormous joy. Aligning our physical body, our conscious mind and the spirit or energy that runs through us, we connect our thoughts and deeds to the core of our being. At the same time, we connect to life itself. Aligning ourselves within, we become aligned with life's larger patterns. Through BodyLearning we learn exactly from our body what is our life to live. And we live it fully.

The 3 Steps of BodyLearning

1. **Develop breath and center.** Develop deep and centered breathing to link body and mind. Developing your center energizes and stabilizes both your physical and emotional condition.
2. **Build a practice.** Dedicate time to developing breath and center. Design a practice that matches your needs and interests.
3. **Grow the practice.** Be open to ways of intensifying, diversifying and applying your practice to daily life.

Getting Started: The Beginning of Practice

Imagine driving in your car, listening to a radio station that's barely in range. A familiar song comes on and, even though you can barely make it out through the static, you still recognize the song and think, "I know that tune." But do you know it well enough to sing along? To learn a song well enough to sing it yourself, you probably want to hear it played more clearly. You might play it over and over until you could memorize all the words. Now you could say you know the song well enough to sing it. But do you know it well enough to play it? That requires more learning of musical instruments and maybe learning how to read music. If you're willing to put in that effort, you'll get to a new level of being able to say—as a band musician might say—"I know that tune." But do you know it well enough to write it or to write another song like it? Writing such a song requires more learning and more knowledge of music, enough to allow the song to grow out of your own experience.

Knowing a song you wrote and knowing a song played on a car radio are completely different experiences, even though we use the same word, *know*. We may say we know something when we've only picked it up through a weak signal. To know more deeply is to participate. We may say we've learned something when we've only learned how to repeat words. To learn more deeply is to participate. Knowledge and learning are not all-or-nothing. Rather, they come to us in stages that reflect our level of involvement.

And so it is with BodyLearning. Which is why this book is about more than reading words. Words or concepts alone are not enough; deeper learning, deeper alignment, is needed for real growth or transformation. Through a physical practice we learn more deeply "in our bones" than through concepts alone. When we choose a physical practice to support a direction in which we want to grow, the practice itself becomes a vehicle for our transformation. That's why a program in BodyLearning can be so effective in helping us reach our goals where conscious willpower alone has failed. But that's also why a book about BodyLearning asks you to do more than read. The real value of this book is not its words; the real value is your own experience, your own application of what these words suggest.

To get the most out of this book and its exercises, you'll need a couple of tools. First, get a notebook. A notebook will let you chronicle your journey through the various exercises in awareness, as well as designing and growing your practice. Collecting your experiences and reflections in one place, you'll compile a useful reference for your practice. Any kind of notebook is fine—spiral-bound, clothbound or loose-leaf—so long as it stays with you as you read this book.

The second tool you'll need for the exercises in chapter 2 is a tape recorder. Scripts are provided for several of the meditative exercises. Unless you have a great memory, these exercises are easier to do if you record the script ahead of time and play it back as you do the exercises.

With these tools, you're ready to begin. The beginning of practice is recognizing that practice is necessary for anything more than superficial knowledge. Real growth, deeper understanding, clarity and certainty require more. We begin our practice when we hunger for more.

The Resistance to Practice

Even once we've decided to begin practice, it doesn't take long before we meet our resistance. Resistance, like learning, comes in all sizes. Mild resistance would have us skim over an exercise, rather than put the book down and do it. We're lazy. I know, sometimes I'm lazy too. I have the same tendency you probably have to read books with exercises in them and think, "Oh, I'll come back to them. I just want to read through the whole book first." But once I get to the end of the book, I'm ready to put it away and go on to other books. Another trick I play is imagining the exercise in my mind, rather than actually doing it. "Yeah, I know what that's like," I tell myself. "I don't need to do that one." Yet countless times I have watched a physical technique in the martial arts and thought I knew how to do it. But when I tried the technique, I found it was much different from what I had imagined. Learning in the body is not the same as learning in the mind. Learning in the body is far more fundamental.

Of course you have to decide what level of learning is right for you. But my advice is to go for all of it. Certainly don't shortchange yourself on the very essence of what BodyLearning is about—which is experience in your body. If you're going to skip over something, skip my words and do the exercises, not the other way around. Some sense of resistance is natural. Be aware of it. Accept it, but don't let it stop you. If it stops you here, it stops you elsewhere.

Bodytherapies Complement Practice but Are No Replacement

We live at a time in which our understanding of ways to heal the body is growing in leaps and bounds as East and West come together in a plethora of new bodytherapies. From Aromatherapy to Zentherapy®, from Acupuncture to Zero-Point Balancing, we are expanding and combining ways of healing, learning much about the body and mind in the process.[2] Dub Leigh, for example, developed his remarkable system of Zentherapy by combining the work of Ida Rolf (aligning the body structurally), Moshe Felden-krais (aligning the body functionally) and Zen master Tanouye Rotaishi (aligning the body's energy).[3]

Having been exposed to Zentherapy, as well as a number of other bodytherapies, I can say without a doubt that they can greatly enhance our learning about the body and our learning through the body. Indeed, a bodytherapy can be an excellent complement to practice for tending to the physical barriers or injuries we may encounter. For example, while I was attending a training session taught by Dub and his partner, Audrey Nakamura, Audrey worked on my hip. She released a muscle knot that had been there for years. For the first time, I could sit (in Zen meditation) flat and straight.

Another time, while I was at the Zen dojo in Hawaii, Tanouye Rotaishi saw me walking rather stiffly and asked what was the matter. Having spent the morning pulling weeds, I answered that I was just stiff from the gardening. "No," he said, "there's an injury in your back." He put his hand on my lower spine, right at the spot where, ten years earlier, X rays had revealed a herniated disk. At that time the doctor had looked at the X rays and said only surgery could correct the problem. He recommended I wait until the pain became unbearable because the surgery would leave me with limited motion. So I learned to manage it. I learned to move in ways that the pain wouldn't grab me.

Tanouye Rotaishi asked a couple of the bodytherapists at the dojo to work on me. "Loosen up the legs and all the muscles connected to the back, and we'll try to reset the spine," he said. They worked on me for hours the first day and hours more the second. After another hour on the third day the spine was ready. Tanouye Rotaishi felt around the area of the injury. "There's a nerve out of place," he said. "We have to reset that first." Running his thumb along my spine, with hands that could feel and move anything, he smoothed the nerve into place. In my lower back I felt the familiar sharp pang and then it was gone. (It hasn't returned since.) He then had me lean over a roll of cushions. As one person pulled my arms, two others pulled my hips and legs, stretching me apart. Starting several vertebrae above the problem, Tanouye Rotaishi gently pushed each one higher, making room for one that had been crowded out. Suddenly it popped into place. "It moved more than a quarter of an inch," he said. And since then, I have found movement in Aikido I hadn't known before.

Without a doubt, bodytherapies can be a powerful and enabling complement to our physical practice. As you encounter injuries or limitations in your practice, by all means, find the bodytherapies and therapists you trust the most. Bodytherapies are not, however, any replacement for practice. Other people can help us, but they cannot do the work for us. To learn deeply through the body, we must do the work ourselves.

Exercise in Breath Awareness

We start with our breath. Even as you read these words, become aware of the next breath that enters your body. Become aware of the breath moving through your body. Maintain awareness of your breath as it leaves your body, slowly and evenly. Watch as the cycle repeats: a new in-breath fills the body. A new out-breath leaves the body. This might be a good time to pause in your reading and follow the next several breaths with your full attention.

Sitting where you are, focus your attention on your breath. Maintain awareness of your breath as several cycles of inhale and exhale move through your body. As you return to your reading, continue to pay attention to your breath.

We notice a shift in our perspective as we watch our breath. Immediately our view broadens as we regard this one-who-is-breathing. Immediately we are invited to a perspective from which we can see more clearly. It is as if we were looking for someone in a crowded room and were suddenly given a chair on which to stand. We rise a level and can take in the whole room. We can see our situation more clearly. This awareness of our breath is awareness itself. The more we cultivate it in our life, the more alive we become. Through our body, we build our awareness.

Continue following your breath. You might think of shining a light on your breath as if to watch it take form. You might think of surfing along your breath, as though it were a wave. You might think of spinning your breath like the finest fiber, a fiber connecting you to life itself. These are only images to entertain the conscious mind; they are not so important as the experience of breath itself. They do help us, however, to focus our thoughts, which otherwise tend to wander. The fact is, we continue breathing whether we think about it or not. Keeping our thoughts focused on something so simple as breathing is not what we normally do. But when we link our thoughts to our breath, we link two parts of our being: those that arise in our conscious mind and those that are deeper than conscious—so-called autonomic functions. We become ever so much more effective and powerful when we align our conscious mind and deeper-than-conscious patterns. Alignment begins with this simple practice.

At the same time, we experience the difficulty in maintaining this awareness. Our mind wants to wander; it's wired for wandering. Our difficulty in focusing here is also our difficulty in focusing elsewhere. We tire quickly of paying attention to our breath; we tire of paying attention to this very moment. We have a tendency to flip our mental channel to something we find more interesting: a desire, a fantasy, a memory, a story in which we're the writer, director, producer, and star. These thoughts are so much more entertaining than following our boring breath. It is exactly this recognition that is the start of our practice. Only when we become aware of our recurring tendency to wander and fantasize do we recognize what draws us away from living fully in this present moment. It's ourselves: the small self insisting on being the center of all things.

Not only is it ourselves, but it's our favorite part: our clever intellect, our inner pep talks, our tireless criticisms, our witty way of putting things, a warm moment lived over and over in our memory, an argument played out to a more satisfying conclusion. Such are the endless delusions and mind chatter that pull us away from the present moment. These are the mental channels we flip to when we won't stay focused in the present. Unfortunately, as we watch these other channels, we are missing the only moment in which we can actually live—the here and now!

Even more unfortunately, another aspect of self is shut out by all this noise. This larger aspect of self has many names: True Self, God-in-us, Christ nature, Buddha nature, spiritual nature—I call it simply the larger self. And while it is our true nature, it is up to us to give it room for expression in our life. At our best, we are a clear channel for this larger life. At our worst, we are so consumed with the concerns of the smaller self that we think that's all there is. Short of aligning with the essential core of our being, we remain fractured into varying degrees of fear, delusion and lethargy.

Further alignment of little self and larger self, further unity of body, mind and spirit, can only happen in the present moment. And it only happens when the mind is in the present moment, rather than lost in its thoughts. So take this moment to be aware of your breath and being. As your mind wanders, be aware that it wanders and gently bring it back to focus on your breath.

Give yourself five minutes to sit quietly and be aware of the breath moving into, through and from your body.

Your breath will develop in a more enriching way if you adjust your posture to allow the breath to deepen in your body. Your spine should be straight but not stiff. It's easier to get your spine into the correct position if you sit near the edge of a seat or on an angled cushion. Your head should be erect with the chin tucked slightly, such that the weight of the head is supported by the spine, not by the neck and shoulder muscles. Invite the tense muscles of your body to relax as you quietly follow your breath with your full awareness.

Many people find it useful starting out in breath awareness to give each breath a count. Breathing in, 1; breathing out, 1; breathing in, 2; breathing out, 2—and so on up till 10. When you lose count, go back to 1 and start again. When you get to 10, go back to 1 and start again.

Sit in this state of breath awareness long enough to experience both its calming effect and its difficulty. Be aware of both. As simple as this exercise is, it is the basis of everything that follows. Through these moments of breath awareness we start along the path by which the promise of BodyLearning becomes our own vivid experience.

STEP 1

DEVELOPING BREATH AND CENTER

2

❦

Energy: Tapping the Infinite Source

"From birth to death, life is a flow of energy."
—Tenshin Tanouye Rotaishi

The Search for Energy

"What I really need is more energy," said Dana, explaining why she came to my seminar on BodyLearning. "I'm so tired. And the less I do, the less I feel like doing." That's a vicious cycle many of us know. The less we do, the less we're able to break our own lethargy, and the smaller our life becomes. How small do we let our life shrink before we feel compelled to recharge it, and what do we choose as fuel?

In Dana's case, life had gotten pretty simple: go to work, put in a long and frustrating day, come home exhausted, make something for dinner, turn on television to unwind, go to bed, get up the next day and do the same thing. Weekends were for recovery, which meant plenty of sleep, plenty of television and the absence of anything challenging. Dana described this life with all the disgust of an indentured servant, as if somebody else had shrunk her life down to these stifling dimensions.

"Where do you get your energy now?" I asked Dana. "Granola bars," she answered jokingly. But, in fact, eating does provide a zip of energy (up to a point, which we sometimes cross over). And our store shelves are stocked with goods that promise the zip: power bars, energy drinks, high-vitamin this and caffeinated that. Some of us go for the more concentrated rush, and any number of drugs, legal and otherwise, are available to deliver it.

Where else do we look for energy? Sex. Exercise. Sporting events. Danger. Anything that gets our adrenaline pumping. Vibrant music. Hot sports cars that surround our body with power and responsiveness that we, ourselves, would like to feel. We also look to one another for energy through anger, indignation, passion and drama. Sometimes we share and build energy in a way that is life affirming. Sometimes we just suck it out of others through petty conflicts and power plays. As a friend of mine once put it, "One thing about being angry, you know you're alive."

The point is, our need for energy is so fundamental that we go after it in ways that run deeper than conscious. And many times we'll settle for an artificial rush—picking a fight or taking a drug—because we don't know how to get the real thing. What we don't realize is that we have access to all the energy we could ever need. We're literally swimming in it, yet like fish in water, most of us are scarcely aware this energy exists, much less how to tap it. The key is learning not to cut off from this infinite supply. This key is learned through our body.

Feeling the Flow: Lying-Down Meditation

Tapping the energy around us and feeling its renewing flow through our body is not an abstract concept. Rather, it is a real experience. And it can be our real experience if we give it time to grow. Unifying and aligning body and mind is not only the key to increasing and focusing our energy in the long run; it is also a wonderful feeling in the here and now.

The following exercise gives you a chance to experience a greater flow of energy through your body by releasing some of the muscular tensions that otherwise block it.[1] To get the most out of this exercise, record the following script, speaking slowly and quietly, and then play it back as you do the exercise. If you don't have a tape recorder, read through the exercise a few times until you get a feel for the progressive relaxation and then put it into your own words (in your mind's voice) as you do the exercise.

Allow ten minutes to make your tape and fifteen minutes of quiet, uninterrupted time to do the exercise. Enjoy.

Before you begin, record the script below. Brackets indicate where you should pause in your speaking for some number of seconds and are not intended to be spoken. If you don't have a tape recorder, read through the exercise enough times to absorb its rhythm and flow, and then do it from memory.

As you do this exercise, lie on the floor with your feet slightly apart. Your arms should rest near your sides, palms down. It's best not to use a pillow or anything under your head, allowing the head to be at the same level as the rest of the body.

[Start Script:] Relax into the floor. Allow the floor to absorb all your body's weight and tension. Tuck your chin slightly so that the part of your head touching the floor is near the base of your skull. Close your eyes. Breathe through your nose. Bring your full awareness to your breath and follow your breath through several cycles. Allowing each cycle to unfold at its own pace, invite the breath deeper into your body. [Pause for 30 seconds.]

Maintaining awareness of your breath, focus your breath-attention on your toes, inviting them to relax. [Pause for 5 seconds.] Focus on the soles of your feet, allowing the tension to ease out through your exhale. [Pause for 5 seconds.] Bring your attention to the tops of your feet, and then to your ankles, inviting each muscle and each tendon to relax. [Pause for 15 seconds.]

Move your breath awareness up along your legs. Imagine you are breathing into your calf muscles, easing apart their tension with the flow of your breath. [Pause for 5 seconds.] Move up into your knees and invite them to relax. [Pause for 5 seconds.] Next come to your thighs, bathing them in your awareness—both inner and outer sides. [Pause for 5 seconds.] Move up into your hips. Invite the hips to relax, as well as the pelvic girdle, the buttocks and the lower back. [Pause for 5 seconds.] Wherever you find tension, spend a few moments warming that tension in the light of your awareness. Continue to breathe slowly and deeply. [Pause for 15 seconds.]

Relax the muscles in your lower abdomen and your stomach; let your breath-awareness bring calm to your internal organs. [Pause for 5 seconds.] Move your awareness up your spine, relaxing the muscles in your back. [Pause for 5 seconds.] Draw your awareness into your rib cage, from back to front. Spend a few moments releasing the tension in your chest area. [Pause for 5 seconds.] Refresh your heart and lungs with full awareness. Relax the muscles in the upper chest and into the upper arms. [Pause for 15 seconds.]

Focus your breath-awareness on your shoulders and upper arms. Invite them to lie even flatter on the floor. [Pause for 5 seconds.] Bring your awareness into the crooks of your arms, your forearms and wrists. [Pause for 5 seconds.] Let your attention rest for a few moments on your palms, releasing tension through your fingertips as you exhale slowly and steadily. [Pause for 15 seconds.]

Move your awareness into your neck and into the base of your skull, where tension often knots. [Pause for 5 seconds.] Spend a few extra moments easing the tension in this area, imagining the muscles thawing and the blood vessels opening freely. [Pause for 15 seconds.] Move your breath-attention up behind the ears and relax the muscles of the jaw. [Pause for 5 seconds.] Let your face muscles drop, and relax your eyes, ears and middle of your brow where there's often a furrow—relax them all. [Pause for 5 seconds.] Relax your scalp; draw your attention to the top of your head and allow any remaining tension to evaporate. Continue following your breath. [Pause for 15 seconds.]

Feel the flow from head to toe as you survey your body for remaining tension. Anywhere the flow feels diminished or the body feels cold, bring your awareness to rest and invite that area to release and expand. [Pause for 15 seconds.] Continue following your breath as you rest with greater ease and connection to the ground. [Pause for 5 seconds.] Continue to feel this flow as you follow your breath, being completely in this present moment. Rest in this state of flow for five more minutes. [End script.]

This is treasured time. You're likely to feel a warmth and lightness in your body, as well as a tendency to become sleepy. (In later meditative exercises you'll keep your eyes open to reduce this tendency. However, if you have trouble sleeping, this is an excellent exercise to do before bed.) As you do this exercise, keep coming back to your breath and to the present moment whenever you find your thoughts have drifted elsewhere. Your mind is likely to be pulled toward some distraction, something you have to do. Be aware of each of these thoughts as they arise. Know that they will come into being, exist for a while and then fade away. You don't have to do anything to chase them away—just continue following your breath.

Perhaps you feel you don't have time to do this exercise. Yet if this chapter were fifteen pages longer than it is, you'd probably spend the fifteen extra minutes reading it, and your life wouldn't know the difference. All time is our time. I invite you to take this time to relax and renew yourself.

What Limits Our Energy?

We are swimming in a pool of boundless energy, with access to all the energy we could ever need. This may sound like a flowery metaphor or wishful thinking because we don't always feel boundless in our energy. But in fact, it's a perfectly scientific account of the physical reality supporting life. For unlike simpler systems— such as clocks and mechanical toys that can only wind down— life is winding up. Ilya Prigogine, one of the great chemists and mathematicians of this century, used the term *dissipative structures* to describe systems (including humans and all forms of life) that are capable of digesting the flow of energy around them to grow or evolve toward greater order.[2]

The energy fueling our life takes many forms. We live on a planet warmed by the energy of the sun and blanketed in an atmosphere that flows through us moment by moment. Blood, with the saltiness of the seawater it evolved from, carries oxygen and nutrients to all pockets of our inner life. All around us are plants and animals that provide energy for our existence. Not only are we sustained by foods, water, air and warmth, but the very process of ingesting them leads to our development over a lifetime and our evolution over generations.

Our ability to absorb energy doesn't stop with our breathing and eating. We also absorb energy through our senses. Light comes into our eye, setting off a chain reaction in our nervous system. Sound enters our body, setting off resonance in our ears and beyond. Every part of our body is in constant vibratory motion. And that motion is amplified when it comes into contact with similar energy. Like so many tuning forks, we literally resonate at various frequencies. And through resonance we absorb energy around us and make it our own. This is why we feel uplifted by a beautiful piece of music. Or stirred by the roar of an engine. Through resonance we feel energized by the people we love.

We are designed to absorb the very energy that has led to our design. That energy is literally everywhere we turn. And yet many of us feel like Dana; we need more energy. How is it we can be surrounded by abundance yet feel lacking?

The answer is twofold. First, we aren't taking in all the energy we have access to. And second, once we get the energy in our body, it's getting stuck. The first issue is a matter of awareness and being in the present moment. When we're off in our mind chatter or absorbed in personal drama, we aren't paying attention to what's present around us. We don't hear the birds chirping. We don't feel the sunshine. We don't hear people the first time they speak to us. We're not able to mine the present moment for its energy when we're really not in it.

The second issue is a matter of how we carry tension in our body. The more tense and rigid our body, the more constricted the flow of energy through it. In the words of Tanouye Rotaishi, "The body of a baby is soft and pliable. The body of a dead person is rigid and stiff. The rest of us are somewhere in between." We almost equate the aging process with the body becoming rigid and brittle, because it is so common in our experience. In fact, the body becomes rigid because of the way we carry our life experience. By using our body to "shoulder our load," or "keep our nose to the grindstone," or "muscle our way to the top," the body becomes tight. We tighten our body to defend ourselves against people who might hurt us and things we "can't stomach." Everything we don't like registers a tension in the body. With every rigid opinion, every unbending certainty that "this is the way it's gotta be," every unfulfilled desire, every attachment to things as we want them rather than as they are, in short, with every grating turn of our imperfect mesh with reality, our body tenses.

Think of the times in your life when you've been under a lot of stress—maybe even now. What parts of your body express that stress? Some people grind their teeth and set their jaw. Some people get constant headaches, so constricted is the blood flow through their neck. Some people get a stiff neck or a sore back. Many (some would say all) the illnesses we suffer are ailments of constriction. Clogged arteries. Clogged blood that causes strokes and heart attacks. Clogged digestive tracts that cause indigestion and lead to infection. Little wonder we experience a lack of energy even when we take in plenty of food. We have a dangerous habit of clogging our pipes.

Through the body we can learn how to reverse this trend. BodyLearning tackles both ends of our energy problem. First, it gives us a practice that brings us fully into the present moment and develops our awareness, allowing us to absorb more energy from our environment. Second, by using our body to develop our breath and center, we allow the energy to move through us. Aerobic activities help us blast out our tension, instead of stuffing it into our muscles. Meditative activities help us relax and build the inner strength that lets us accept life as it is. Through a BodyLearning practice we learn to open the gates and unclog the pipes, and swim freely in the flow of energy that is our true life.

Becoming Aware of Our Energy Blocks

In this exercise, you'll be able to develop some awareness about where you store tension in your body. As you become aware of where you're holding tension in your body, you can focus your breath-awareness into those areas, inviting them to relax, and allowing more energy to flow. As with the previous exercise, you'll find this exercise easiest to do if you prerecord the script and play it back. Allow ten minutes to make your tape and ten minutes to do the exercise. You'll also need your notebook for reflecting on the last part of the exercise, so have it handy.

This exercise is done lying on the floor (as in the previous exercise) with your feet slightly apart. Rest your arms at your side, palms down. Follow the script below, observing the pauses indicated in the brackets.

[Start Script:] Give your weight and tension to the floor, relaxing your body completely. Tuck your chin slightly, elongating the back of your neck. Close your eyes. Breathe through your nose. Bring your full awareness to your breath and follow your breath through several cycles. Allow each breath to drop deeper into your body. [Pause 60 seconds.]

Survey your body with your breath-awareness, inviting the tight places to relax. Relax your hips and lower back. [Pause 5 seconds.] Relax your stomach and chest area. [Pause 5 seconds.] Allow your shoulders to drop; allow your body to lie more flatly on the floor. [Pause 5 seconds.] Relax your face and the tension in your brow. [Pause 5 seconds.] Count your breath cycles from 1 to 10. With each exhale, feel the flow of energy through your body. [Pause for 4 minutes.]

Now bring to mind a difficult conversation you've had recently, a time when you've felt very angry or frustrated. [Pause 5 seconds.] Start at the beginning and run through in your mind how that conversation went. Be specific. Review every part you can remember. What did the other(s) involved say or do? What did you say or do? [Pause 30 seconds.] What did you feel at the time? [Pause 20 seconds.] Put yourself back in that moment: What would you like to have said or done? [Pause 60 seconds.]

Now stop. Check your body. Where does it feel tense from replaying the difficult conversation? What's different? [Pause 5 seconds.] Where does your body feel most tight or anxious right now? [Pause 5 seconds.] Relax that area. Bring your full attention back to your breathing and let out a deep sigh of relief. Notice what relaxed. [Pause 5 seconds.] Breathing smoothly and calmly, bring your breath awareness to your stomach and invite it to relax. [Pause 5 seconds.] Bring your awareness into your chest and shoulders, inviting them to relax. [Pause 5 seconds.] Survey your neck and jaw for tension, releasing any you find. [Pause 5 seconds.] Bring your awareness into the muscles of your face and forehead, relaxing them once again. [Pause 5 seconds.] Once you've returned to a relaxed state, roll to the side and get up slowly. [End script.]

After you get up, get your notebook and write down the places in the body where you noticed tension following the imagined conversation. Wherever you found a muscle that needed relaxing after the imagined conversation, take note: this is where you stuffed the tension when this event actually happened. And you probably stuff tension here as a matter of habit.

Blocking Energy May Be Dangerous to Your Health

In the previous exercise you had a chance to become aware of the tension generated by a recent conflict. In daily life we're generally not so aware of the gradual accumulation of tension until it becomes so severe that it causes us problems. One set of problems, as we've discussed, is that we experience a lack of energy. If this lack is serious enough we become lazy, lacking in confidence, and embroiled in conflict because we never quite feel up to the situations we face.

Tension also causes problems with our health. The places where we carry tension in our body become weak links in the body's energy flow and therefore likely targets for health problems. This understanding is not only the basis of our New Age of holistic health practices in the West; it is also the basis of the oldest systems of healing in the East. Chinese medicine and such therapeutic methods as shiatsu and acupuncture aim at restoring the body's health by restoring the flow of vital energy through the body. This vital energy—what the Chinese call "chi," the Japanese call "ki," and we in the West might call the body's flow of electrochemical currents and fields—both affects and reflects our overall state of health.

As we go about our day, holding up under pressure, holding in our feelings, or just trying to hold on, all these "holdings" create trouble in our body because they not only build dams of tension against our feelings (or against the outside world), they also block the healthy flow of energy. If a little bit of holding makes our posture stiff or our expression grim, more holding makes us downright sick. What starts as "not being able to stomach" situations may end up as colitis. What starts as "sticking our neck out" may end up as spinal problems.

M. Scott Peck, who's been "sticking his neck out" through an entire career of integrating psychology and spirituality, relates the story of coming to terms with his back and neck illness, a condition called spondylosis. After experiencing paralyzing pain and realizing that recurring surgery to treat this condition would become life threatening, Peck asked himself whether there was any way he might be feeding his illness:

> As soon as I was willing to ask that question, I immediately realized there was. I realized that for most of my life, I'd been walking on the cutting edge of my profession, and I'd always been fearful of generating hostility. I had run into some hostility, though never as much as I anticipated, so my fear had a basis. But I had been going through life with my head and neck hunched down like a football player about ready to buck into the defensive line of the Pittsburgh Steelers. Try holding your head and neck that way for thirty years, and you too will know something about what causes spondylosis.[3]

Even more common are our efforts to protect our heart, to hide or manage our feelings in some way that makes us feel less vulnerable. It's no coincidence that more people die of heart disease and heart attacks than from any other cause. Even before we die, many of us are living in a way that is strangling our heart.[4]

Stan, a friend of mine, had a very cold and troubled relationship with his father while he was growing up. He protected himself, as many a resourceful child would, with an armored heart. Now he struggles with his adult relationships. He has met a woman he loves as much as he's capable of loving—but his heart will only open a crack, and often she cannot feel the warmth. He wants the warmth of friendship, but he holds people at bay with his sharp tongue. These patterns of protection, which might have been essential at some early point in his life, no longer serve him as an adult. Indeed, they oppose what he consciously desires. Stan's father died relatively young of a heart attack. Not even forty years old, Stan has a partially blocked heart and seriously high blood pressure.

This way of looking at Stan's heart condition, or health problems in general, is not to ignore the role of traditional medical factors such as heredity, diet or exercise. Rather, it recognizes that all health factors have a physical and psychological component and play into a network of chain reactions. Heredity shows up in our genes, for example, but also in our attitudes and behaviors. One of our behaviors may be to constantly protect our feelings, which also has ramifications in our physical body. What makes holistic health whole is recognizing that the body-mind is one whole system.

Flowing Energy versus Holding Tension

Counteracting our tendency to hold on to life's big and little dramas is the simple fact that flowing energy *feels* a lot better in our body than holding tension. Flowing energy makes us feel more vital and joyful, more powerful in a positive way. You can experience this for yourself in the two exercises that follow.

The first exercise, which is more of a demonstration (not something you'd do on a daily basis), is called "Unbendable Arm" and comes from Aikido. Even first-time students experience a remarkable difference in their strength when they do this exercise by "extending *ki*," instead of by tensing. This exercise takes only a minute. To do it, you need a partner, preferably one of about your strength.

Stand with one foot ahead of the other. Extend the arm corresponding to your forward foot, allowing it to rest on your partner's shoulder (see figure on page 30). Bending your elbow slightly (in other words, *don't lock your elbow*), have your partner place both hands in the crook of your arm. To get a sense of contrast in your strength, first do the exercise wrong by tensing or holding your arm nearly straight, while your partner tries to bend it. (Remember, *don't lock your elbow*.) If your partner is near the same strength as you, your arm will eventually give way.

Next do the exercise properly by flowing, rather than holding. Instead of tensing as your partner tries to bend your arm, imagine your arm as a firehose that you want to send as much water through as possible. The water, of course, is your energy or *ki*; you want to imagine it as flowing through your arm rather than freezing in your muscles. A good way to check whether you're extending your energy correctly (rather than tensing) is that you should be able to wiggle your fingers as you maintain your extension. If your partner is near the same

strength as you, and you've developed a good sense of this flow, your arm will not give way.

In the following exercise, you can further experience the difference between holding and flowing in your entire body. As with the earlier exercises, it is best if you prerecord the script and play it back as you do the exercise. Allow yourself eight minutes to make your tape and ten minutes to do the exercise.

This exercise is done lying on the floor as before, hands at your sides, palms down.

[Begin Script:] Close your eyes. Give your weight entirely to the floor, allowing your body to relax. [Pause 10 seconds.] Draw your awareness to your breath and follow your breathing with your full attention, breathing through your nose. [Pause 5 seconds.] Feel each breath moving into your body and then—slowly and easily—leaving your body. Invite your breath to sink deeper into your body, eventually moving to and from your center. Place a hand on your lower abdomen to help guide your breath to this area. [Pause 1 minute.] Once your breathing has settled, return your arm to your side, palm down. Continue breathing deeply and slowly. [Pause 1 minute.]

Beginning with your feet and ankles, tense these muscles and joints as tightly as possible, holding your breath and tension for the next few seconds. [Pause 3 seconds.] Now release the tension completely as you exhale through your feet and ankles. Imagine your breath itself flooding through the released muscles. [Pause 5 seconds.] Next hold your breath and tense both feet and legs from the knees down. Tense and hold as hard as you can [pause 3 seconds], and then release completely. [Pause 5 seconds.] Your tension should feel like a tourniquet, stopping the flow of blood, breath, energy—whatever can flow. As you release completely, feel the gush of warmth reentering the area, rushing toward the toes. You might think of freezing the water in a pipe and then instantly melting it into a warm river rush. Now tense the entire length of your legs from your hips down, holding your breath at the same time. [Pause 3 seconds.] Release completely. [Pause 5 seconds.]

Working the trunk of your body, tense the abdomen and buttocks. [Pause 3 seconds.] And release. [Pause 5 seconds.] Tense all the muscles of your back. [Pause 3 seconds.] And release. [Pause 5 seconds.] Bring your awareness into your chest area. Tense all the muscles in your chest. [Pause 3 seconds.] And release completely. [Pause 5 seconds.] Go back to an area where you didn't feel much difference between tensing and releasing. Work that area several times, tensing and releasing more with each cycle. This area is probably one where you normally carry tension. [Pause 15 seconds.]

Next, bring your awareness to your hands, freezing them with tension. [Pause 3 seconds.] Relax your hands completely. [Pause 5 seconds.] Tense your forearms and hands together. [Pause 3 seconds.] Release completely. [Pause 5 seconds.] Tense both arms all the way to the shoulders, holding with everything you've got. Hold, hold, hold, and then release completely, allowing the rush of warmth to flow toward your fingertips. [Pause 5 seconds.]

Tense your neck and throat area. [Pause 3 seconds.] Then release. [Pause 5 seconds.] Tense your jaw as tightly as possible [pause 3 seconds], and then release. [Pause 5 seconds.] Tense every muscle you can find in your face. Feel tight, tight, tight—and then let go. [Pause 5 seconds.] Tense your entire head [pause 3 seconds], and then release. [Pause 5 seconds.] Feel the flow down from your head, into your neck and body, as you let go of your tension.

Follow the trail of warmth down from your neck. Imagine it flowing down through your body, out both arms and legs, leaving your fingertips and toes and returning to the top of your head, where it reenters and flows down again. Now tense your entire body—head to toe—stop the breath, stop the flow, freeze the pipe, hold, hold, hold. And let go. Let go completely and feel the gush down through your body and out your fingertips and toes. Follow this flow with your breath awareness. Resume your quiet, deep breathing to and from your center. Imagine your exhale guiding this flow through your entire body.

Feel the aliveness of this moment, in this place of no-holding. Invite your body to be rejuvenated by the passing flow. Continue, for several minutes, to follow the flow through your body with full breath awareness. [End script.]

For most people the feeling of flow in these exercises is unmistakable and very pleasant. Yet most people are scarcely aware of this flow as they go about their busy, active lives. That's why we need to set aside time to practice in this way. The more we practice developing breath and center, the more we experience the flow of energy in our body—and the less willing we are to give way to our habitual patterns of tension that cut the flow.

To Change Our Energy Level, We Change Our Breathing

When Phil first came to my Aikido class, he stepped off the mat after the first twenty minutes, panting and exhausted. "Gee, I didn't realize how out of shape I was," he said when I came over. "We're never in exactly the shape required by new activities when we start them," I told him. "So we try to compensate by throwing ourselves into it and tensing everything. The problem is that you're holding your breath and tensing on every throw. And that's why you're getting so exhausted." He rested for a bit and then rejoined the class. But during that class and several that followed, he was frequently off to the side, trying to catch his breath. I kept telling him to relax and breathe as I watched him struggle through his earliest throws. He kept holding his breath and tensing.

He did notice that other beginners could make it through the class while he couldn't. His frustration grew, and he might have quit altogether if he hadn't paid for a whole month. Although we practiced breathing exercises at the start of every class, he couldn't apply the same feeling to his Aikido. After a few weeks he stayed after class one night and asked me what I meant by "all this breathing stuff." We did a few minutes of a breathing exercise, and then I attacked him. Instantly he froze. We went back to the breathing exercise and I told him the next time I attacked him to do the throw (which we had practiced in class) with the same feeling of exhale and ease as he currently felt. I attacked; he stumbled and fumbled but did a little better. More breathing. Another attack. Breathing. Attack. Eventually he got the hang of it.

Of course, by the next class, most of his old habits had returned. But now he had a reference point, and he worked toward returning to it. It wasn't long before the improvement was obvious—even to him. Not only was he able to make it through two hours of regular class, but his movements began to flow with much more vitality. Naturally, he started enjoying Aikido more and learned more quickly, which further energized his practice. He commented to me some months later about how "that breathing stuff" really worked on his Aikido. "Now put that same feeling," I told him, "into the rest of your life."

The way we breathe has a great deal to do with the energy level in our body. It also colors our thoughts and emotions. For example, when we let out a deep sigh—try it—our body drops a bit of its tension. Our shoulders are likely to drop. The tiny worry lines in our face are likely to soften. We call it a "sigh of relief," as a real sense of relief and relaxation spreads through our muscles, thoughts and emotions. We are relieved of a bit of the muscular tension that otherwise constricts the flow of energy through our body and, by extension, through our life.

By contrast, when our breathing is very rapid and shallow, like a tired dog's on a hot day—try it for a few seconds—it's not long before we feel hyper and anxious. Our energy level drops when

> *"Breathing in, I calm body and mind.*
> *Breathing out, I smile.*
> *Dwelling in the present moment*
> *I know this is the only moment."*
> —*Thich Nhat Hanh*

our breathing becomes high and tight in the chest, because energy gets dissipated pumping muscles that are relatively inefficient (compared with the center) in drawing air. Tightness in the chest hampers the heart's ability to send oxygen out after it gets in.

To raise our energy level, we drop our breathing into our center. We drop our breathing by paying attention to it. Immediately we relax a bit. With a few more slow, deep breaths, we ease the tension out of our chest; our heart rate slows down and our breath drops physically lower in our body. This relaxation and settling continues until our breath moves smoothly to and from our center. As we breathe deeply and slowly into our center, our center radiates a vital energy that spreads through our body.

Initially our breathing will develop in this enriching way only if we pay attention to it. Eventually it will become second nature. Initially however, our conscious mind has to get into the act of undoing the patterns of breathing that have become our habit up to now. That is why the first step of BodyLearning is to focus on our breath and center, allowing the breath to deepen and the center to develop.

Lying-Down Meditation and Setting the Center

The exercises presented up to this point are intended to give you a feel for the flow and relaxation possible through breath awareness, and you should feel free to return to them as often as you like. This exercise, however, is the start of recommended daily practice: the start of your everyday attentiveness to the wisdom of your body. Regardless of what ongoing practice you design as you work through later chapters, this exercise lays the foundation of deep, centered breathing that you can then bring to the other things you do. Try it now and do it again tomorrow, and the day after that, and so on until you read far enough in the book to select another activity for your practice. Begin now to carve out the twenty minutes a day that makes more energy possible. By making this exercise your practice for now, you'll protect this sliver of time, into which you can later slide other BodyLearning exercises and eventually your own ongoing practice.

"The only joy in the world is to begin."
—Cesare Pavese

In the first part of this exercise we practice centering our breathing. In Part II we further develop the vital energy in our center, the area the Japanese call the *"hara."*[5] We do this through a process called "setting the *hara.*" Only after you're comfortable with centering your breathing in Part I of the exercise does it make sense to go on to Part II. As with the earlier exercises, this one works best when prerecorded on a tape. Allow 20 minutes to make your tape; a script with suggested timing follows. However, if the script begins leading you into Part II before you're ready (which you'll know if your breath still feels up in your chest or stomach area, rather than down in your center), simply turn off the tape as Part II begins and continue working on Part I. Spend twenty minutes doing this exercise. Your tape can serve as your timer once you can move from Part I to Part II without shutting it off.

[Part I: Centering the Breath. Start Script:] Lie down on the floor with the soles of your feet touching a wall and your knees rolled slightly toward each other. [Pause 5 seconds.] Keep your eyes open and, using your peripheral vision, see 180 degrees around you.

Bring your awareness to your breath as you breathe through your nose. Place your right hand on your center and your left hand on the middle of your chest. Continue following your breath, inviting the chest area to relax and the breath to flow smoothly to and from your center. [Pause 30 seconds.] Gradually invite the motion of your breath more into the hand on your center and less in the hand on your chest. [Pause 30 seconds.] Breathe quietly in this way, bringing your mind to your breath and your breath to your center, for the next several minutes. When your mind wanders, gently bring it back to your breath. As your

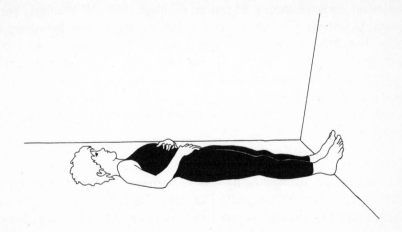

breath becomes centered, your left hand on your chest becomes still. [Pause 4 minutes.]

[**Part II: Setting the *Hara*.**] Now that all the motion of your breath is at your center, you're ready to begin setting the *hara*. At the start of your next exhale, roll the base of your spine ever so slightly up and toward your navel. The small of your back will flatten slightly onto the floor. Gently push the wall through the balls of your feet. Continue pushing the wall slightly through the entire exhale; then release, relax and allow a new breath to flow in naturally. [Pause 15 seconds.] As inhale turns to exhale, set the *hara* by slightly moving the base of the spine toward the navel and pushing through the balls of your feet. Continue in this way, setting through the exhale, releasing on the inhale. [Pause 15 seconds.]

Pay attention to the motion of your body as felt by each of your hands. As your breath comes into your center, feel your center rise like bread, your hand with it. As you set and exhale, let your center hold its rise for part of the exhale. [Pause 15 seconds.] What you should feel with your hand on your center is that, rather than sinking immediately, the center maintains its shape for part of the exhale. [Pause 15 seconds.] The muscles in your chest, felt by your left hand, should remain soft and relaxed. If they feel tight, relax. The only point of tautness should be below your navel as you press gently against the wall during your exhale. [Pause 30 seconds.]

Continue breathing in this way: at the start of the exhale, set, and exhale through your feet, putting slight pressure on the wall and maintaining a slight roundness in the *hara*. At the end of the exhale, release and relax; air will naturally fill the body. Begin mentally counting your breath: breathing in 1, set, breathing out, slowly, o–n–e. Breathing in 2, set, breathing out, slowly, t–w–o. Continue counting in your mind's voice up to 10. If you lose count, go back to 1. Once you get to 10, go back to 1. Continue developing your breath and center in this way. [Pause 12 minutes.]

At the end of your next exhale, roll to the side and come up slowly. [End script.]

Developing and strengthening this pattern of breathing takes some time. Be patient with yourself. The payoff is enormous. By breathing this way you're learning to relax the diaphragm. Through alternating tension and release in the lower abdomen, we create a kind of pump. Similar to our heart pumping blood, this breath pump in our center sends vital energy throughout our body.

Steps in Lying-Down Meditation

Lie on the floor with your feet against a wall. Breathe through your nose. Keep your eyes open and look 180 degrees.

1. **Center your breathing.** Bring your awareness to your breath and your breath into your center. Your chest should be still, and the motion of your breath should be felt in your center.
2. **Set your** *hara*. *On exhale:* Roll your tailbone ever so slightly toward your navel. Gently push the wall through the balls of your feet. *On inhale:* Relax completely.

Give each breath a count from 1 to 10. Make your exhale at least twice as long as your inhale.

Be Here Now

"Boy, there's a lot more to this meditation than I thought," said one of my students after learning this exercise. "I've done meditation before," he continued, "but we never concentrated on setting the center and breathing into the center. We just relaxed and let go of our tensions. This is a lot more demanding."

He's right. Paying attention to our breath and developing our center is more difficult than just sending our mind off into space. Indeed, it places a very difficult demand on our mind: Be Here Now. We can mine only the present moment for its energy. We cannot draw energy from the future or the past. Yet our mind would almost always rather be somewhere in the future or the past, in a worry or a hope. Be Here Now—this is the heart of practice, breaking the pattern of mind wandering that cuts us off from the present moment and the genuine sources of energy that could revitalize us.

Be Here Now—this breaks a pattern of tension and holding that constricts the energy flow within us. By bringing our mind to our breath and our breath to our center, we forge an essential connection between mind and body. Through this connection we slowly dissolve the internal tensions and conflicts that otherwise dissipate our energy, moving ever closer to full power. Be Here Now—this is how we draw our personal vitality from the infinite well.

Tapping an infinite well of energy may sound grandiose, but in practice it's very simple: If you want to raise your energy, lower your breathing—meaning lower the rate at which you breathe and allow your breath to drop physically lower in your body. You can't do this by forcing it. (If you force, you become tense and the breath is unable to sink.) And you won't remember to do it by chance. (You might remember today. You might even think of your breath tomorrow, but soon it will be a faded memory.) The only way to change your breathing is with a steady practice.

> "Better to live one day of steadfast energy than a hundred years idle, without energy."
>
> —Suttapitaka

"But isn't that a lot of work?" asked Dana, once she understood the idea of a practice for developing more energy. "That's the question you need to settle," I told her. In one sense, it's no work at all. You invest an effort, to be sure, but the return on your investment is multifold. In another sense, there are easier ways to go after a zip of energy: eating, driving aggressively, picking a fight. There are easier ways to take the edge off of tension in our day: drinking alcohol and watching television are coast-to-coast favorites. But after the car is parked, the argument ends, or the drink wears off, we still have the same old life and the same low energy. Unlike these "easier" methods, a practice doesn't plaster over the condition of our life. It fundamentally changes that condition—from inside out.

The question for Dana, and for anyone who wants more energy or a better life or better health, is simply this: How badly do you want it? When you want it badly enough, you'll open a crack in your life to get it.

3

❦

Awareness: Waking Up to the Present

*"Right now a moment of time is passing by! . . .
We must become that moment."*
—Paul Cézanne

Living and Learning

"Max doesn't have twenty years of experience," one of my colleagues said of another. "He has one year twenty times." If somewhat biting, the comment had the seed of truth in it. Max did seem stuck in a repeating loop, making the same errors in judgment over and over. For example, every time he was given a new assignment and told to coordinate his work with the group across the hall, he would do the work by himself and only show it to the other group once he was finished. When he finally showed it to them expecting their rubber-stamp approval, they always had new ideas about how he should change what he did. Thinking the assignment was complete, Max was no longer open to new ideas, so he would end up frustrated that nobody respected his work. Meanwhile, the other group was frustrated that he didn't work with them earlier.

Over the eight years I knew Max, this cycle was repeated several times a year. "Insanity," one of my psychologist friends points out, "is doing the same thing over and over and expecting different results." What makes some people able to learn and grow from their experience, while others, like Max, are stuck in a pattern of commonplace insanity?

Awareness is the difference. Along with energy, awareness is the second benefit you can realize through BodyLearning. As soon as you pay attention to your breath, you suddenly shift into the present moment with added awareness of what you're doing. This shift is subtle, yet it changes everything. From this perspective, you get a better view of what's really happening. You get a choice about whether to be sucked into daily dramas or to be present in calm awareness. Perhaps most important, with this awareness, connecting mind to body and body to the world, you strengthen the link between living and learning.

By contrast, when our mind is absorbed in its chatter, chasing its stories, replaying a past insult or a hoped-for conversation, we are not truly present in the moment in which we're living. Whatever learnings that moment offers are largely or totally lost. We aren't paying attention. Like having a poor connection on a phone line, we lose most of life's learning in the transmission. We repeat mistakes and cycle around the same problems. Without awareness, we essentially live the same day over and over.

> *"To be aware is the uniting of knowing and doing."*
> —*Seymour Kleinman*

While we can get away with not paying attention much of the time and still be functional or even successful in the world, we never approach our full strength until we develop awareness. Awareness is learned through the body, by paying attention to the breath and senses and all that the moment presents. A question you might ask of your present life is this: How much is your body learning awareness now?

Exercise in Awareness: What Might Your Body Be Learning Now?

Reflecting on your own habits and experience, you can get a better idea of how much awareness (i.e., awareness of the present moment) your body is currently learning. You can also develop greater awareness of other lessons that come through one of the main activities in your present life. This exercise gives you a chance to do that. It also introduces the thought process we'll use later in designing a practice that matches the lessons you'd like to work on. This exercise takes about twenty minutes, and you'll need your notebook.

Think about your typical day. Think about how you spend your waking hours: moving around your home, sitting at a desk, driving in a car, eating meals, exercising, whatever. Write down the top few time consumers in your day; that is, the activities you do most often. From your list select the one activity you probably spend more time at than the rest. Use that activity as the basis for the following survey.

In the next step of the exercise, you'll survey various senses and parts of your body for what they contribute to this dominant activity in your day. To give you an idea of the process, I'll work through an example from my own life in which writing (no surprise) is presently the most common activity. First I'll survey a number of body witnesses for what they put into or get out of writing. Then (in Step 2), I'll put their responses in the order of who's most involved in this activity. My answers are in the table on the following page.

Now try this for your activity. You want to capture immediate reactions—ten words or so from each body witness. If some parts of the body aren't particularly involved in the activity, just say that and move on.

1. Draw a table in your notebook like the one on the following page. Fill in the left column with the nine body witnesses you'll query. Ask each witness what it either puts into or gets out of the activity you've selected. Fill in the table with immediate, uncensored responses. Phrase your responses as if that part of the body were speaking. (Ignore the "Order" column for now; we'll use that in the next step.)

2. Of the body witnesses who had something to say about this activity, select the area or sense that had the most to say or is most emphasized by doing this activity. Assign it the number "1" in the "Order" column and then number the remaining areas in roughly de-

Body Area or Sense	Involvement in Activity (Writing)	Order (Step 2)
Feet (and legs)	Cold, we often get cold. And we move often to find comfortable positions.	8
Chest area (heart and lungs)	We get off pretty easy. Not much strain in this.	6
Hands (and arms)	Type, type, type. We frantically try to keep up with the words.	2
Lower abdomen, "gut"	Centering this mess. Practicing the exercises.	5
Ears	Listening: Raindrops, traffic, and the steady hum of the computer. Listening for the right phrase.	4
Skin (touch)	Not a lot of new input moment by moment.	9
Nose and mouth (smell and taste)	Coffee, we taste a lot of coffee. And water and juice.	7
Eyes	Sometimes bleary from too much computer screen.	3
Head (thoughts)	Words, words, words.	1

scending order of involvement in this activity. Give your highest number to all the areas that had nothing to say about this activity.

3. Based on your table, rate this activity somewhere along the 5-point scales by asking yourself the following questions:

a. To what extent does this activity "put me in my head"?

| 1 | 2 | 3 | 4 | 5 |

Completely   Sometimes   Not at All

Example: If "Head" was your No. 1 witness, and several other parts didn't report in, give this activity a 1.

b. To what extent does this activity "put me in my body"?

|1   2   3   4   5|

Not at All   Sometimes   Completely

Example: If all nine areas are solidly involved in this activity and Head isn't No. 1, give this activity a 5.

c. To what extent does this activity awaken my senses?

|1   2   3   4   5|

Not at All   Sometimes   Completely

Example: Give a point for each sense that plays a significant role in this activity.

d. To what extent does this activity make me feel alive?

|1   2   3   4   5|

Deadens Me   Neutral   Enlivens Me

Example: If the activity deadens and enlivens you about equally, or doesn't do either very much, give it a 3.

Add your four scores.

If this activity scored 15 or higher, it's a good source of awareness in your life. In fact, it's probably a great BodyLearning activity, and awareness is one of the lessons it's teaching.

If this activity scored in the middle (10–14), which is where my example of writing ends up, it's fairly neutral with respect to developing awareness of the present moment. Given that you spend considerable time doing this activity, you might consider how you could do it in a way that is more alive to the senses and enriching.

If this activity scored less than 10, it's not building a habit of greater external awareness in your life. Indeed, it may be reinforcing the opposite pattern: less awareness and greater disconnection between mind and body. That doesn't mean you should stop doing this activity—you may not have that luxury or desire. Perhaps you can do it less; perhaps you can do it differently. Even being aware, however, that it's reinforcing a pattern on the dull side underscores the need to bring other activities into your life to foster awareness.

Regardless of whether the most common activity in your waking life is teaching you to be more aware, it is undoubtedly conveying some set of lessons. In the next part of this exercise, you'll have a chance to consider what they might be. By way of example, I'll start with offering a few lessons that writing day after day is teaching me:

- How to type better (i.e., how to correct my typing errors faster)
- Writing skills
- Learning to listen
- Managing my day so that I use my best writing hours for my most challenging work
- How to finish—projects, papers, chapters, books
- How to sit for long periods in a way that doesn't hurt my body
- How to navigate the publishing world
- Developing an eye for information layout and computer graphics
- Learning to keep plugging away, even when progress seems lacking

Now develop a similar list for your activity.

Reviewing your table of responses from the body's witnesses, consider what habits your body-mind is developing from doing this activity over and over again. What are the lessons being learned? These lessons don't have to be obvious while you're doing the activity, and perhaps they're just a side effect. Write them down anyway. Take about five minutes to jot down as many lessons as come to mind.

In the next part of the exercise, you'll summarize the lessons learned in terms of single words and feelings. To continue my example, here are my one-word summaries of lessons and feelings drawn from sitting at my desk, writing.

Lesson	One-Word Summary	Feeling
How to type better	Speed	Hyper
Writing skills	Communication	Ease of Expression
Learning to listen	Listening	Openness
Managing my day to use best writing hours for most challenging work	Time Management	Efficiency
How to finish	Finishing	Closure
How to sit for long periods in a way that doesn't hurt my body	Correct Posture	Balance
How to navigate the publishing world	New Directions	Competence
Developing an eye for information lay-out and computer graphics	Artistic Sense	Creativity
Learning to keep plugging away, even when progress is lacking	Perseverance	Persistence

Now go back over your lessons learned and pick one or two words for each that capture the essence of the lesson: What are you getting a chance to practice as you do this activity? Alternatively, or in addition, state one top-of-mind emotion you associate with each lesson. For each lesson ask, "How does learning this make me feel?"

While my experience of writing is mixed with respect to developing awareness, it's certainly teaching lessons on a daily basis. Most of them are lessons I'm glad to learn. At least one in this example—feeling hyper from typing—is not a habit I want, yet I can see how my pattern of work reinforces it.

Reflecting on your lessons and feelings, decide whether, on the whole, this activity is teaching more good lessons or bad habits. If you're not happy with your conclusion, you might consider different ways of approaching this activity that would change your lessons and feelings. For example, if I don't want to reinforce the hyper feeling of jumping my fingers all over the keyboard, I could learn to type correctly (actually using more than four fingers) and slow down. Remember, you spend more waking hours at this activity than anything else. If it is reinforcing patterns you really don't want in your life, change something.

The thought process you went through to arrive at one-word summary lessons or feelings is the inverse of the process we'll use later to design a practice. Here, you started from something you were already doing and derived the lessons it was teaching. Later you'll have a chance to consider what lessons you'd like to learn and identify the kinds of BodyLearning activities that would teach them. The better you understand yourself and the habits reinforced in your daily life, the better able you are to adjust your activities to the lessons you sincerely want to learn.

Of course, the extent to which you learn from any experience comes back to a matter of awareness. If you're not fully present, you don't fully absorb the positive lessons from what you do. Rather, you reinforce the bad habit of being lost in your thoughts. That's why BodyLearning entails a *practice*—a time in your day when you make the effort to be fully present. In this way you build the awareness that lets you learn not only from your BodyLearning practice, but also from other activities in your day.

Say Again

My friend Henry never hears me the first time I speak to him. "Say again?" is always his first response. I repeat what I said, and when I'm about halfway through, he finishes my sentence for me. At first I thought Henry had trouble hearing, so I raised the volume of my voice. "Say again?" he still said. Then I figured maybe he didn't know I was talking to him, so in my opening sentence, I started with his name. "Henry, how have you been?" "Say again?" A long pause followed as I stubbornly refused to restate half of my simple question. "Oh-h-h," he finally said, "I've been fine."

"Earth to Henry," I want to say. "Come in, please." But Henry only makes obvious what all of us do some of the time and some of us do all the time: stall for time while we drag our mind out of the thoughts we're lost in and into the present moment. Those thoughts may come from our own mind on automatic, or we may be absorbed in an activity, a book or a television show. The more engrossed we are, the more likely we are to respond like Henry when something actually happens around us. "What's that?" we say. "Pardon me." "Say again?"

The problem is that life doesn't happen twice. It's one thing to get people to repeat what they're saying to us. Other than generating a bit of irritation, we probably can get away with it much of the time. But if our pattern is always to need a second chance to catch things a first time, we miss the opportunities or dangers in the present moment. There's no point in saying to the driver whose car we just rear-ended, "Could you repeat that business about applying your brake lights?" There's no point in saying to the person who just ran off with our wallet, "Could you repeat that? I'd like to do something differently." When the show must go on at 3:00, there's no point in saying at 2:59, "Could we repeat the last half-hour so I have a chance to get ready?"

Ready or not, the fact is that life is a string of firsts. Even when we can get people to repeat what they tell is, the second time is really its own first, because it comes later in time (meaning other things could have happened) and with a new reaction (such as irritation or an impression that we're slow) to the very fact that we asked for a repeat. There really is no second chance to make a first impression.

When we're not squarely in the present moment, we miss the natural timing of situations. In the commonsense wisdom of our day, those who hesitate are lost. This is made especially evident in activities requiring split-second timing, such as sports or martial arts. I certainly felt the impact of my own sluggishness when I began training in martial arts. My earliest experiences were in karate. In sparring matches I was painfully slow and ineffective. While I couldn't admit it at the time, I was afraid of getting hit. Like a doe in the headlights, I was stuck in my fear, which was all the more realized. Always "behind the curve," I was denying the attack at some level until it was too late. Missing the timing—BAM!—I'd get hit.

Now if Henry got hit every time he said "Say again?" and had people repeat themselves, he'd probably break the habit. Martial arts training demands that we do break through our resistance to deal with situations as they happen. Indeed, that's one of the ways the martial arts work to develop our awareness and one of the reasons they're such good BodyLearning activities.

In everyday life, however, the consequences of our denial or inattentiveness are less obvious. Indeed, our limited awareness does have a payoff: it gives us the illusion that life is a little closer to the way we want it to be. A little slower. A little less at odds with our preconceived notions, as we fail to notice the things that don't fit. A little less ugliness that we choose not to notice as we look on the bright side. There's a bit of comfort in our bad habit, which is how it becomes so much a part of our life.

While the punch is slower to land than in a karate match, the consequences of our limited awareness are potentially even more damaging. We set ourselves up for greater difficulties when we won't deal with early warning signs. When we ignore the signs of a problem brewing, we often end up with a crisis to handle. When we miss the opportunities to act when our options are many, we become ensnared in the problem when our options are few. This happens over and over in the lives of individuals, families and organizations. We buy a little bit more and more on credit until we're deeply in debt. We tune out a little bit of abuse from someone in our life until the whole relationship and maybe we ourselves are at the breaking point.

At our workplaces we often let problems fester until all the best options for dealing with them have expired. Mitch, who was not a bad company president by most measures, had a blind spot when it came to one of his longtime managers. The manager had been with the close-knit company for more than thirty years and had developed into a bitter, tyrannical boss to the people under him. His sense of direction for the department was hopelessly out of date. He would trash any initiatives to change direction and publicly denounce their proponents who were, by all accounts except his, rising stars in the company. If the truth be told, even Mitch was somewhat intimidated by this man's abrasive nature. Yet he shrugged it off as "no big problem" and encouraged those who came to him with complaints to do the same. Finally, when the three most talented people under this man left the company,

Mitch saw his business in jeopardy. By that time, the frustration in the department was so high that people were demanding the resignation of Mr. Abrasive. Not only was that scenario fraught with difficulties, but even if Mitch could retire this troubled manager, the three best people to fill his shoes had already left.

The second and even more insidious side effect of limited awareness is the inner brokenness left behind when our mind denies what's

> "Most of all we deny what we know in our bones."
>
> —Marilyn Ferguson

knocking on the doors of our senses. A perception of slow change in a rapidly changing world is a delusion. A perception of "no problem" when a real problem exists is a delusion. The only way we can maintain these delusions is, in effect, to lie to ourselves. At a conscious level, we may not know we're doing it, but it's damaging our integrity just the same. The more the mind denies what the body is sensing, the more we create disconnections within. Doubt arises in these cracks, making our actions more tentative and ineffective. Energy is drained through these cracks, as we pour more energy into resisting life than into living it. We cannot act with clarity and decisiveness when our day-to-day comfort-seeking habits create a muddle.

Most of us don't wake up in the morning saying "What I really need today is more awareness" (as we might say about energy). Yet if we want to live our lives fully, with greater joy and less suffering—riding the current, staying off the rocks, and dealing with whatever life throws our way—what we need today really is more awareness. And the way to more awareness is through the body.

Exercise in Awareness: Listening to the Senses

Awareness begins in your senses. When you pay attention to something—your breath or the sounds or sights around you—you give it more conscious space, more room in which to deliver its goods.

To do this exercise, you'll need your notebook and a watch. Give yourself one minute to answer each question. You want to capture first thoughts on these questions, not long-labored responses. This isn't a race, but write your answers down as quickly as they come to mind, without censorship. (If you don't have one of the senses queried, skip that item and go on to the others.) It's best if you write your answer to each question as you come to it without reading ahead. Ready? One minute. Go.

1. List as many sounds as you remember hearing within the past day.

How many sounds could you remember in a minute? The rate at which ideas come to your mind—or whether they come at all—is related to how much you've stocked your sensory pond with answers, in this case, sounds. In developing your answers, did you spend more time writing or thinking? If you had plenty of ideas and were writing them down as fast as you could, you probably had ten or so items. If you spent a fair amount of time trying to remember what you did recently, where you went, much less how things sounded, you probably had just a few items. That's fine. You have another shot at it. Give yourself a minute for the next question.

2. List quiet, subtle sounds that you've heard within the past day; i.e., sounds that another person going through your day with you might not have noticed.

This list is probably shorter. Maybe you weren't able to think of anything that wouldn't have been obvious to others. Or maybe you recalled several sounds that caught your attention, though most people would have missed them. They resonated with you and you took note of them. One can imagine many other lists that could be developed by others going through your day with you but having different sensitivities. Something we often appreciate in fine writers or storytellers is their ability to add subtle but salient detail to the scenes they create. Such people catch what others miss—and then draw our attention to it. This is awareness.

Give yourself a minute to query a second sense.

3. List as many odors and aromas as you can remember smelling in the past day.

You might compare the length of this list to your list for sounds. Given the same amount of time to answer, which sense has more to report? Most people seem to have an easier time recalling sounds. Because smell is our oldest and most primitive sense, aromas reach us at a deeper level and we seem to have to dig deeper to bring them up to a conscious level. But once we do, we tend to experience richer, fuller memories around smells. Sometimes a smell, reminiscent of an earlier time, puts us right back in that earlier place. The smell of bread baking will always take me back to Mrs. Garra's second-grade class and the day twenty-eight pairs of doughy little hands—including mine—shaped four loaves of bread.

Now cover this first list of smells, and give yourself another minute to answer the following:

4. List aromas and odors you smelled in the past day that were subtle; i.e., someone else going through your day with you probably would not have noticed them.

It's not surprising if your second list is shorter than the first; recalling the subtle smells in your day forces you to dig a bit deeper, beyond the obvious exhaust fumes on the freeway or popcorn-air at the movie theater. What I find remarkable is that in digging deeper for subtle news from our senses, we almost always come up with answers in our second (subtle) list that we missed in the first. Our second list also probably has items in it we don't notice much of the time. But when we do take time to listen to our senses, we're rewarded with a richer experience of life itself.

Give yourself a minute for each of the following questions:

5. Think of the street that runs in front of where you live. List the things you noticed that were different the last time you walked or drove down that road.

6. List things you noticed for their distinct color within the past day.

Reflecting on your lists of answers, where did you overflow with ideas and run out of time? Where did you run out of ideas and have to wait for the time to expire? The more awareness you bring to your normal day, the more you'll notice what's distinct or different about it. Surely there are many things you could have noticed in the past day for their distinct color—a flower, package, outfit or automobile. Surely there are many differences you could have picked out along the road in front of where you live: the vintage Volkswagen, the license plate from Alaska, the spider web stretched between two branches, and so on. And since you gave yourself as much time to answer these questions as for naming sounds and smells, you know how many answers you're able to write down in a minute—if you know what to write.

But if you're like most people, your list of answers to these last two questions is considerably shorter than your list of sounds or smells. These questions are harder because they're asking not only what you saw but also what you saw with fresh eyes. In some sense, everything is always changing and every day is distinct and different. But how much of the new do we notice? When I give this exercise in seminars, the average list is two or three items. Five is doing great. What I notice among people who seem most aware is that they keep digging for items for the entire minute. A surprising number of people actually give up and wait out the last thirty seconds, as if knowing there's nothing more to report. In a curious twist of logic, it's as if they decide what they can't recall didn't happen (and besides, they seem to think it's a dumb exercise).

Don't be discouraged if you found little to report in these questions. This isn't a contest. No one's judging. What is certain is that if you practice awareness, awareness will grow. The more you ask of your senses, the more they report. Paying attention is the very audience requested by your senses. If you give them an audience, your senses give you the moment at full strength.

Developing Awareness in the Ordinary

The sense of aliveness we feel when we do extraordinary things is our awareness being sparked. Skiing a dangerous, invigorating slope. Dining on an exquisite meal, where even the tomato soup surprises and delights the taste buds. Listening to a profoundly moving piece of music, where the low notes quake at our very center. In falling out of the same old patterns, the special events peppering our life stimulate our awareness.

But if we confine the development of our awareness to the extraordinary events in our life, our awareness will not have much chance to develop. If I develop my awareness only when I order the tomato soup at a four-star restaurant maybe once a year, that's hardly going to be habit-forming. In his wonderful book *The Miracle of Mindfulness*, Thich Nhat Hanh suggests instead that we use the very ordinary events of our lives to develop extraordinary awareness. On the ordinary event of washing dishes, he writes:

> While washing dishes, one should only be washing the dishes, which means that while washing the dishes one should be completely aware of the fact that one is washing the dishes. At first glance, that might seem a little silly: Why put so much stress on a simple thing? But that's precisely the point.
>   . . . If while washing the dishes, we think only of the cup of tea that awaits us, thus hurrying to get the dishes out of the way as if they were a nuisance, then we are not "washing the dishes to wash the dishes." What's more, we are not alive during the time we are washing the dishes. In fact, we are completely incapable of realizing the miracle of life while standing at the sink. If we can't wash the dishes, the chances are we won't be able to drink our tea either. While drinking the cup of tea, we will only be thinking of other things, barely aware of the cup in our hands. Thus we are sucked away into the future—and we are incapable of actually living one minute of life.[1]

What Thich Nhat Hanh means by "actually living" is more than registering a pulse. It is registering an awareness of the moment and the wonder of our own existence within it. Being aware of life in the present tense connects us to the only moment in which we can actually live. All other points on the time line can entertain our thoughts, but they cannot engage our body or its actions. Consequently, being anywhere other than the here and now splits us between a body that's in the present and a mind that's off somewhere else. Any time we split our attention or intention, we are weaker than when we're whole.

As Thich Nhat Hanh points out, awareness watered daily has the best chance to grow. If we can wash the dishes in full awareness, or clean the house or drive the car in full awareness, we have a way to build awareness into our every day. This is exactly what we do in BodyLearning. Devoting a time in our day to be fully present in the present moment, we give our awareness a daily shot of growth. In this sense, what we choose as our practice is less important than the fact that we choose something. Breathing exercises, meditation, tennis, watercolors, needlepoint, cleaning the house or taking a walk can be the basis of a fine practice—so long as when we do them, we are totally present, here and now.

On the other hand, we might wonder why, if awareness is such a good thing to develop, we don't just start doing everything in full awareness. Why make a special practice out of it and call it BodyLearning? While it would be great if our practice mindset could expand to fill our entire life—and indeed the third step of BodyLearning is expanding our practice—a well-defined practice is the only way to get there from here. Trying to do everything all at once is too much: we overload and give up. It's simply not possible to change our entire pattern of living on a dime. The body doesn't work that way. It takes time to expand the links to our senses, to lower the barriers that create resistance to new ideas or ways of doing things. Our body-mind circuits have many patterns of split performance, of inattentiveness, of places where our conscious mind goes on "automatic." If we want to walk the path toward greater awareness, we need to train these patterns out of our body and replace them with new patterns.

Through a BodyLearning practice we begin building a new set of awareness habits, twenty minutes at a time. While it's not realistic for most of us to be here and now twenty-four hours a day, we can do it for twenty minutes. If we have a well-defined activity in which to practice this heightened awareness, we'll remember to do it day after day. By contrast, if we just tell ourselves we'll remember to do something in full awareness but don't have a specific activity in mind, it's amazing how soon we'll forget. Like it or not, that's how we are. Knowing that's how we are, we're wise to build a practice.

Walking Meditation

Nowhere can we experience the contrast of awareness so sharply as in ordinary activities done in extraordinary awareness. Nowhere do we find such fertile soil for our practice as in the things we do every day. Walking is such an activity. In this exercise, you have a chance to experience the renewal and richness of walking in full awareness.

"Walking meditation is learning to walk again with ease."[2] Many of us do a fair amount of walking during our day, but generally, we're in a hurry to get somewhere, and we don't pay much attention to walking as an end in itself. In walking meditation, we do pay attention. Walking *is* the point.

In our normal way of walking, we're usually absorbed in our thoughts, carrying on a conversation if we're with someone else and carrying on an inner conversation if we're by ourselves. We don't generally notice much that is going on around us—because there's so much going on within us. In walking meditation, you take your senses out for a walk, shutting down outer conversation or inner chatter, allowing your senses to open into more conscious space. It is far easier to maintain awareness of your breath and posture and everything around you when your attention is not pulled into a stream of words.

Walking meditation is walking in full awareness of breath, body and everything the senses present. It is not an aerobic exercise—though it

> "The press of my foot to the earth springs a hundred affections."
> —Walt Whitman

would be a fine lead-in to aerobic walking. Rather, walking meditation is done slowly and consciously, with each step fully feeling the earth. During this precious time, body and mind come together, joined in the present moment. Although the benefits of walking meditation will deepen over time, even from the start, you can experience some measure of the relaxation, balance and quiet energy that builds through this practice.

Walking meditation can be done anywhere. If you have a favorite place to walk, that's probably the place to start. If walking is not the way you normally get around, adapt this exercise to your own method of mobility. For example, in a wheelchair the use of arms and legs is different, but the same principles of breath and centeredness apply.

Since we want to open all our senses during walking meditation and not isolate our hearing to headphones, I don't recommend prerecording this exercise. Read through it a time or two, and if you don't think you can remember it, make a couple of notes to remind you as you walk. Allow twenty minutes to do this exercise—though more time is great. The awareness exercise that follows in the next section (p. 59) should be done right after you finish walking meditation. In this way, you'll get a sense of how much more your senses present during this precious time.

Begin by walking your normal walk a little more slowly. Become aware of your breath, breathing through your nose, and count the number of steps that go with your inhale. Count the number of steps that go with your exhale. Continue for several minutes in this way, blending your breathing with your walking, and your walking with your breathing.

Drop your shoulders and keep your back straight. Let the tension in your body fall to your center, where it blends with your breathing. Let your breathing sink to your center as your muscles relax. Use the same kind of breathing pattern as you practiced in lying-down meditation: relax on the inhale, set the *hara* at the start of the exhale. Practice bringing this rhythm into your walking. To set the *hara* for walking, place your hand on your lower abdomen (below your navel). Keeping your knees slightly flexed, tuck your tailbone ever so slightly forward. This should have the effect of rocking your hand slightly upward, creating a sense of roundness in your lower abdomen. Don't tuck too much, otherwise walking will be uncomfortable. With the slightest tuck, imagine your center becoming a perfectly round globe, which then becomes the center of your walking motion.

Our tendency is to carry our tension high in our body, in our neck and shoulders and chest area. This makes our balance more "tippy." When we walk very slowly, we experience this tension as unstable steps. Work to drain this tension down to your center, get it under your belt where you can manage it with balance. By setting the *hara* at the start of each exhale, you bring more awareness to your center, which allows it to become more the physical center of your motion.

Allow the number of steps that go with each breath to increase as feels natural; as your body relaxes, your breathing will tend to slow down. In particular, let your exhale lengthen, growing two to three times as long as your inhale. Don't force your breath to lengthen; simply invite it to stretch out. Continue to breathe with your walk, allowing your body to move evenly from your center.

Feel your feet touch the earth. Feel the stability of each step as your weight rolls from heel to toe, from heel to toe.

Allow each step to touch the ground with care and stability, leaving a beautiful imprint. Feel the earth greet each foot, and each foot greet the earth. By maintaining your balance at your center, each step rolls smoothly and evenly. If your feet are clomping on the ground, landing heavily and flatly (rather than rolling from heel to toe), your weight is too far forward. If your heels are hammering the earth, your weight is too far back.

Keep your head erect. Don't watch your feet or the ground as you walk. Let your eyes take in all that is around you, keeping your vision as broad as possible. Rather than focusing narrowly on each object with the center of your eye, see everything all at once by using peripheral vision. Take in the sounds, the smells, the beautiful, the not-so-beautiful: take in everything evenly—and be caught in none of it. If you find your attention wandering off, come back to your breath and blend it back with your step. Come back to your center. Come back to your feet feeling the earth. Come back to your senses.

Continue to walk. Enjoy your breath, body, and mind—moving together in this simple harmony, alive in this moment, and awake to what this moment offers.

Awareness develops through this special time of walking as you throw wide open the apertures of your senses. Broaden your vision to see 180 degrees—using the kind of peripheral vision that you're tested for when you get a driver's license. Listen to the messages from all parts of your eyes, including the motions catching the corners.

Although it's easiest to describe for the eyes, all your senses should be similarly opened during walking meditation. Hear all sounds, not just a single melody. Pick up all the scents carried in the air, not just your favorites. Feel all sensations the day brings to your skin. By accepting the inputs from all your senses evenly, without censorship, you take in the whole picture. You can be aware of the thoughts or feelings triggered by your senses, but you don't need to ride off on any of these inner trails. If you can simply watch with your breath, each thought or feeling will arise and fade on its own.

Walking meditation is a particularly powerful practice because it builds on something that's part of almost everyone's everyday activity. If you can set aside some time during the week to practice walking meditation, you will soon be able to blend your practice into other times when you walk. Soon the awareness from this time of practice will begin seeping through the rest of your day.

> "The real voyage of discovery consists not in seeing new landscapes but in having new eyes."
> —Marcel Proust

If you prefer walking meditation to the lying-down meditation that was suggested as the start of practice in the previous chapter, substitute it as your daily practice for now. Better yet, practice the lying down meditation once or twice a week (in which it's easier to develop the breath cycle that develops the center), and then apply that same breathing in your walking meditation on the other days.

Steps in Walking Meditation

1. **Connect your walking to your breathing.** Keep your spine straight and shoulders relaxed. Count your breath with your steps. Your exhale should be 2–3 times longer than your inhale.
2. **Focus on your center.** Create a sense of roundness at your center by ever so slightly tucking your tailbone forward. Imagine this rounded center as the center of your walking motion.
3. **Open your senses.** Keep your eyes level and focused 180 degrees.

Exercise in Awareness: The World after Walking Meditation

This exercise should be done right after walking meditation. The fresher the experience is in your mind, the more you'll see the difference between answering these questions and the lists you did earlier.

To do this exercise you'll need your notebook and your watch. Give yourself one minute per list to answer each of the following:

1. List things you saw on your walk that you don't normally see.
2. List subtle smells that you noticed along your walk.
3. List things you felt (either externally or internally) that you don't normally feel when you walk.

Do you notice a difference in generating these lists as compared with the earlier exercise? When I give this exercise in seminars, people generally find that it's much easier than the earlier questions. Their lists are longer and produced more fluidly. They run out of time before they run out of ideas. They find twenty minutes of walking meditation produced more grist for the mill than had the entire day they reflected on earlier. Of course, part of that is the freshness of the experience. But part of it is simply giving the senses the space and time to be heard.

Once we give space to our senses, they almost certainly will bring back news. How could they not? The page of our mind will fill with something. When that something is not the litany of our usual chatter, the senses will stretch to fill it. They not only fill us with news of the world but also (as you may have experienced in the last question) put us more in touch with our inner condition and feelings. Once we can develop awareness of our feelings as just another set of sensations—not something we have to be totally sucked into—we gain a new perspective. We can experience the effects of our biochemistry without amplifying every sensation into our entire being. What freedom! We can experience anger without becoming anger machines. We can experience fear without letting it stop us. The more we're aware of what's going on in the moment—inside and out—the more appropriate our moment-by-moment actions become.

Essential Awareness

Developing awareness may seem like something of a New Age luxury: something we do after the bills are paid and the kids are in bed—if there's time. In reality, it is the most essential and practical thing we can do. Far from being the luxury of a comfortable life, awareness is most needed when we're faced with conflict and suffering. For it is exactly our lack of awareness that leads to our troubles. Our conflict and suffering provide exactly the motivation we need to wake up and see our difficulties for what they are.

Many of our troubles arise because we don't live and learn. We just live. Without awareness of our outward situation or inward condition, we stumble along vaguely familiar paths that end up repeating past problems. Think of how soap operas manage to create their drama and endless stream of difficulties. As viewers, we're always given a little more awareness about situations than the characters themselves have, so we know when they're being set up. Their world is very limited, scripted by lies and half-truths, innuendo and blind reactions—the very opposite of genuine awareness. And look how much trouble they can make for themselves and one another carrying on that way. Not only that, but their stereotypic lives look pretty much the same season after season, show after show. Like my colleague Max with his "one year of experience twenty times," our lives repeat like a soap opera when we cannot connect living and learning. Awareness is the link.

We make trouble for ourselves when we refuse to see what's going on. Scary movies often have a point in them where the heroes enter some huge dark place with only a flashlight. We know something's going to get them from the shadows. Yet we often go into the dark rooms of our lives with only a flashlight of awareness because we're too lazy or afraid to turn on a more powerful light.

Sometimes what we don't see does hurt us. And when we're not willing to look at it, it can hurt us doubly. Not only does it land its punch of difficulty; it also leaves another crack of brokenness within us, between some deep part of us that feels the impact and a thinking mind that refuses to deal with it. Awareness turns on the light in our life, bringing reality into view with all its beauty and all its warts. Awareness builds our inner integrity as we quit fooling ourselves into thinking what we don't see doesn't happen.

We make more trouble for ourselves when we're not ready for life in the present tense. Dithering on decisions that cannot wait, not dealing with issues until it's too late, coming up a "day late and a dollar short" time and again—these number among the symptoms of missing the here and now. When we're lost in our thoughts, we're lost to the present. "Say again?" as my friend Henry asks of life and everyone in it. But life rarely indulges our requests for an instant replay. The only way we can act clearly, decisively, creatively, and appropriately in the moment is to be in the moment already.

How do we develop confidence in our ability to do the right thing moment by moment? Many of us don't. Many of us try to patch together our confidence for handling any situation through careful planning and contingency planning. My father tells a great story of how, as a young man and first-time father-to-be, he wanted to be certain about the fastest way to get my mother to the hospital when the time came to deliver my sister. So he planned a route and drove it ahead of time, timing carefully. He then realized the route crossed a set of railroad tracks, which would never do should a train decide to come at the same time as my sister. So he found an alternate route and timed that. Then he found backups to his backups. He laughs about it now, how nervous and plan-ful he was. But he needed the plan to have some confidence about knowing what to do.

We often get stuck when life doesn't go according to our plan—or any contingency plan we've been able to think of. What if my father had gone out to the car when the time came, and it didn't start? What if the neighbor he'd normally call on in such a jam wasn't home? No matter how rich our contingency planning, sooner or later we're in situations where we just have to go "live" and do the best we can. Awareness equips us with the essential wisdom for those essential points in our life.

This essential wisdom is an aspect of the awareness we cultivate through daily practice. It is not a lengthy chain of reasoning but rather an instantaneous knowing, an intuition as clear as light. There is no doubt in this knowing, no tentativeness in the actions that spring from it. Developing awareness, connecting mind to body through the breath and body to the world through the senses, we develop this knowing. There's no plan that can match it. It's the difference between carefully planning ahead of time how to navigate a white-water river and simply being the river.

This gift of awareness comes to us twenty minutes at a time—one practice session after another. Awareness is both the seed and harvest of BodyLearning. It is what we put into our time of practice; it is what we get back multifold. Far from being an extra luxury in our lives—something we work on once everything else has been taken care of—developing awareness is the very way we reduce our troubles and increase the joy and wisdom in our life. How important is awareness?

> There's the story of the disciple who went to the master and said, "Could you give me a word of wisdom? Could you tell me something that would guide me through my days?" It was the master's day of silence, so he picked up a pad. It said, "Awareness." When the disciple saw it, he said, "This is too brief. Can you expand on it a bit?" So the master took the pad back and wrote, "Awareness, awareness, awareness." The disciple said, "Yes, but what does it mean?" The master took the pad back and wrote, "Awareness, awareness, awareness means—awareness."[3]

4

❧

Focus: Developing a Sharper, Clearer Mind

"Not to stop the mind anywhere is the aim
and is of utmost importance.
Put nowhere, it will be everywhere."
—Takuan Soho

What We Do for the Body, We Do for the Mind

Jack is hardly what you would call a product of the New Age. To him, meditation was "something the people in airports did when they weren't selling flowers." It wasn't what normal people did, certainly not successful American businessmen like himself. Besides, Jack was too busy for something as slow as meditation; he was too busy successfully driving himself to a heart attack by the age of forty-eight.

Fortunately, it was not severe enough to kill him, but it was severe enough to get his attention. When his properly Western doctor suggested he do some meditation as part of his recovery, Jack agreed to give it a try. He bought a book on how to meditate, tried it out while he was convalescing at home, and took the practice back to work with him a few weeks later. Having previously warned his secretary and group that "the first twenty minutes are my own," Jack would arrive at the office twenty minutes early (a very honest man), close the door, and start his day with quiet breathing. Not only did Jack realize the benefits in his health, but his practice also had a side effect he hadn't expected. "I'm surprised how much it quiets me down," he said. "Not only does my heart quit racing, but so does my mind. I'm able to think much more clearly. And problems that had no solution at the end of yesterday are much easier to handle today."

In addition to developing energy and awareness, paying attention to our breath has the most remarkable focusing effect on our mind. Connecting mind to body through our breath allows our mind to absorb and transform to a mental condition the same relaxation and stability we experience in the body. Freeing up the blocked energy in the body also frees up what we experience as mental blocks. Quieting the body has the effect of quieting our mind chatter. It's no coincidence that Jack and so many others have found that when they improve their physical condition, their thoughts and feelings improve as well. After all, the mind and body dine on the same biochemical soup (even as they create its ingredients). As sociobiologist Marilyn Ferguson observes, "Changes anywhere in the mind-body loop must affect the whole."[1]

Not all people turn to quiet, meditative activities to improve their condition. "I need to go out and smash something," Chris would announce as she was headed out to play tennis on her lunch hour. We worked in the same laboratory in graduate school, spending much of our day staring through microscopes and absorbed in tiny, exacting work. Sometimes it felt as if our whole world had shrunk to tight little knots in the middle of our foreheads. "I can't think anymore," Chris would say, pushing away from the lab bench and reaching for her tennis bag. "Tennis opens me up again. There's something about blasting that ball across the net that makes you feel bigger." Chris was very good at her game. Without a doubt, her game was very good for her work.

From countless anecdotes to careful studies, the fact that improving our physical condition also improves our mental condition has been well established.[2] We know, for example, that many of the physical effects of exercise correlate with improved mental-emotional states, such as more relaxation, less anxiety, greater alertness, more energy and even the endorphin-induced "runner's high."[3] Likewise, many studies have linked meditation with greater mental acuity, reduced anxiety and more stable patterns of electrochemical activity in the brain.[4] Whether we favor quiet, meditative activities or dynamic, aerobic activities, what we do for the body most assuredly extends to the mind.

BodyLearning adds something of utmost importance to the mind-body connection. Borrowing from Zen training, there is a particular focus to BodyLearning activities, different from the way most people approach exercise or meditation (or anything else they do). This unique focus—focusing on breath and center, focusing through our senses and being fully present in the present moment—develops a condition of mind that moves freely with penetrating insight. Far beyond the general feel-good side effects of ordinary exercise or meditation, this condition is our mind at its sharpest and clearest.

Mind Moving Freely

What is meant by a "mind that moves freely"? One way to understand this better is by contrast. Our language is stocked with phrases that express the opposite of a mind moving freely: "I'm stuck on this problem," we say. Or "I'm bogged down in these details." "He's hung up on his way of doing things." Or "She's in a rut." The imagery is always the same, describing something stalled, snagged or somehow stopped in its tracks. When the mind stops, we stop.

By contrast, a mind moving freely is more like water, less like ice. It conforms to circumstance and penetrates the tiniest openings. A mind moving freely is spontaneous and creative. "Put nowhere, it can be everywhere," says Zen master Takuan. Going everywhere, it can handle every situation.

Earlier, I told the story of my father and his planning and contingency planning for getting my mother to the hospital when she was pregnant. He was concerned he might get stuck if he had only one route, so he worked out two or three options. Having contingency plans, his mind was a little more free to act than if he'd had just the one plan. He wouldn't have gotten flustered or stuck if one of his contingencies had been called for. But if something happened that he hadn't planned for—such as the car breaking down—he might have gotten flustered and stuck in the problem for a moment. Our plans can expand the range of situations we're prepared to handle, but they can't prepare us to handle every situation, since they're limited in number. A mind moving freely is like having an infinite number of plans and being able instantly to call upon the appropriate response in the moment.

> "Mind that abides nowhere must come forth."
> —Diamond Sutra

A mind moving freely is a mind of infinite flexibility. The analogy to plans breaks down at some point, since spontaneous response in the moment is not a rational, step-by-step process. My father, with his plans for driving to the hospital, might have reasoned, "If the train blocks route A, I'll take route B." But something spontaneous such as water doesn't reason, "If the rock goes here, I'll go there." It just goes. The infinite flexibility of water does not develop by adding together so many finite trajectories. Likewise, a mind moving freely is not a patchwork of so many contingency plans. It is beyond all plans and all need to plan. It is not a reasoned response, based on experience. Rather, it is a knowing based on awareness and being a part *of*—not apart from.

Let me give another example from the martial arts of mind moving freely. Being physically attacked, whether it's on the battlefield or in a blind alley, is a fear-prone event in which many people get stuck—if only for a moment—and don't know what to do. It takes only a moment of frozen, startled fear for an attacker to gain the advantage. In the Japanese samurai tradition of fighting sword-to-sword, a split second of stuck mind meant instant death. So in that tradition, as in military traditions around the world, warriors trained vigorously in ways to handle a wide variety of attacks. Each area developed its school or tradition of techniques—its set of contingency plans, so to speak. "If the attacker moves this way, cut that way." The more techniques they knew, the more attacks they could counter without hesitation. If they relied purely on technique, however, it was only a matter of time before they lost to a novel attack that was outside of their playbook.

It was no coincidence that Zen flourished in the samurai culture. It was exactly through the kind of focus developed in Zen—and that we cultivate in BodyLearning—that the most successful samurai were able to graduate from technique to the condition of mind moving freely. Being able to move freely and spontaneously in the moment, they were never caught off guard.

The samurai recognized this condition of mind was far more

valuable than the particular techniques that had been the stepping-stones of their development. This shift in emphasis beyond technique (*jitsu*) is expressed in the Japanese word *do*—a Way. A Way for the human spirit. A Way for the profound development of a mind moving freely. Many of the Japanese martial arts and fine arts that are still practiced today—Aikido, Judo, Kendo, Shodo (calligraphy), Chado (tea ceremony)—express this larger purpose.

As individuals coming to train in these arts, each of us more or less repeats this history in our own development. When students first come to train in Aikido, for example, they don't know any techniques, and almost any kind of attack will fluster them. Even such simple physical instructions as "Put your left foot forward" stymie many people for a second or more (sometimes much more) until they can distinguish left from right.

One attack and one throw at a time, students gradually build up their Aikido vocabulary. As the training progresses, responses to more difficult attacks are learned—more contingency plans—including facing attacks using weapons or from multiple people. By the time students are approaching black belt level, they have to be able to handle a wide variety of attacks with at least five different "free" responses. But most people at this stage in their training are not moving freely, they're just stuck in a larger plan. A practiced eye can see them mentally calculating while they're on the mat: "First I'll move this way, then I'll go that way, just like I practiced a zillion times." But eventually, as the Aikidoist faces four, five or six attackers, all plans break down. The best Aikidoists graduate from planning to the condition of a mind moving freely. Of course, even this development has stages. As Tanouye Rotaishi—a superb martial artist as well as a Zen master—tells his students, "First you learn the technique. Then you graduate from the technique. Then you graduate from graduation."

Exercise in Awareness: Creative Thinking

Another example of mind moving freely that is commonly taught in business and personal development seminars is creative thinking. A number of techniques and exercises have been developed to foster creative thinking in individuals, teams and even large organizations. In this exercise you'll have a chance to experience how the most commonly known method—brainstorming—frees the mind to think in new ways.

The essence of brainstorming is to suspend judgment. In brainstorming you make no attempt to evaluate the merits of the ideas as you generate them. We can only judge based on our experience. If we keep returning to what we know so as to judge each idea as we think of it, it's harder to move our mind very far from the original framework of the problem. On the other hand, if we keep leapfrogging one idea after another, our mind can move in new directions, and may get into a region where we hit pay dirt.

For this exercise you'll need your notebook, watch and about ten minutes. This exercise, by the way, is adapted from one that NASA Administrator Dan Goldin used to stimulate creative thinking among the employees at NASA. The technique of reframing the question (used in the latter part of the exercise) comes from creativity expert Mark Kiefaber.

Imagine you're in the business of making coat hangers, and suddenly the demand for coat hangers has disappeared—people have found some other way to hang their clothes. You're sitting on an enormous surplus of millions of coat hangers. Give yourself two minutes and brainstorm as many ideas as you can think of for other ways to use coat hangers besides hanging clothes. Go.

Did you run out of time or ideas? If you couldn't think of any more ideas after the first few, that's the experience of your mind getting stuck. If it was just one idea after another until the time expired, that's the mind moving freely. Most people experience ideas coming in bursts, punctuated by moments of getting stuck as they change mental gears. Don't feel bad if you got stuck. The trick is in learning to unstick quickly.

Look over your list of ideas and consider what it reveals about the way your mind tackled this question. What patterns do you see in your answers? For example, if you tackled the assignment by asking "Where else have I seen coat hangers in use?" you might have answers like "car door openers" or "marshmallow cookers." If you thought of the question in terms of "What else can be hung on coat hangers besides clothes?" you might have answers like "stocking dryer" or "fish hook." If you thought primarily about the shape of the coat hanger, your answers would suggest other items of similar shape, such as "dip sticks" or "plant stakes." If you thought primarily about the material of coat hangers (my coat hangers were metal), your list would have other uses for that material (in my case "antenna" or "wire").

Answers of these types may be clever and have potential for actually solving the coat hanger problem. From the point of view of creativity, however, they're fairly conventional inasmuch as they preserve many of the qualities and relationships of ordinary coat hangers. To get more ideas that are less conventional—or more ideas, period—we need to change something about how we frame the question. We do this in the next step.

Without thinking about coat hangers specifically, brainstorm around the word *hanging*. Hanging expresses a relationship between two or more objects. What other possible relationships can you think of? Take two minutes and write down as many verbs as come to mind expressing how two objects can relate.

Connecting, extending, sensing, supporting, extracting, cleaning— these are among the alternatives to hanging that made my list. Surely some form of a coat hanger could be used to do any of these things. We explore that next.

Pick what seem to be your most promising relationship verbs and brainstorm how a coat hanger could be used as an object in that action. After you've come up with two ideas for that verb, move on to another one. Try to cover as much of your list as possible in two minutes.

Jumping from verb to verb, as we did in the last part of this exercise, is one way to unstick the mind from its conventional knowledge about coat

> "The creative mind plays with the objects it loves."
>
> —C. G. Jung

hangers. We could take the exercise further and brainstorm around different shapes or materials. We could generate lists of objects and brainstorm how coat hangers could be used with each of them—you get the idea.

Reflect on how your mind worked during each part of this exercise. Were you able to think more freely in one part than in the others? If one of your lists is considerably longer than the others, that's an area where you were able to think more freely. Perhaps you were able to experience intervals when your mind moved freely, as well as points where it got stuck. Having both experiences, you can appreciate the joy of a mind moving freely as opposed to the frustration of a mind stuck. These corollary emotions are no coincidence. Every point of frustration in our life is a place where our mind has stopped. If we want more joy and less frustration in our life, we have to learn how to keep the mind moving freely.

To Train the Mind, We Use the Body

Can we train the mind with the mind? If we want the mind to move freely, can we simply train it intellectually by doing creativity exercises and the like? If we did creativity exercises over and over, without a doubt we would get better at generating lists of ideas. But this kind of training doesn't go deeply into most of the areas that stop our mind in the first place. Fear, greed, desire, ambition, defending our ego—these are the rocks on which we get seriously stuck. Calisthenics for the frontal cortex are not deep enough to unseat brainstem reactions. Moreover, if it's *our* mind training our mind, who trains the trainer? In other words, how can our mind train itself to be sharper or clearer than it is? To try to tackle the question intellectually leads to a dilemma—if not a headache.

> *"If you work on your mind with your mind, how can you avoid an immense confusion?"*
>
> —Sosan

"To train the mind, we need the body," my teacher, Hosokawa Roshi, explains. "If we try to focus the mind with the mind, we just create more disturbance." The approach that does work deeply enough is to connect the mind into the body using our conscious awareness—and then train the body.

From this we derive the two core principles of BodyLearning: (1) connect the mind into the body, using the breath and being fully present for our practice; and (2) train the body, developing the center, and building moment-by-moment awareness through all our senses.

When the mind connects to the body, the body can teach the mind. When the body is connected to life itself through every sense opened for insight, it's much smarter than "we" are (if "we" are identified with our thoughts). It can be a wise teacher indeed. All the better if the body learns from physical activities that, by their very nature, have evolved as a Way to free the mind, guided by teachers who have covered great ground before us. But regardless of what we select as a BodyLearning practice, the principles of developing breath and center and building awareness will move us in the direction of a mind moving freely—and the joy that goes with it.

Two Principles of BodyLearning
or how the mind learns from the body

1. **Connect the mind to body,** using the breath and being fully present for your practice.
2. **Train the body,** developing your center (*hara*) and building awareness through all your senses.

Exercise in Awareness: Focus Means Focus Out

"People have a misconception about focus," Hosokawa Roshi responded to one of our questions about Zen training and what it meant to focus the mind. "They think it means focus *in*, like a laser beam illuminating only one tiny spot. Focus, the way we use it, doesn't mean focus in. Focus means focus *out*. See everything. Take it all in." This exercise gives you a chance to experience the difference. For this exercise, you need your notebook, watch and five to ten minutes.

Sit in a comfortable position. Pick a single item of interest in the room and stare at it for one minute. As soon as you're done, write down your first, top-of-mind answers to the questions below. Your answers don't have to make sense, and it's best if they're not premeditated. Just write the first thing that comes to mind after you've stared at one point for a minute.

1. If your mind were a circle right now, how big would it be across?
2. If your mind were a musical instrument right now, what would it be and what would it sound like?
3. If your mind were something you see in nature—alive or otherwise—what would it be?

I almost feel dizzy after staring at one point awhile. For what it's worth (and certainly our answers don't have to agree), after I've stared at one point for a minute, my mind feels about one inch wide. It's making the rather dull sound of a violin bow scratching back and forth across one string, and it reminds me of a bee buzzing.

Gently massage your eyes and forehead, making sure you rub out any creases that have furrowed your brow.

Raise your hands up to eye level on either side of your head and draw them apart so that your fingers are just barely in range of your peripheral vision. Wiggle your fingers slightly and notice that you can bring your hands even farther back and visually sense their motion, although you don't actually see them (as in the figure opposite). Hold this position for one minute and take in the whole room between your wiggling fingers. Keep listening for and sensing your finger motion the entire time.

When the minute is over, immediately answer the same three questions that you answered before.

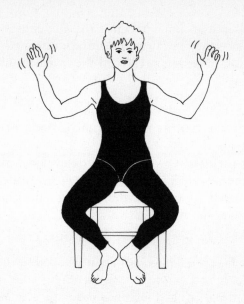

4-1. Looking 180 degrees

Do you notice a difference in your answers? Most people experience a sense of expansiveness when they focus out. Their second sets of answers are larger. The mind is now "six feet across" or "thirty feet across." The sound of the mind is richer: "a big drum" or "a full symphony." And the images from nature are larger: "a big bubble" or "a sunrise."

If you had something of this experience yourself, you now have a basis for understanding that how we use our eyes—or any of our senses, for that matter—is important in shaping our consciousness. Our mind cannot move freely when our senses are stuck on one point. We want to focus our senses broadly as much as possible in our BodyLearning practice. In particular, we want to see 180 degrees. While we won't be able to do this at all times, if we keep coming back to this kind of vision whenever possible, we develop the pattern of focusing our mind out, not in.

I teach the following breathing exercises at the start of most of my Zen and Aikido classes because they effectively, in the span of a few minutes, settle and focus the mind. They are excellent to do on their own or as a prelude to exercise or meditation. Give yourself about fifteen minutes to do the three exercises. A prerecorded tape is not so important for these exercises (as it was for earlier ones), since they're fairly short and illustrated. If you would find a tape useful, however, prerecord the instructions, omitting the figure references.

Breathing Exercise No. 1: Deep Breath, Wide Breath

This exercise is the easiest way I know to develop a sense of breathing down into the center. Alternating between two different breathing patterns, it also lets us practice the expansiveness and 180-degree vision that focuses the mind outward.

Stand with your feet shoulder-width apart with knees relaxed and your weight comfortably settled in your center. Bring your hands together at your center, palms up, and interlace the fingers as in Figure 4-2a.

The first breath pattern begins with a deep, relaxed inhale as you raise your hands up to the level of your solar plexus (see Figure 4-2b).

4-2a. Starting position

4-2b. End of inhale

As inhale turns to exhale, set your *hara* and turn your hands over so the palms face the floor (as in Figure 4-2c). Exhale deeply as you push your hands back down to your center (as if they were a piston pushing your breath down). Press the floor through the balls of your feet, keeping your knees relaxed. At the end of the exhale—which should be two to three times longer than your inhale—your hands should be back at your center, as in Figure 4-2d.

4-2c. Beginning of exhale

4-2d. End of exhale

The second breath pattern begins with a relaxed inhale as the arms—fairly straight and with palms out—lift in a circle until they're overhead. As your arms move upward (Figure 4-2e), keep your shoulders down and relaxed. At the end of the inhale (Figure 4-2f), maintain a sense of your weight at your center, not up in your shoulders.

As inhale turns to exhale, set your *hara*. Separate the fingers and let each arm slowly carve an arc back to your center as you exhale (see Figures 4-2g and 4-2h). Again, press through the balls of your feet, and make the exhale two to three times as long as the inhale. Use your peripheral vision to see 180 degrees, keeping your hands in sight as they carve downward.

Repeat the first breath pattern, followed by the second, alternating on odd and even breaths. Invite your breathing to grow slower and deeper as you continue this pattern for several minutes.

4-2e. Halfway through inhale

4-2f. End of inhale

4-2g. Halfway through exhale

4-2h. End of exhale

Breathing Exercise No. 2: Three-Step Breathing Focusing on the Center

This exercise strengthens the *hara* and further develops the pattern of breathing deeply to and from our center. Normally we think of breathing as a two-step process: inhale and exhale. In this exercise, we add a third step between inhale and exhale where we focus on setting the *hara*.

Step 1: Inhale. Begin by standing with your feet slightly wider than shoulder-width apart, knees slightly flexed. Your arms should be relaxed at your sides, as in Figure 4-3a.

4-3a. Starting standing position   4-3b. Mid-inhale   4-3c. End of inhale

Bending your elbows, bring the backs of your hands together in front of you and raise your arms toward the ceiling as you breathe in through your nose (see Figure 4-3b). Develop the feeling of the breath filling from the bottom (i.e., *hara*), rather than rising up in the chest. You want to maintain your sense of center, even as you stretch upward. At the end of the inhale, you should be stretched upward, even onto your tiptoes (as in Figure 4-3c)

Step 2: Set. Fairly sharply, let out a bit of air through the nose as if you were compressing it into your center. At the same time, set the *hara* and drop your weight down onto your full feet (also see "Tips for Setting the *Hara*," page 80). Drop your shoulders by opening up the arms into a wide V, elbows down, as in Figure 4-3d. The arms pause for a moment at this point.

4-3d. Set position

Step 3: Exhale. Breathing through the nose, exhale slowly and steadily, allowing the pressure to cook in the lower abdomen. The arms continue their downward half-circle (as in Figure 4-3e) until they meet in front of your center at the end of a long exhale (Figure 4-3f). The exhale part of the cycle should be about three times as long as the inhale.

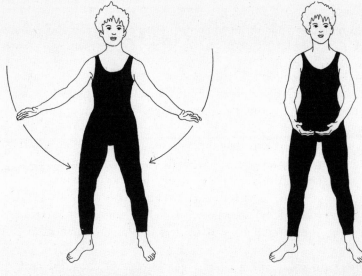

4-3e. Mid-exhale   4-3f. End of exhale

Leading from the fingers, draw the backs of the hands together as you begin the cycle over again. Relax completely to begin another inhale. Repeat the exercise for several minutes. Each breath should be powerful and punctuated by a strong "set" between the inhale and exhale.

Breathing Exercise No. 3: Two-Step Breathing, Focusing Out

In the previous exercise, setting the *hara* between the inhale and exhale was a strong, distinct step in the breath cycle. While this develops the *hara* and leads to very powerful breathing, this cycle is more intense than we use for extended periods of meditation. In this exercise we combine the body motion and expansiveness of the previous exercises with the quieter, two-step breath cycle we use in sitting, walking or lying-down meditation.

Step 1: Inhale. Begin by standing with your feet slightly wider than

Tips for Setting the Hara

Imagine inflating a balloon. If you let go of the balloon, it collapses immediately, sputtering out all its air. If instead, you close the neck of the balloon, it maintains its round shape. The same applies in developing the *hara*. Physically what closes in setting the *hara* is the sphincter muscles. Here are some tips for finding the right position.

Standing or Lying Down: Stand with your heels and back of your head against a wall or lie down on the floor. Flexing your knees, rock your pelvic area forward so that your lower back (i.e., the "small" of your back) flattens ever so slightly against the surface. Back off from the flattening until you feel the larger stomach and hip muscles relax.

Sitting: Push your tailbone (i.e., your lowest vertebra) forward and up toward your navel ever so slightly. If you push too far, the larger muscles of the stomach will tense. Back off until they relax.

Try these postures until you feel a roundness in your *hara* that you can maintain as you exhale. The most common mistake people make in learning to set the *hara* is tensing too much. Think of the balloon and how little pressure is needed at its neck for it to keep its shape. You need no more pressure than that.

shoulder width, knees slightly flexed. Your body should be relaxed and centered with arms at your sides (see Figure 4-4a).

Bring the backs of your hands together and stretch toward the ceiling during a smooth inhale. In contrast to the previous exercise, keep your feet flat on the floor, even at the top of the inhale (see Figures 4-4b and 4-4c).

Step 2: Exhale. Round the corner of your inhale with a quiet, subtle "set" that begins a long, slow exhale. Keep the intent of the "set" as practiced in the previous exercise, but make it quieter and gentler now. Let your hands flow continuously from overhead, back to your center, timed with this outbreath (as in Figures 4-4d and 4-4e). Keep your hands within peripheral view, focusing outward 180 degrees. As before,

4-4a. Starting position

4-4b. Mid-inhale

4-4c. End of inhale

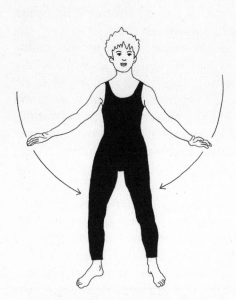

4-4d. Mid-exhale

4-4e. End of exhale

the exhale should be about three times longer than the inhale. Maintain a roundness in your center throughout the exhale.

As exhale turns back into inhale, relax completely, releasing the pressure in the *hara* and allowing air to flow in naturally.

Repeat this exercise for several minutes, allowing each breath to flow more quietly and smoothly than the one before.

By alternately setting and releasing the *hara* with each breath, we develop the pattern of centering our breathing. This pattern stabilizes our emotions and connects our thinking mind to the very core of our power. Not only does this kind of breathing generate a great deal of energy (notice how much warmer your body starts to feel), but it also enables the mind to flow freely by quieting it down and connecting it through the body to the present moment.

This quieting effect comes about partly by lengthening the exhale, which is the part of the breath cycle that relaxes the body. Partly it develops as we change the way we're inhaling so as not to agitate the upper body. By putting slight pressure into the *hara* on the exhale, we create a low-pressure area above it. As soon as we release the *hara* pressure, air naturally flows in. In other words, we learn to breathe in a way in which the inhale simply happens without generating tension or agitation in the chest.

As an example of the way this breathing works, imagine holding a sponge between your hands and submerging it in water. As you apply pressure with your hands, the sponge compresses. As soon as you release the pressure, the sponge immediately expands by itself. You don't have to fill it by stretching it apart or stuffing water into it. The very process of compression sets up the condition for effortless expansion. That's how our breathing develops.

By not having to apply effort to inhale, our body quiets down. By making our exhale longer and slower, our body quiets down further. By connecting our conscious mind into this quieter body, the mind quiets down. And finally, by opening our senses, the quieter mind focuses outward and learns to flow with the present moment.

Through these exercises we can develop this fine quality of breathing and then apply it to other forms of meditation or practice. Not only does this breathing deepen our sitting meditation, it also enriches our sitting at a desk or sitting in a car. We need a different kind of breathing for highly aerobic activities, but this two-step breathing can be applied to any of the meditative (i.e., nonaerobic) activities we might select for our BodyLearning practice.

Sitting Meditation: A Time to Focus

Most of us spend much of our day sitting. Like Jack, who began meditating in his office after recovering from a heart attack, if we redefine even twenty minutes of that time as our time to focus, we will find a remarkable difference in our mind's condition that, in my experience, grows more remarkable over time.

You need a chair for this exercise. Most chairs will do, as long as they're firm enough that you don't feel as if you're going to slide off when you sit near the edge. This exercise is best done right after the two-step breathing exercise, as it applies the same kind of breathing. I suggest that you read through this exercise a couple of times and then put the book down. Give yourself twenty minutes to do the exercise. Start with a few minutes of two-step breathing and then sit on your chair.

Sit near the edge of your chair with the balls of your feet touching the floor and your knees comfortably apart, as in the figure below. Your

hips should be slightly higher than your knees, so that your thighs angle downward.

Straighten your spine as if you were trying to make yourself taller from the very back of your head. Grab your knees with your hands to position the upper body and then release the grip, allowing your hands to rest on your knees. Imagine your spine and your two arms forming a stable pyramid.

Bring your awareness to your breath and—without moving the arms this time—begin the two-step breathing pattern practiced in the previous exercise. Relax completely on the inhale; quietly set; exhale slowly with set *hara*. Give each breath a count from 1 to 10 (if you lose count, just go back to 1. If you get to 10, just go back to 1). Let your eyes take in 180 degrees and similarly open all your senses.

Give yourself this time—twenty minutes—to quiet and focus the mind in the wonder of the present moment.

Without a doubt, what we do for our body through exercise or meditation extends benefits to the mind. But the general relaxation or refreshment that we normally associate with a good workout is just the beginning of the benefits possible through BodyLearning. The special focus that we bring to BodyLearning activities—connecting the mind to the body and then training the body—develops a condition of awareness in which the mind moves freely.

Learning to unstick the mind from its chatter and from the rocks of our various attachments—greed, desire, defending our ego, and so on—we can learn to act with the spontaneity of water. Able to go anywhere, a mind moving freely is able to find a way through every situation. Beyond the limits and reason of contingency planning, a mind moving freely acts with instantaneous appropriateness because it is acting as a part of the present situation—not apart from it.

> "Wisdom is knowing what to do next; virtue is doing it."
> —David Starr Jordan

There are many techniques for approaching this priceless condition of mind. What they have in common is developing breath and center and awareness through our senses. The three meditation forms—

lying down, walking and sitting—together with the three breathing exercises in this chapter form an excellent foundation to practice. Draw from all of them. And draw daily. You may decide when it comes to designing a BodyLearning practice that a more active or aerobic set of activities suits you better. That's fine. But practice the fundamentals once a day for now. The more you can apply this breathing, this centeredness and this awareness to whatever you select as your practice, the more your practice will turn the promise of BodyLearning into your own actual experience.

5

❧

Alignment: Moving Beyond Self-Defeating Patterns

"A house divided against itself cannot stand."
—Gospel of Mark 3:25

The Myth of a Balanced Life

"On the one hand, I really like my job," Bill said. "And I want to do well at it. I'm in line for a promotion, and I know if I put in just that little bit extra, I'm going to get it. I've been moving up in this company since I got here, and that's important to me." Bill was attending a management development program I was helping to teach. As we met privately to review his feedback, he outlined his career dilemma.

"On the other hand, I'm really losing ground at home. I want to spend more time with my wife and kids, but when I come home early [read: anywhere near normal quitting time], I feel guilty about all the things left hanging at work. And it's not like our time together is so great. We usually end up arguing about why I'm not home more. I guess I can't have it all."

How can Bill or any of us "have it all" when all that we want conflicts? On the one hand, we want a successful career. On the other hand, we want a fulfilling personal life. On the one hand, we want to lose weight. On the other hand, we want to eat chocolate. On the one hand, we want to be in loving relationships. On the other hand, we want to be invulnerable. And on and on it goes—all the apparent opposites we try to balance in our life.

Most of us want to do it better. The question I hear most often as I work with individuals in personal and management development programs is "How do I find better balance in my life?" While this seems like a good question to ask—and any number of smart people have tried to answer it—the very question conceals part of the problem. If we picture a balance, such as the sign of Libra or the scales of justice, we see it has two sides. It has two trays in which to weigh two piles of stuff. To balance something, we have to be thinking in pairs, i.e., in dualistic terms, either-or.

A balanced life in this respect is a myth. As soon as there's a need to balance, life has already been fragmented. As soon as there are fragments, circumstances will eventually bring them into collision. Too much work, not enough time at home. Too much materialism, not enough meaning. Whatever the specifics of our balancing acts, the fact is, they divide our energy. So long as we're trying to balance the realm of fragments, we aren't operating from the power of being whole.

A much richer alternative lies beyond the myth of a balanced life. And that is a whole life: one life aligned in body, mind and spirit. BodyLearning conducts us along this path of wondrous alignment. Moreover, by developing breath and center, we connect our mind to the core of our body's power. By strengthening our center, which is physically our center of gravity, we develop a stronger sense of balance. As we become better integrated, this increased balance extends to our physical, emotional and mental well-being. We do not achieve a balanced life by becoming adept at balancing acts. We achieve a balanced life by becoming—ourselves—better balanced and aligned. To do this, we have to begin with the body.

Exercise in Awareness: Balance Begins in the Body

We've so abstracted words like *balance* from their physical meaning that sometimes we forget they have one. In this simple exercise you'll have a chance to be reacquainted with the physical aspect of balance and how this can extend to the rest of your condition. To do this exercise, you need a watch, your notebook and about five minutes.

Stand up. Check the time on your watch. Lift one foot a few inches off the ground and stand on one foot. As soon as you have to catch your balance, note the time and how long you were able to stand on one foot. (Note: if you are able to stand for more than a minute, you can make the exercise more challenging by also raising the heel of the foot on the floor.)

As soon as you catch your balance, immediately draw a squiggle on a blank page of paper depicting what you would guess your brain waves looked like during the exercise. Don't worry that you don't know how to draw brain waves exactly. Just imagine if your brain were a line, what it would look like over the seconds that you did this exercise. Start the line when you first lifted your foot off the floor and end it when you caught your balance. Turn the paper or page in your notebook over, facedown.

You may already know a number of tricks for maintaining your balance on one foot. If so, ask yourself why these tricks work— What effect are they having in the body? Whether you could hold your balance for a long time or only a few seconds, ask yourself where in the body you felt the most weight. In the second part of the exercise, we use the trick of focusing our weight in the center.

Practice this posture once or twice before timing yourself. Standing on one foot, bend your supporting knee so that your center is vertically aligned with the ball of your supporting foot, as in the figure opposite. (If you lifted the heel of your supporting foot on the first part of this exercise, do the same on this part.) Sink your weight into your center as you begin a long, slow exhale. Look 180 degrees and focus on your center as you breathe deeply and slowly.

After you've gotten the feel for this posture, check your watch and time how long you can maintain your balance on one foot.

As soon as you put your foot down, draw a squiggle on the back side of the paper depicting what you would guess your brain waves looked like during this part of the exercise. End the squiggle when you put your foot down.

5-1. Balancing on one foot

If your weight felt physically lower and more centered in the second part of the exercise, almost certainly you were able to maintain your balance for a longer period. Although the exercise was brief, you may also have noticed a settling effect mentally or emotionally when you were able to do the exercise with greater balance. Compare the squiggles on the two sides of the page. When I give this exercise in seminars, people usually draw a more stable line in the second part of the exercise (i.e., fewer bumps and sharp turns). Even the blip where they catch their balance tends to be less spiked in the second drawing. If this was also your experience, you can better appreciate not only that balance is physical, but also that the physical extends to your entire frame of mind.

More Goals Than We Need

Some of us make a New Year's resolution every year. Some of us are always expressing our goals, writing them down or talking them up at every opportunity. Others of us don't ever think about goals.

As my young friend Jason put it, "I don't like to set goals. I like to live each day as it comes." Yet, if we watched Jason live each day as it comes, we'd see he acts with a great deal of intention. When he drives, he's always in a hurry. When he speaks with people, he's always trying to charm them. Valuing his independence, he makes a point of not committing too deeply, whether it's to projects at work or people outside of work.

Whether we declare them vocally or don't like to make them, in the broad sense that I'm using the term, we all have goals. Many of our goals stretch us toward change for the better: a new job, a better marriage, a safer neighborhood. Other intentions reflect conditions that we don't want to change. If our job is already good, we don't want to lose it. Likewise with our good marriage or good neighborhood, or any number of conditions that shape the comfortable patterns of our life.

Our comfort zone has many dimensions. Physically, we are comfortable within a certain range of temperature. Psychologically, we have a comfort zone around how much we like to be with people versus being alone. Some of us are more comfortable with novelty while others are more comfortable with routine. Like the thermostat in our home, we may hardly be aware of these silent sentries until they are triggered by a change in our life. But when we are pushed out of our comfort zone, these quiet comforts become loud and clear goals.

Among the goals we consciously set, the intentions we unknowingly express and the comforts we seek to maintain, we have more goals than we need. Many of them are deeper than conscious, poorly focused and in conflict with reality or with one another. If we are of a mind to set goals, often we are not of one mind-body in the goals we set. A new goal inserted into our accumulated record of experience and desire may be at odds with something else we hold dear.

> *"Though he should conquer a thousand men in the battlefield a thousand times, yet he, indeed, who would conquer himself is the noblest victor."*
> —*Shakyamuni Buddha*

Accumulating over a lifetime of experience, our goals have been shaped by every stage of our development. Cast in our youth, deeper-than-conscious intentions have been stored in our body. Regardless of whether they make sense in our adult life, many of these intentions have made it to this day. In my own case, I was mesmerized by the space program as a child and wanted nothing more than to be an astronaut. Thirty years later, working at NASA and knowing up close and personal what the job entailed, I knew it wasn't right for me. But a part of me could never let go of that goal. Another part of me could never quite embrace it.

Adding to our inconsistencies is our tendency to split ourselves internally. The barriers of tension we throw up to block our feelings (and block the healthy flow of energy within us) also serve to carve us into compartments. In its extremes, we might call this condition schizophrenia or split personality. But well short of the pathological extremes, many normal people describe their lives in very split terms. "I'm torn," some of us say. Or "I have to find a better balance." Or "I'm of two minds on this matter." The result is that we act in ways that are self-defeating because there's not a single self at work.

Even when our goals are not warring with one another, they may be out of touch with reality. The goals produced by a mind off in its own world lack the reality check of genuine awareness through the body. At some gut level, in the wisdom of our body, we know this. And knowing the goals are without basis, we can never summon the full intention of our mind-body working together to achieve them.

Exercise in Awareness: A Goal Going Nowhere Fast

What is your experience with setting and reaching goals? Even if you have been fairly successful, there's a great deal of insight to be gained in examining a goal that hasn't quite come together. You may find that it's being held hostage by conflicting intentions. In this exercise you have a chance to consider such a goal. You'll need your notebook and about twenty minutes.

Take stock for just a moment. Sit in a comfortable position and bring your awareness to your breathing. Follow your breath deeply and slowly into your center for a few cycles, inviting your body to relax.

Think of a goal in your life that you've been unable to reach. This doesn't have to be your "life's goal," but try to pick a goal that you've had for some time or that keeps drawing you back. Write it down in your notebook.

I'll also work through this exercise to give you an example of the thought process. The goal I'll focus on is to get back to playing piano. I've had this goal for a number of years, and I'm no closer to it now than when I set it. Specifically my goal has been to get a baby grand piano in my living room that I could play almost every day.

I'm assuming that you, like me, could write down many good reasons why your goal is important to you. What we'll focus on in this exercise is what seems to be holding us back.

Consider the following as regards your goal: What conditions do you place on reaching this goal? Think of at least five answers to complete the following phrase: "I want this goal to happen as long as I don't have to . . ."

I can think of a number of conditions I place on playing piano. I want this goal to happen as long as I don't have to—

- give up writing, Aikido or Zen
- settle for less than a baby grand
- take piano lessons again (which I don't like)
- become frustrated, knowing I used to play better
- frustrate those around me because I don't play better
- keep moving a piano all over the country.

What are the possible complications or downsides to this goal being realized? What would become more difficult if this goal became true? Think of at least five answers to complete the following sentence: "The complications of reaching this goal would be . . ."

I can already see some of the downsides of my piano playing when I look at my conditions. The complications of reaching this goal would be—

- I'd have to move a piano all over the country.
- I'd have to get a piano to fit in my living space.
- I probably would annoy the people around me with my playing.
- If I didn't take lessons, I probably would become frustrated with not being able to play better.
- I'd have less time for writing, Aikido, Zen and the other things I already enjoy doing.

Now consider the changes you would have to make to come a step closer to this goal. What would you have to give up or do differently? You might want to query different parts of your body (center, heart, head, hands) for what they would have to do to realize the goal. Think of at least five answers to the following sentence: "The changes I'd have to make to reach this goal are . . ."

To continue my piano-playing example, the changes I'd have to make to reach this goal are—

- buy a piano (baby grand, of course)
- somehow get the piano into my second-floor apartment
- make time for playing the piano
- get my fingers back into playing shape
- remember how to read music
- remember old music I used to play
- learn new music

Looking over my conditions, complications and changes, I can see the mixed signals. Little wonder I'm not making rapid progress in reaching this goal. As long as I tie my piano playing to having a baby grand, and as long as I live in places like second-floor apartments, I'm going to be pretty much at a standstill on this goal. As long as I shun the idea of piano lessons, I probably will frustrate myself and others with my clumsy playing.

Do you likewise detect any mixed signals in your own answers? Can you see why progress toward your goal has been slow?

Look over your three lists and pick the condition you're most willing to relax, the complication you're most willing to accept and the change you're most willing to make in the interest of furthering this goal. Mark up to one item on each list; if there's nothing you're willing to accept on a list, don't mark anything.

Now put yourself in the perspective of the wise, objective "You." Mark the item on each list that would have the greatest positive effect on reaching the goal. Which condition (if relaxed), complication (if accepted) or change (if you made it) would give the goal the absolute best chance of being realized? Mark those items on each list.

In my piano case, I would be most willing to relax the condition and accept the complications of moving a piano around the country. In the area of changes, I'm probably most willing to do the exercises that would get my fingers back in shape—although that's hardly the most important step to furthering this goal. Wise, objective me knows that if I were serious about playing piano right now, I'd relax the condition that it has to be a baby grand and buy a piano that would fit into my apartment. I'd accept the complication of taking lessons, and I would make time for playing.

Compare your two sets of marked items. If they're different, this goal is likely to remain at a standstill. If what you're most willing to do is not very relevant to the goal, or conversely, if you're not willing to do something that you feel would be most effective, then—face it—this goal is not of overriding importance to you. You may want it, but not badly enough.

You may discover that your long-held goal is going to be on hold indefinitely. That's certainly my conclusion about piano playing. What I'm most willing to do is basically irrelevant to the goal; what I know is the most direct course of action, I'm not willing to do. That's OK. At least I understand why I'm not making any progress on this goal. If I ever want it badly enough, I know what I have to change to make it happen.

Two Steps Forward, One Step Back

Doubt arises in the space where our goals conflict, either with one another or with reality. Even when we're consciously committed to a new goal, if deep-down inside, some part of us knows the goal is irrelevant, unrealistic or incompatible, a disconnect arises. A bit of doubt. Even if our goal is a worthy one, we will not be able to pursue it effectively, which is to say, wholeheartedly, so long as we harbor this doubt.

Doubt cuts our energy. It robs us of the crucial concentration that comes only with clear intention. Our effective-

> "Doubt picks a man's pocket."
> —Noah benShea

ness is vastly reduced when we send and spend our energy in mixed signals that largely cancel one another. As a simple example of how our effectiveness changes with the clarity of our intention, imagine you're approaching a door to a building you don't want to enter at all. Perhaps you're showing up for a tax audit, thoroughly dreading it. You've gotten caught in traffic, you know you're late, and you're almost hoping the building is closed for the day. Approaching the door, you see other people go through it, but it looks as if they might have had keys. When you try the handle, the door doesn't want to give. "Phew," a part of you breathes a sigh of relief as you start mentally preparing your alibi for having missed your appointment.

Now imagine you're approaching the same door, but this time it's a door you really want to enter. Maybe it's a hospital, and you've learned your child or best friend is injured inside. Approaching the door, you see other people go through it ahead of you. Yet when you try the handle, the door doesn't want to open. You jiggle the handle, pull, push and jiggle some more. There's no way you're going to take a stuck door for an answer. Eventually the jiggling pays off, and the door opens.

Most of us can recognize times when we've played out our own versions of these scenarios. When we're strong and clear in our intent, we'll sail right through minor obstacles. When we're not clear and committed to what we're doing, we'll give up at the first opportunity. If we're something of a muddle inside, with many conflicting goals and intentions, doubt and tentativeness can become a dominant pattern in our life.

Every point of doubt is a point where our mind is stuck. Stalled in the moment, we're not certain what to do. Our uncertainty is expressed through our body and into our actions. We can get in this jam over the simplest matters, such as leaving a grocery store and suddenly remembering we forgot an important item. We ponder, "Do I keep going? Do I go back?" While we sort through these mixed signals, we're doing a tentative two-step in the parking lot. First, we turn back toward the store, thinking, "I have to go back; no, maybe I don't want to go back." Turning toward our car, we decide, "The lines were too long." We take another step and reconsider, "But I really need that stuff." And now we're heading back toward the store. If it's a real borderline case, we might change our minds and our footwork two or three times before settling on a course of action. And this is for the simple stuff. Think how much harder it is to have clear intention when we're trading off the big stuff—strong desires and buried fears—some of which lie far below the surface of consciousness.

Moving beyond the Muddle

To understand how BodyLearning moves us beyond this muddle, it's important to understand how much this muddle has to do with our body. Through many centuries of healing arts in both East and West, and reflected in the poetic and commonsense expressions of many ages, we've recognized that different parts of the body are associated with different elements of our character. The *hara*, or center, is associated with our core power and vitality. As psychotherapist Ron Kurtz and cardiologist Hector Prestera observe—

This belly center may be viewed as having a "mind" of its own. This "mind" includes the consciousness of our basic instinctual drives, our sense of hunger and satiation, our sexual drives, our "gut" awareness of ourselves and of our environment.[1]

The head is associated with intellect and is often the only "mind" we acknowledge. "I think; therefore I am," proclaimed the famous philosopher and mathematician René Descartes, influencing more than 350 years of Western rational thought. Our head has its own ideas about how to satisfy our needs, which are often at odds with our gut-level knowing.

Between the two lies our heart "mind," the seat of our emotions. Feelings of love, generosity and openness are associated with this area, as are feelings of vulnerability and protectiveness. "He's brokenhearted," we say of someone who has suffered a great loss. "She's openhearted," we say of someone who expresses compassion. The heart area can also be a battlefield for warring factions. As Kurtz and Prestera summarize—

> Often, the conflict which arises between the belly mind and the head mind is expressed by the emotions of the heart and chest. Our belly mind might feel sexually fulfilled once weekly, whereas our head mind pushes us to have more. Our chest mind, caught in between, experiences this as an unbalanced desire. Sex, lust, jealousy, envy, gluttony all begin to find expression as deep heartfelt emotions.[2]

How do we move beyond the muddle of warring factions, self-defeating patterns, competing goals and balancing fragments so as to truly bring our life together? The same way we zip up a jacket: connect at the bottom and go from there. By connecting our thinking mind to our *hara*, or center, it is as though we're fitting the base of a zipper together in the light of our awareness. Aligning at our center, we establish the most stable, powerful starting point from which to align our whole being. By developing breath and center—the first essential step of BodyLearning—we tether our intellect to our gut-level knowing and align from there. Of course zipping up a jacket takes a second or two, while aligning our mind, body and spirit can be the work of a lifetime. Yet there's nothing to do but start. To put off starting is simply to prolong the patterns of self-defeat.

The benefits from BodyLearning described in earlier chapters also help tackle the challenge of alignment. By increasing our energy, which we experience as increased flow through our body, we reduce the tension and barriers that otherwise divide us into separate parts wanting separate things. By building awareness through our senses, we give our goals and intentions a regular reality check and opportunity for larger alignment. By learning to keep our mind moving, we more quickly notice when we've stalled on doubt, and we're able to restart with less hesitation.

The more of our body we involve in our practice, the more extensive the opportunities for alignment. We can do activities that actually increase the physical alignment within our body. And by simply involving more of the body in what we choose as a practice, we connect more of ourselves into an integrating activity, more broadly enabling the process of alignment within us.

Breathing Exercise No. 4: Full-Body Breathing

Alignment begins in the body. In this exercise you're invited to take a few relaxing moments to experience this sense of alignment in your own body. Alignment is a quiet process that we notice only with vivid attention; it doesn't blast through our bodies like a powerful drug. But as we build it slowly and deliberately, neither does it wear off like a drug.

In the next two exercises, you have a chance to recruit your body fully into your breathing process. Using your entire body as a bellows, you can change your posture in ways to draw and expel your breath deeply and without effort. If you experience any back pain while doing these exercises, stop. Many people have injuries or tension in their backs that make bending difficult. These exercises should not hurt. If they do, they're not right for you at this time. They are best done while wearing comfortable clothing and without shoes. Read through each exercise a couple of times first, and then allow about five minutes to do each one.

1. Inhale: Begin by standing with your feet shoulder-width apart, hands at your sides (see Figure 5-2a). Letting your arms drop behind you, breathe in through your nose as you make a circular motion with both arms until they meet overhead, palms together, at the end of your inhale (Figures 5-2b and c). Keep your focus on your breath and center: don't rise up into your shoulders even though your hands are overhead.

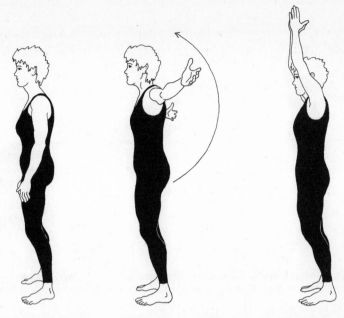

5-2a. Starting position   5-2b. During inhale   5-2c. End of inhale
During the inhale, arms circle back and up.

2. Exhale. Breathing through your nose, begin a long, slow exhale. Let your hands sink slowly down the center of your body (Figure 5-2d). As your hands pass your chest, bend at your waist, bend your knees, and continue to follow your hands down to the floor (Figure 5-2e). Place your palms on the floor in front of you as you get low enough to reach it (Figure 5-2f).

As your knees reach the floor, continue your smooth, long exhale, moving closer to the floor (Figure 5-2g). Keeping your back straight, let your hips and head come down as low as possible (Figure 5-2h). In this fully bowed position, invite the last bit of air to escape.

5-2d. Start of exhale   5-2e. Continuing exhale   5-2f. Mid-exhale
During the exhale, hands drop slowly, reaching and finally touching the floor.

5-2g. Late exhale   5-2h. End of exhale
This exhale ends in a full bow.

3. Secondary Inhale. Breathe in through your nose and slowly raise your body toward the vertical (Figure 5-2i). Using your palms, gently push your weight back onto your feet as you continue to rise and inhale. Keep your knees slightly bent. Return to the starting position (Figure 5-2j).

5-2i. Secondary inhale   5-2j. Return to starting position
On the secondary inhale, return to standing.

4. Secondary Exhale. Set your *hara* and exhale slowly into your center while maintaining the starting position.

Repeat the cycle four more times in full breath awareness, allowing each breath to develop more slowly and deeply than the one before.

As you bow forward in this exercise, you naturally recruit the diaphragm into the breathing process, assisting the lungs from underneath. You don't have to tense or force the diaphragm to work; your very posture enables it. (That's why it's easier for you to catch your breath when you hunch forward, such as in a football huddle.) Eventually the diaphragm will stay involved in your breathing, even when you're not tilted forward. Through this simple exercise, you wake it up to its job.

Breathing Exercise No. 5: Expand and Compress

In this exercise your breathing is coordinated with full-bodied expansion and compression. You expand on the inhale, opening to the whole universe, as it were. On the exhale, you compress the whole universe into your center.

1. Inhale. Stand with your feet shoulder-width apart, hands placed on your *hara* (Figure 5-3a). As you breathe in through your nose, stretch your arms up and away from your center, extending back behind you. Fully open the chest area, as if you were trying to bring your shoulder blades together in your back (Figures 5-3b and c). At the end of the inhale you should feel fully opened up.

5-3a. Starting position   5-3b. End of inhale—front 5-3c. End of inhale—side
Arms open fully during the inhale.

2. Exhale. Set your *hara*, which slightly flattens the lower back and moves your hands into the range of your peripheral vision (Figure 5-3d). Begin exhaling slowly into your center as you compress the volume of air between your hands and body (Figure 5-3e). The feeling you want to develop on the exhale is that of compressing a huge bubble into an ever-more dense, powerful core at your center. As you reach the end of your exhale, you should be back to the starting position (Figure 5-3f).

Repeat this cycle four more times, allowing the body to expand and compress more fully with each breath.

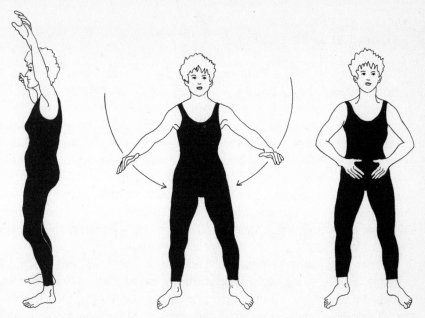

5-3d. Set position—side   5-3e. Mid-exhale   5-3f. End of exhale
Arms compress toward the center during the exhale.

These exercises can be a wonderful refresher in your day. Not only
do they feel good in the present moment, but they're also building
a pattern of alignment, bringing more of "you" into the present
moment, connected and whole. By doing exercises such as these,
your body becomes better balanced over time. You'll notice it becomes easier to reach the
arms back or reach the floor
without having to catch yourself. The very process of becoming more balanced and
graceful is a process of alignment. You eliminate all the
useless tensions and motions that take you off center. When you're
no longer having to catch your balance, you know you've captured
some enduring stability.

> "Man is an animal who is split halfway
> up the middle and walks on the split
> end."
>
> —Ogden Nash

Learning at Different Rates

"I can't believe I'm so stupid," said Paul, during one of his first Aikido classes. "I've known left from right since kindergarten, but I can't seem to get the right foot forward on this throw." Paul wasn't unusually stupid or uncoordinated. Indeed, he learned faster than most. But we can all feel stupid when it comes to learning in our body, at least judging by the standards of our mind. Conceptually we can learn very quickly, but that doesn't mean we've learned deeply or for the long run. Children, for example, don't take long to grasp the concept of riding a bicycle. But they still go through wild swerves and a topple or two before they learn in their bodies how to ride.

Learning involves change. And not all parts of our body can change at the same rate. Our thinking mind, associated with our brain, is wired for change. It hops from one thought to the next in a matter of seconds. Reconfiguring around a new concept may take but a moment. Our body, on the other hand, and the deeper consciousness that goes with it, changes more slowly. It may take weeks to change our resting blood pressure after we've started a fitness program. It may take years to change our posture after we've started moving and using our body in a new way. Probably the most familiar example of excruciatingly slow change in the body happens when we're trying to lose weight. Even though the mind can conceive of losing thirty pounds in a flash, it takes much more than a flash for the body to make that weight loss a reality.

The fact that the body changes more slowly than the thinking mind has both an upside and a downside. On the downside, the differing rates of change make it difficult for the body and mind to stay on the same page of music. Even if they get to the same song eventually, the mind can race ahead. The body's slower timetable means that it poses what often feels like resistance to the latest scheme of the conscious mind.

Absorbing change quickly in some parts of our body-mind and slowly in others results in times when we're uncoordinated, or we know one thing but do another. Paul, for example, clearly knew the concept of left and right, but putting it into physical practice was more difficult. Whenever we try new physical activities, we go through a phase of uncoordinated swerves—trial, error and overcorrection.

Swerving occurs not only in physical activities but in everyday life situations as well. For example, we may know in our heart that a person we're romantically involved with is not good for us, but our head may see an advantage in the relationship, and our body may long for physical contact. The result is likely to be mixed signals, first drawing the person near and then pushing him or her away, thus generally swerving through the relationship.

Because change is always entering our life and our body-mind adjusts at different rates, alignment is an ongoing process. If we develop a conscious connection of body and mind through which alignment can proceed, we will swerve less and stabilize sooner. It is not the case, however, that we can align ourselves once and for all and forget about it. As long as we have a body, we need to keep the channel open by which body and mind come together.

The upside of this state of affairs is that BodyLearning, specifically body memory, is more enduring. When we learn in the body, we learn deeply and for the long run. As with riding a bicycle—we don't forget easily. Moreover, sometimes the latest scheme of the conscious mind is not right for us. At such times the thinking mind gains essential balance through access to the deeper, more enduring wisdom of the body.

Connecting mind to body through our breath, we open a channel by which the patient process of alignment can proceed. Sometimes alignment means changing the body to agree with the mind. Learning to ride a bicycle, for example, our body aligns with what our mind has already grasped. Sometimes alignment means stabilizing the mind to agree with the body. For example, we may become less capricious in our career as our mind aligns with our body's sense of a gut-level, heartfelt calling. In either direction, alignment creates a condition of greater balance and harmony within.

Aligned Walking Meditation

In this exercise you'll have a chance to experience walking meditation with greater focus on alignment, slowing down a bit and paying attention to details. This exercise is useful not only as a practice but also as a model for the kind of attention that aligns more of your body in the process of practice. Even if you don't expect to make walking meditation your practice in the long run, by doing this exercise you can gain important insights into how other aerobic, artistic or everyday activities can be done in such a way as to develop alignment.

In aligned walking meditation you combine several of the exercises you've done in place and put them into motion. This exercise is adapted from a walk used in the ancient martial art of *Hojo*.[3] You set the *hara*, allowing your walk to move forward evenly from your center. You also pay attention to your breathing, blending your steps with a relaxed inhale and smooth, set exhale. As your concentration and balance develop, your step will become quieter, lighter and yet more stable. Practicing in this way, you can learn to walk with a sense of oneness with the earth itself.

Begin this exercise where you left off with "regular" walking meditation (p. 55). Take a few minutes to reacquaint your body with the basics of walking meditation.

1. Connect your breathing with your walking. Straighten your spine and drop your shoulders.
2. Set your *hara* on the exhale, maintaining a sense of roundness at your center, which is also the center of your walking motion. Relax on the inhale. Invite your exhale to lengthen two to three times longer than your inhale.
3. Open your senses; keep your eyes level and focused 180 degrees.

After you've gotten the feel again for walking meditation, slow down a bit and pay attention to these details:

1. Aligning Your Feet. To walk in a straight line forward, your feet need to point straight forward. Your center will not be able to move straight if your footstep is toe in or toe out. (You can experience this for yourself. If you walk with your toes out like a duck, you'll waddle like a duck; that is, your center will waver from side to side.) Point your feet straight in the direction you want to walk and step evenly from heel to toe. On each step feel your weight roll straight from the back of the foot to the front.

5-4a. Aligning the center in walking meditation

5-4b. Right way—
aligning the head

5-4c. Wrong way—
head too far forward

2. Aligning Your Center. Place your hands on your lower abdomen (i.e., on your *hara*, as in Figure 5-4a). Feel with your hands whether your center is holding its shape (i.e., roundness) during each exhale. If you imagine a light emitted from your navel, its beam should never waver. Through the whole step-breath cycle, it should be focused ex-actly forward—never off to the left or right, never moving up or down. As you continue to walk, align your center on steady forward motion.

After you've gotten the feel for moving smoothly from your center, you may want to take your hands off your center and let them move freely. If you feel yourself wavering, bring your hands back to your center until you stabilize.

3. Aligning Your Head. Position your head so that it's squarely over your spine (Figure 5-4b), rather than hung out in front of your body (Figure 5-4c). Depending on how rounded your posture has become through your habits, it may not be possible to align your head in the first attempt. But know what you're aiming for and keep moving the head closer to this aligned position. Only when the weight of the head is supported by the spine can the muscles of the neck and shoulders relax.

From years of sitting round backed in chairs and staring forward, many of us have distorted our posture to where our head hangs far in front of our body. In the extremes, our whole spine bends forward and we hobble at a fraction of our full height. Don't be discouraged if you find it difficult to walk straight and maintain your balance the first time you try it. Pick one thing to align and work on it until you experience some progress, and then go on to another area. Continue making subtle adjustments in your prac-tice—stretching what's tight, straightening what's off—and over time your body will align. Remember, some of what you're working to change will only change slowly. Have patience and give it time. Be clear on your aim, and eventually you'll get there.

As you perfect your prac-tice of a well-aligned walk, you perfect the posture that anchors your centered breath-ing, and you perfect the bal-ance that is your posture in motion. The last step is pruning what's not needed.

> *"When walking, just walk.*
> *When sitting, just sit.*
> *Above all, don't wobble."*
> —*Ummon*

4. Get Rid of the Extra. Simplify your walk. Move straight from your center, allowing your weight to roll straight forward from the back to the front of each step. Let your breath awareness survey the inner workings of your walk for extra tension that doesn't need to be there. You might ask, "Which muscles are working that don't need to be working?" And relax those. You might ask, "What impression am I trying to convey through my walk?" And let go of that impression. Just be. Be aware. Be present. You don't need to be anything else.

To some extent, we've all developed a stylized walk: a wiggle, a shuffle, extra gestures that express the habits stored in our posture and the quirks in our personality. Aligned walking meditation invites us to take the quirks out of our walk and simplify it to the straightforward essentials: nothing more, nothing less. Moving straight from our center, we drop all the extra gestures and tensions that spend our energy uselessly. Through this simple practice we align what's essential to our intent (which in this case is to walk straight forward) and drop the rest.

Consider ways you could bring this same principle of alignment to other things you do: driving the car, chopping onions, shopping for groceries, washing the floor. By aligning your entire mind and body on exactly what each situation requires and dropping the rest of the useless gestures and reactions, you move clearly and at full strength.

---

4 Steps to Alignment
in Walking Meditation and Other Activities

1. **Align your feet.** If you want to move forward, point them forward.
2. **Align your center.** Move straight from the center, not wavering up and down or side to side.
3. **Align your head.** Move the weight of your head squarely over your spine.
4. **Get rid of the extra.** Let go of the unnecessary gestures and reactions.

Pulling It All Together

One of the reasons I think superb athletes capture our admiration is that they model for all of us the ability to singlemindedly, wholeheartedly achieve a goal of peak excellence. Yet even among professional and Olympic-caliber athletes, some are clearly more successful at achieving their goals than others. Some athletes, for example, come to the Olympics predicted to be the best; they perform at their peak and leave with gold. Others come in top rated but clutch in the crucial performance. Some enter the Olympics as underdogs and surprise the world, performing beyond their normal levels.

One would guess all Olympic athletes arrive at the games consciously committed to performing at their best. But does the body unfold fearlessly at just the right instant on the ski jump? Does the heel catch the bar on the pole vault? The conscious mind may know the goal, but is every ounce of the body driven by this intention more than by anything else? Shreds of doubt, unhealed injuries, subtle misgivings that repel the responsibility of success, distractions of the ego wondering on what cereal box the photo will appear, a body that is tired of all this training and ready to move on to something else—any number of deeper difficulties can interfere with the conscious goal to win. When we see people pull it all together and perform flawlessly, we share in their triumph. We know that, beyond the particulars of their sports, what they've mastered is themselves.

How well we're aligned with what we do shapes how well we do it. Conversely, when we get steady feedback on how well we're doing a physical practice and keep adjusting to do it better, it helps us become better aligned.

In Aikido, for example, if we're not aligned when we do a throw, it comes out clumsy and forced. When we don't know what we're doing, we tend to tense everything and throw our energy around like seed in the spring. The process of training works to refine our energy and motion to what's essential for each technique. No more. No less. Over and over we practice aligning our mind and body, aligning our feet, hips, eyes and fingertips exactly on the technique at hand. The effectiveness of the throw tells us instantly if we're on target.

The fact that alignment is measured in our effectiveness is true not only for sports and other physical activities but also for the many nonphysical goals and intentions we carry through our day. Whether we want to become more successful at work or develop a more enriching home life, lose weight or become a safer driver, our goals can only be realized through our actions. And our actions come through our body. Our condition of alignment will be revealed in the clarity of our actions—or in the muddle we make when we're not clear.

Regardless of our goal, alignment will help us get there. Our difficult goals are achieved only when we're aligned from brain to bone. A practice in alignment—twemty minutes a day—will begin to zip together our body-mind into a more unified whole. Moreover, the alignment we develop through BodyLearning doesn't stay confined to the quarters of our original practice. It begins to spread to all corners of our life. The more of our body we engage in our practice, and the more wholehearted our intent, the more channels for alignment we open within us.

In this chapter we've added tools for practice that emphasize bringing more of the body-mind together. You might take a few minutes to consider where these activities could be added to your own twenty minutes of practice. For example, if you're currently doing walking meditation a few days a week, you might designate one of those days to do aligned walking meditation. If you've been doing breathing exercises first thing in the morning, you might add the two new breathing exercises to your routine.

Practice these exercises daily, and you'll discern ways of bringing greater alignment to other things you do. The very best opportunities for alignment come through activities that—

- involve your total body;
- give you feedback on your progress; and
- you love doing!—and therefore do wholeheartedly.

As we'll see in the next step of BodyLearning—designing a practice—these are among the criteria that distinguish an activity as a way for BodyLearning. Regardless of the specific activities you choose for your practice, in this first step of BodyLearning, you've experienced the basic ways to practice: developing breath and center, aligning your motion with your breath, moving from your center, fully opening your senses and being vividly aware in the present moment. This is how you make balance something you have rather than a juggling act that you attempt to do. This is how you take your piecemeal self and make it whole.

STEP 2

BUILDING
A PRACTICE

6

❦

Inner Strength: Building Bedrock Confidence

"The body is the place for transformation."
—Mirka Knaster

Affirmations Are Not Enough

"Do you want to go through life on a bicycle or a tank?" Zen master Tanouye Rotaishi asked in a lecture years ago. I flashed back to the previous winter when I had been crossing Michigan's Mackinac Bridge in heavy side winds, driving my tiny Volkswagen, which was being almost equally driven by the winds. A Volkswagen is more stable than a bicycle—less than a tank—but it was still a white-knuckle crossing. In a similar sense I was somewhere between a bicycle and a tank in terms of my stability in daily life. In low winds, I was fine. But I thought back to a number of situations that had cracked my confidence and filled me with fear. As I listened to Tanouye Rotaishi, his powerful presence overfilling the room, he was the very embodiment of strength and fearlessness. He was not a bicycle. Or a Volkswagen. He gave us his bottom line: "Me, I'll take the tank."

Many of us try to build more inner strength and confidence so that we can live our lives with greater effectiveness and less fear. Any number of smart people have hit the bookstores or lecture circuits with good advice on ways to become more confident and successful. Following in the tradition of such greats as Dale Carnegie and Napoleon Hill, they maintain that the key to success is a positive mental attitude, and the way to a positive mental attitude is to keep telling ourselves positive things over and over. We call these affirmations. And we apply them liberally.

"I'm great," Jan was taught to say three times a day in her sales training program; "I can do anything." "I am Woman," Helen Reddy sang to us in the '70s; "I am invincible." We buy books with affirmations in every margin and calendars with affirmations for every day. Most of us started young in the practice of affirmations, being given positive examples in our early childhood: "I think I can, I think I can . . ." said the Little Engine That Could.

Affirmations and a positive mental attitude are not bad things. But if we're using them as something of a slick ad campaign that we plaster over an otherwise fractured self, they simply won't hold up. If we believe in our gut that we cannot do something, trying to convince ourselves at the surface that "I think I can, I think I can" mostly leads to denial and disillusionment. We can liken it to riding a bicycle in stiff winds: if the weight of our conviction is centered high in our heads, we're easily bowled over. A false positive mental attitude, which is nothing more than a smiley-face facade, is hardly worth the effort it takes to maintain it.

On the other hand, the bedrock confidence of a genuinely positive mental attitude does help recruit and align the entire body, mind and spirit through our actions. Bedrock confidence is built on the genuine power we experience by connecting to the core of our being. A truly positive mental attitude is one that grows out of a positive, connected condition within. More like a tank, if the weight of our conviction comes right from our core, we're more stable and harder to throw off.

> "The highest kind of skill is shown in the long run by a 'letting it happen' . . . For this power to take effect there must be an anchorage in hara where there is no ego."
> —Karlfried Graf Dürckheim

Inner strength and bedrock confidence are grounded in the body. Hence, they are learned through the body. Through a BodyLearning practice in which you connect your conscious mind to your center, your mental attitude becomes a true expression of what's true for yourself. Unstoppable strength and unshakable confidence develop from bottom up: from your center, through your heart, informing your intellect.

To develop this essential connection of mind and center, we need a practice. The best kind of practice for developing this steady connection is one in which we consciously focus our mind into our center for a steady period of time. This is easier to do in meditative activities than in aerobic activities, as the latter tend to draw our attention into the mechanics of what we're doing. Among the meditative activities, this steady connection is easier to foster in sitting than in any other position. In walking meditation, with all the nerves firing and muscles moving to enable our walking, the body doesn't reach the same point of quiet as it does in sitting. In lying-down meditation, the body can get too quiet, meaning it's easy to drift off into sleep. Sitting meditation is an optimal middle ground in which it's possible to maintain complete concentration and complete relaxation at the same time. For developing inner strength and bedrock confidence, there's nothing like it.

Sitting Meditation: *Zazen*

Sitting meditation, called *Zazen,* is the heart of Zen training. The form presented here comes from the Rinzai Zen tradition.[1] Appendix A provides a more detailed description of *Zazen* for later reference and refinement of your practice.

A quiet room is best for getting started in sitting. Eventually you'll be able to sit anywhere and maintain your concentration. But initially, sounds will be distracting, so try to find a place that minimizes them. It's best not to accept routine interruptions, for if you accept them, they will surely come. If you live with other people, it is best to tell them ahead of time that this time is different. It is yours with *no* interruptions. For these twenty minutes you don't need to be answering the phone or resolving minor family disputes.

Zazen is traditionally done sitting on one or more small cushions (called *Zafu*), which themselves rest on a large flat cushion, approximately thirty inches square (called a *Zabutan*). Sitting on cushions is generally more stable and grounded than is sitting in a chair, and it allows more energy to build in our center. A folded blanket or throw rug works fine for the base cushion. For the smaller cushions, it's best if you try a number of options to see which works best for you. My preference is a cushion stuffed with buckwheat hulls, which are becoming so popular, you can now find them in discount stores. Alternatively, you can use one or two firm pillows set into a wedge so that the back is higher than the front.

Many people express interest in Zen. They've read about it. They've heard about it. They sense its pure tone and clarity. But for all their reading about Zen, few people actually experience its benefits, which is too bad. It's like reading menu after menu and never tasting the food. Zen can nourish us only when we taste it. Rather than settle for the menu, please cook this meal for yourself. Allow twenty minutes.

1. Position of cushions and legs. Your base cushion, which may be a folded blanket or rug, should be large enough to support the base of your spine and both knees. Depending on your flexibility, you'll need more or less height in the small cushions to be able to sit in a stable posture. Ideally, you want enough cushion height so that your hip joints are slightly higher than your knees (similar to the way you sat in a chair earlier). To find the best height and placement of cushions do the following four steps—

i) Place your small cushions on the base cushion and sit on them. Move one leg completely out of the way and fold the other into a cross-legged position, as in Figure 6-1a.

ii) Adjust the cushions until the knee of the folded leg comes down toward the ground. If the knee is up in the air, try sitting on a slightly higher cushion. If a higher cushion doesn't help, just pick a height that feels most stable. Make sure the cushions are in a wedge shape, higher in back than in front.

iii) Fold the second leg into cross-legged position (Figure 6-1b). Better yet, if you can, place the foot of your second leg on the thigh of the first for half-lotus position (Figure 6-1c).

iv) If either of your knees is off the floor, fill the gap with a secondary cushion or small towel so that the knees are in contact with something, as in Figure 6-1d.

The most stable sitting position is full lotus, shown in Figure 6-1e. Ideally, you want to work toward this position over time.

6-1a. Move one leg out of the way to adjust cushion height.

6-1b. Sitting cross-legged   6-1c. Sitting half-lotus   6-1d. Extra support under knee

6-1e. Sitting full lotus

Don't be discouraged if your legs are initially stiff. My teacher, Hosokawa Roshi, shares the story that when he first started sitting, his stiff knees were so far off the ground he put weights on them to bring them down. He doesn't recommend this approach, to be sure. But if you watched him sit now, you'd think his legs were made of rubber. However slowly it changes, the body is very malleable. If you sit, your legs will eventually adjust to sitting. However, if sitting on cushions is so uncomfortable you won't do it, then use a chair for sitting meditation, as described on page 83.

2. Position of the Spine. Your spine should be straight but not stiff. Most people have a tendency to round the upper back and hunch the shoulders forward. To counteract this, work to keep the upper back as flat as possible and the shoulders rolled down and back as far as possible. To find the right position, try touching your shoulder blades together behind your back, and then relax, keeping the upper back flat. Open up the chest area, but don't thrust it forward. Allow the chest to be as relaxed as possible. Your tailbone should be pushed ever so slightly forward, so that the *hara* can be set on each exhale. Keep your chin tucked and pull your head back as far as possible, allowing its weight to be supported by the spine rather than by neck muscles. If you get pain in your neck when you sit, your head is dropping too far forward.

Imagine the triangle formed by the base of your spine and your two knees. Moving forward from the hip joint (not bending any vertebrae in the back), place your hands on your knees and pull slightly; this move should position your upper body in the center of the triangle. Return your hands to your center. The correct position for sitting is shown in Figure 6-1f opposite. A couple of common mistakes, hunching too far forward (Figure 6-1g) or leaning too far back (Figure 6-1h) are shown in contrast.

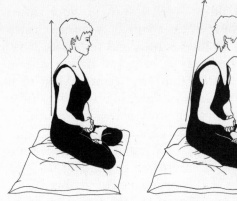

6-1f. Correct posture 6-1g. Incorrect posture: 6-1h. Incorrect posture:
Hunched too far forward Leaning too far back

3. Position of Hands. Join your arms in a circle, encircling the first knuckle of your left thumb (not the whole thumb) into the palm of your right hand (as in Figures 6-1i and 6-1j).

6-1i. Right hand takes knuckle of 6-1j. Final position of hands
left thumb

Rotate your joined hands so that the blades of the hands (i.e., edges alongside the little fingers) press slightly into your lower abdomen. This rotation rolls the shoulders down and back, further opening up the chest area. This hand position also allows you to keep checking that your *hara* is setting properly on each exhale.

4. Position of Eyes and Face. Relax your face muscles. Rest your tongue on the roof of your mouth and gently close your teeth. Your eyes should initially look straight ahead and take in 180 degrees. Dropping the pupils only (not your neck and head), bounce this same 180-degree vision off the floor several feet in front of you. Completely open up your hearing. The feeling you want to develop is to "See through your ears; hear through your eyes."

This is the posture you maintain or work toward in your sitting. Your posture is to your breathing as the shape of a musical instrument is to its tone. If a violin or flute is bent and distorted, it will not play well. Likewise, if your body is bent and distorted, your breathing cannot properly resonate from your center. Most of us recognize the proper shape for a violin or flute, but we're less aware of what proper shape looks like in our own body.

> "The posture itself is satori."
> —Taisen Deshimaru

What it looks like is this posture. Depending on your starting point, getting to this posture may take some time. If you cannot straighten your spine initially, work toward that. If you cannot tuck your chin to position the weight of your head over your spine, work toward that. If your knees are too high to allow your back to straighten, work toward lowering them. From wherever you start, you will find some benefits. At the same time you are building and reinforcing a new pattern of posture and hence a new pattern of breathing, which will yield greater benefits downstream.

5. Breathing. Breathe through the nose, using the same pattern as practiced earlier: relax on the inhale, set and maintain the roundness of the *hara* through the exhale. Bring your awareness to your breath and develop this pattern. Relax on the inbreath. Set on the outbreath. The exhale should be two to three times longer than the inhale. Be aware of each breath leaving your body as a steady, quiet stream. As you relax the set feeling in your *hara* at the end of the exhale, air should naturally flow in, forming the inhale.

Give each breath a silent, slow and steady count from 1 to 10: in 1, out 1, in 2, out 2 and so on up to 10. Let your mental count stretch out as long as the breath itself: o-o-o-o-o-n-n-n-e. If you lose the count, return to 1 and start over. Once you get to 10, return to 1 and start over.

Maintain awareness of your breath through your count. Be aware of your thoughts, feelings and impulses as they arise, neither fighting with them nor

> *"We should count our breaths, 'One, two . . .' with all our might, as if trying to penetrate the earth."*
> —Omori Sogen Rotaishi

riding away with them. Maintain the body's stillness during sitting meditation. Through this stillness, the mind will also quiet down. When the impulse to fidget arises, watch it as you would any other thought, but don't give in to it. Otherwise, such impulses will never quiet down and neither will your body-mind.

Following your breath to and from your center, and opening your senses to the present moment, sit quietly for twenty minutes.

6. When You're Done Sitting. It's not uncommon for a leg to fall asleep, even during a short sit. Neither is it a problem, so long as you stand up carefully, pushing your weight evenly onto your feet and making sure both ankles are straight. If a leg has fallen asleep, you can wake it up more quickly by pushing your awareness into your sleeping toes.

Our awareness during sitting meditation is critical. Some people have a misconception that *Zazen* is a time to shut off or escape to oblivion. Nothing could be further from the truth. Our time of sitting is a time to penetrate the present moment with our thrown-wide-open awareness. It is a time to connect our mind into our center and build the wholeness that underlies inner strength and unshakable confidence.

Some of us will find this sitting to be the most peaceful and pleasant twenty minutes we enjoy during the day. Most of us, however, will experience some initial discomfort. It's not uncommon, for example, for our legs to hurt or fall asleep, even during a brief sit. The first time my sister sat with me, she was certain her right leg had snapped off of her body within twenty minutes. An unlikely circumstance, to be sure. But it's not at all unusual for us to feel this way. When we have lost feeling in one or both legs, it's important that we push our awareness into our legs before we put weight on them. As we stand up, we need to make sure our ankles are straight.

Most of the discomfort from sitting comes from a deeper source. We do well to consider it for the insights it contains.

Steps in Sitting Meditation

1. **Position cushions** in a wedge so that knees are as low as possible; sit cross-legged, half- or full lotus.
2. **Straighten the spine and tuck the chin;** locate the upper body in the center of the triangle formed by the knees and the base of the spine.
3. **Position the hands** with the blades pressed slightly into your center.
4. **Look 180 degrees,** see through the ears and hear through the eyes.
5. **Breathe to and from your center,** setting and maintaining the *hara* on every exhale, relaxing on the inhale.

What Happens When We Sit?

Some people sit quietly, follow their breath, and find the time restful and invigorating. Some people sit semi-quietly on the outside while a war of wills is raging on the inside. Difficult thoughts arise, the legs feel cramped or have lost feeling altogether, and everything is tense. No wonder people in the second group would rather read about Zen than do it. What fun is this?

The truth is, most people start out in the second group. Don't be the least bit discouraged if you're one of them. We can find the will to persevere if we can see the resistance for what it is: self-defeating patterns that we are always carrying inside, whose face we are at last invited to see. Whenever we try new things, we almost always start out trying too hard, tensing too much and exerting all the wrong muscles. The feedback we get from our practice tells us where things aren't working. This is the very guidance we need to learn how to relax and align our body-mind in the moment.

In sitting, we bring up further resistance because we're also training our thinking mind to think differently: to follow our breath and be present in the present moment, rather than running off with its own story line. Initially, most thinking minds rebel at this notion—they love their own drama. They delight in their own story lines. In their rebellion, they may throw up lots of uncomfortable thoughts or images. One woman I know said that the first time she sat, she saw the devil. That was all it took to get her to stop. How clever of the ego, I thought, to conjure a frightening image that would end the sitting and allow its game to continue.

Other people see God when they meditate and think they must have arrived at enlightenment (from which they conclude they can stop sitting—another clever trick). It's not uncommon for people to experience tricks of the eye, hallucinations or feel transported out of their body. These are examples of what the Japanese call *makyo*: delusions. These thoughts and feelings arise naturally in the way we're put together; there's nothing particularly wrong with them. It's just that we shouldn't take them seriously. All we have to do is acknowledge that they happen and let them go. If we ever use them as an excuse for not sitting, we can bet our bottom dollar that a threatened ego was behind them.

Even if we're not steeped in delusions when we sit, we may be steeped in an internal battle. The nose itches. The leg hurts. The mind's asking, "Why are we doing this?" Meanwhile it ticks off a shopping list of things we should be doing instead of sitting. On and on it goes. Uncomfortable as it is, this battle itself is instructive. We might ask these questions: Who is this who wants to sit quietly? Who is this who wants to do anything but sit quietly? And why aren't we together? If we split our intention here, we split it elsewhere.

Sitting *Zazen* does not create our problems; it simply reveals them. It does not make matters worse; it simply shows us how bad things are in terms of our inner brokenness and pain. Put another way, once our sitting is strong and centered, our life is strong and centered. Once we quit fighting ourselves on the cushion, we quit defeating ourselves in other aspects of our life.

> "We should sit hard and sit a great deal."
> —Omori Sogen Rotaishi

Entering Zen is something like wading into an expansive body of water with sharp rocks and stones along the shore. When we first get started, we encounter all these sharp edges that can very well deter us. But if we have the will to persevere past the shoreline, we get past the rocks to the soft sand of deep relaxation. By learning to bring ourselves together in the stillness of sitting, we learn to bring ourselves together in action.

Nevertheless, sitting is not for everyone. If you try it, hate it, and know that you won't stick with it, do something else. Some people simply cannot sit still. That's fine; they should do something active instead. But if you can sit still, you will see things in the stillness that you have missed for years in the flurry. Ironically, sitting still can be the most powerful propulsion in our lives. Tanouye Rotaishi once said in a lecture, "Sit twenty minutes a day and it will change your life." Large as that may sound, I have never known that not to be the case.

The Missing Ingredient

Hal could be the poster child for personal development seminars. He's attended virtually every one that has come to the large city in which he and I live. He travels around the country, attending weekend seminars and week-long retreats in beautiful places that promise beautiful changes in one's life. I was listening to Hal not long ago recount the laundry list of seminars he's managed to pack into the past ten years of his life. He's covered the waterfront from thinking himself healthy to becoming more assertive and finding the warrior within. But Hal is still Hal. If the truth be known, he doesn't do these things better now than he used to.

In the afterglow of each seminar, Hal gets wonderfully excited about the new possibilities in his life. He discovers new habits for effectiveness. He learns how to increase his wealth, extend his influence, and balance his polarity. For about one day he's ready to become whatever he's just been taught.

But then Hal goes back home. And on Monday he goes back to work. The new formula doesn't fit into the old patterns of his life. Day by day his good intentions slip away. The euphoric sense of possibility fades, and soon it's nothing more than a fond memory. The only way Hal knows to get the good feeling back is to find another seminar. Yet for all his personal development seminars, he is not developing.

It's not the fault of the seminars. No matter how wise the speaker or well planned the program, nobody can change our life but us. And there's no changing the facts of our biochemistry. All thoughts and emotions have a natural lifetime. No matter how strong they are at the start, they don't last forever. No matter how powerful the seminar, and how revved up we feel coming out of it, if we do not anchor our motivated feelings through the physical commitment to change, we will eventually lose our motivation. If we do not make space in our life for a new activity—a new physical pattern—to embody what we've learned, the learning will not go very deep. What doesn't change us physically doesn't change us deeply. If our good intention simply remains a thought, it will fade with the chemistry that created it.

The difficulty of this fade is recognized in the personal development business, and it is often answered with longer, more intense learning experiences, refresher seminars, or sustained programs. Most religious traditions, in sending out their message on how to be a better person, discovered long ago that we needed a booster shot at least once a week. Intense, repeated exposure to the message does help with integrating it into our system of beliefs.

But the new message—another belief, shaping another set of intentions in our conflicted maze of intentions—may still not be strong enough to transform us. It may just be another case where we can "talk the talk" but can't "walk the walk." Even though we seem to know the right answer, we can lack the will to act on it. It's one step to learn a message well enough to repeat the words. It's a thousand more steps to experience fully its meaning in our life. For us to experience fully the truth of a message, it needs to change us physically.

The missing ingredient in most of our efforts to change or grow is the physical vehicle: a physical practice that reinforces the change, integrating the change into us. Making the physical commitment to change is a visible sign of how unified we are in our intention to change. In Hal's case, the fact that no new patterns turn up in his life as a result of his seminars is a good indication that while part of him intends to change, another part intends not to change. And on the whole, Hal is getting exactly what he wants from his search: a temporary lift and the need to keep searching.

In BodyLearning, we feast on the ingredient missing in so many other approaches. Whatever we want to learn, whatever change we want to integrate into our life, the body can help. And a well-designed physical practice is the path to take us there.

A well-designed practice begins with the basics: developing breath and center, building awareness and being in the present moment. As we'll see in the next chapter, a well-rounded practice combines meditative and aerobic activities. While we'll consider a wider range of such activities later, in truth there's no better meditative practice than one that uses the tools we've learned already, namely the breathing exercises and meditation. Next we look at how to combine these tools into a powerful program that builds the basics.

Designing a Program in the Basics

Basic to BodyLearning is developing breath and center. Breath is immediate; it is here and now. Using our breath to connect our conscious mind to our center, we realize both the near-term benefits of greater energy and calm, as well as the long-term benefits of greater wisdom and wholeness.

Our posture is our body's memory of how it has breathed up till now. Like the shape of a musical instrument, our body's condition determines how breath flows through us and the tone that results. A centered posture, which is where the weight is carried low in *hara*, rather than high up in the chest, shoulders, or head, makes us more stable, more tanklike and more confident. This stable posture is the foundation for everything else we do. It allows us to anchor the pattern of good breathing in our body, where we'll remember it for the long run. Once this added stability and confidence becomes part of who we are, what we do reflects this same stability and confidence—whether it's driving the car, teaching the children or negotiating with colleagues.

Breathing exercises and meditation are the most straightforward way to develop breath and center. Even if you decide on a more aerobic practice eventually, the foundation you build through these meditative programs will improve the more active elements of your practice. After all, everything you do requires motion and breathing. Once you learn to move from your center, your motions have more balance and power. Once you change how you breathe, you've changed everything.

Forms of Meditation for BodyLearning Practice

1. **Lying-Down Meditation (pp. 34–37):** Lying on the floor with your feet against a wall, place your right hand on your *hara* and your left hand on your chest. Bring your awareness to your breath and transfer the breath to the *hara*. Practice setting the *hara* with each exhale, pressing slightly against the wall through the balls of your feet. Relax completely on the inhale.

2. **Walking Meditation (pp. 56–58; 106–109):** Walk a little more slowly than normal, with your back straight, head erect, and eyes looking 180 degrees. Pay attention to your body's alignment. Move straight from your center, not wavering from side to side. Keep your feet straight and roll your weight evenly from heel to toe. Set your *hara* on each exhale; relax on each inhale.

3. **Sitting Meditation (pp. 83–84; 118–124):** Sitting on a chair or, better yet, a wedge of cushion(s), flatten your upper back and drop your shoulders. Join your hands in a circle at your center. Keep your chin tucked and look 180 degrees, bouncing your vision off the floor several feet in front of you. Set and maintain your *hara* on each exhale; relax on the inhale.

I recommend twenty minutes a day for working the body basics. The following programs outline different ways to combine the breathing exercises and meditation forms (summarized in the boxes) depending on your preferences, your condition and what you're working on. I'd suggest starting with one of these programs and then blending in more dynamic, aerobic activities later on.

The programs are planned on a weekly schedule, allowing twenty minutes of practice per day and one day off per week. If your days get crowded, it is better to cut down the time of practice than to skip days altogether. These exercises take root when they become habit-forming. As you blend other activities into your practice, you can substitute them for these exercises several days a week. Better yet, make a habit of doing these each morning (or evening), and find another time during the day for another element of your practice.

Breathing Exercises for BodyLearning Practice

1. **Deep Breath, Wide Breath (pp. 74–76):** Stand with feet shoulder-width apart, hands at center with the fingers interlaced. On the first inhale, bring your hands up to your solar plexus. Set the *hara,* turn the hands over (palms down) and exhale pushing the breath down into the center. On the second inhale, bring the joined arms straight overhead. Set the *hara,* separate the hands and let each arm carve an arc back to the center during a slow exhale. Look 180 degrees. Alternate these two patterns of breathing.

2. **Three-Step Breathing (pp. 77–79):** Stand with feet shoulder-width apart. (1) Bring the backs of your hands together and raise them straight overhead as you inhale. Stretch all the way to your toes. (2) Set the *hara,* dropping your weight down onto your feet and opening your arms into a V. (3) Exhale, maintaining a roundness in your *hara,* as your arms slowly arc back to your center.

3. **Two-Step Breathing (pp. 79–82):** Same as above except (1) don't stretch to your toes on the inhale. Also, the set is not treated as a separate step. (2) At the start of the exhale, quietly set the *hara* and maintain its roundness through the exhale.

4. **Full-Body Breathing (pp. 98–101):** Stand with feet shoulder-width apart, arms at side. As you inhale, let your arms drop behind you, then meet palm to palm overhead. As you exhale, let your hands slowly drop. As they pass below your chest, begin bending at the knees and waist, separating your hands with palms facing the floor. Touch your hands and then knees to the floor, and continue exhaling as your head reaches the floor. After you've exhaled completely, inhale as you push yourself back up into standing position. Exhale standing. Repeat the cycle several times.

5. **Expand and Compress (pp. 101–103):** Stand with feet shoulder-width apart, hands at your center. As you inhale, draw your arms up and back as far as you can. Your body should be arched slightly back. Set the *hara,* which slightly flattens the back, bringing the arms into peripheral view. Continue exhaling as you compress the breath into your center. Your hands should feel as if they're surrounding a huge bubble that is compressing into your center.

If you listen carefully to your body, it will guide you toward the program that is best suited for you, that is, the program that will help your mind, body and spirit together take the next step along your way of development. To select among the basic programs, ask yourself the following two questions:

1) Have I yet gotten the feel for breathing to and from my center?
If your answer is "no," start with the Centering Program, which is the best place to start for most people. You may want to do this for several weeks until the body learns the new depth at which breathing is possible. After you've really gotten the hang of centered breathing, or if your answer is already "yes," ask yourself the following:

2) Have I given sitting meditation a try, and do I think it would help me?
The only way really to answer this question is to try sitting. If you answer the question intellectually, the answer will almost always be "no," for just the reasons we talked about earlier: the thinking mind generally wants its game to continue, even if it's making our life a mess. But if you actually sit and give the process twenty minutes to cook, you might hear a different voice. Just the other day I was teaching a friend of mine how to sit. She told me afterwards that five minutes into it, all she could think was "I can't possibly do this. Everything feels awkward." But fifteen minutes into it, she started thinking "Hey, I am doing this. And I'm starting to quiet down." The test of whether sitting can help us is not that it's easy from the start. Rather, it's that something deep within us resonates with the need to do it.

If your answer to this question is "yes," start with the Sitting Program. If you have tried sitting and don't feel it would help you (or know you just won't do it), start with the Walking Program.

Centering Program. Relaxation and centered breathing are the focus of this program. If you're still working on centering your breath in the *hara* or setting your *hara* on every exhale, this is the place to start.

Days 1 and 4: Do twenty minutes of lying-down meditation with your feet against a wall. You might start by inviting the body to relax, using either the method of surveying it with your breath awareness, or alternately tensing and relaxing each muscle group. Then, placing the right hand on your center and left hand on the chest, transfer the motion of your breath to your center. Set the *hara* on each exhale by pressing the wall through the balls of your feet. Relax completely on the inhale. As you continue, allow the breath to deepen and lengthen.

Days 2 and 5: Do breathing exercises for about five minutes. While you can blend in any of the five exercises you wish, close with a couple of minutes of Three-Step Breathing (exercise No. 2) followed by Two-Step Breathing (exercise No. 3). Transfer the quiet, Two-Step breath cycle to sitting meditation and continue for the next fifteen minutes.

Days 3 and 6: These are days devoted to breathing exercises. Do each of the breathing exercises in order, spending several minutes on each one.

Sitting Program. Once you're accustomed to breathing to and from your center, you can devote more of your practice time to meditation. This program emphasizes the development of energy, confidence and awareness.

Days 1–5: As you feel the need, warm up with breathing exercises, especially the Three-Step and Two-Step Breathing (exercises Nos. 2 and 3), and then do twenty minutes of sitting meditation.

Day 6: Do five minutes of breathing exercises Nos. 1, 2, and 3, followed by fifteen minutes of aligned walking meditation.

Walking Program. Once you've developed the feeling for breathing to and from your center, and if sitting meditation is not for you, try this program. This program emphasizes moving from your center and developing awareness.

Day 1: Do twenty minutes of lying-down meditation, as in Day 1 of the Centering Program.

Days 2, 3, 5 and 6: As you feel the need, warm up with breathing exercises, especially the Three-Step and Two-Step Breathing (exercises Nos. 2 and 3), and then do twenty minutes of walking meditation. Pay careful attention to your body's alignment and balance while walking. Open up your senses and be completely present in the present moment.

Day 4: Devote this day to breathing exercises. Do each of the breathing exercises in order, spending several minutes on each one.

These programs are suggested starting points. If you find a combination of exercises and meditation forms that suits you better, by all means follow it. As your body's awareness develops, your body's voice will become more clear as to where you need to spend your effort. Spend your effort well. The quality of your life is shaped by these basics.

Confidence Is Contagious

Genuine confidence is built on something deeper than heady affirmations. If confined to the surface of our intellect, a positive facade is subject to cracking when the going gets tough. On the other hand, a positive mental attitude that grows out of a solid, connected inner condition gives us a tanklike stability. By learning strength and confidence through the body in a meditative practice, we connect to and from the core of our being. Our present moment becomes more powerful and clear, as does our presence in the world. The gifts of our practice are not confined to ourselves. As the quality of our life changes, we change in the ways we affect other people.

Confidence is a good example of one of the contagious benefits of BodyLearning. Some people positively inspire confidence in others. If you think about the best leaders you've known or seen portrayed in movies, they have the quality of being able to convince others—mostly through the strength of their own conviction—that the difficult is easy and the impossible is in reach. Gene Krantz, who was the flight director for Apollo 13 and whom I had the privilege of knowing during my time at NASA, was this kind of leader. It's not that he was naive or blind to difficulties, but his overriding conviction that "failure is not an option" captured others in its momentum. Not only do others gain confidence in following such a strong leader, but they may also pick up the pattern themselves.

One of the greatest gifts we can give one another as we strengthen ourselves is a sense of fearlessness. A sense of power. Confidence is contagious. And when we spread it, we take some of the fear out of the world. We replace "can't do" with "can do." We replace victims with players. We replace the mindless and often destructive striving for dominance with a sense of tanklike stability that no longer needs to prove itself. We build this confidence first in ourselves. Then it grows.

> *"You should not lose the frame of mind attained through sitting in tranquility and calmness, but true Zazen is to be able to act freely in the movements and changes in this world."*
> —*Vimalakirti*

So please know, as you design your practice and dig through your day for the time to devote to it, that the difference it makes starts at the center of your life and extends boundlessly from there.

7

❧

Personal Inventory: Discovering Your Needs and Interests

"My belief is in the blood and flesh
as being wiser than the intellect."
—D. H. Lawrence

Finding Your Bliss

"I've tried meditation before," said Bob, a participant in one of my seminars. "And I just can't sit still. I feel like I'm going to jump out of my skin. I've got to do something active." At the other extreme, there was Joan, who couldn't stand exercise. "Don't tell me I've got to jog to do BodyLearning," she said. Like Bob and Joan, you may have some strong preferences when it comes to designing a BodyLearning practice that's right for you. The good news, as I tell my students, is that I won't tell you to do anything. I can help you organize the messages, but by listening deeply to your own body, mind and spirit, you'll tell yourself what is the right practice for you.

Joseph Campbell, the great scholar of mythological and religious traditions, advises "follow your bliss" in finding a way for your enrichment. And so we follow his good advice in further crafting a practice in BodyLearning. To start, you assess your interests, because you're most likely to stick with a practice when you sincerely enjoy it. You'll also examine your patterns and needs to identify specific areas you would most like to develop through your practice. In this chapter you'll collect all the information you need to tailor your own BodyLearning program in the chapter that follows. Through a personal inventory and step-by-step process, you'll be able to identify two to four activities that would be a powerful program in BodyLearning, best matching your own needs and interests.

Before examining the field of activities from which you can design your practice, let's review the essential qualities that make an activity a good candidate for BodyLearning.

The Essential Qualities

Each of the earlier chapters has explained at least one essential quality of BodyLearning activities. Now you'll consider those qualities together and the full spectrum of activities that meet most of them. While each activity you choose for your practice may include only some of these qualities, it's best to combine activities so that your total program includes every essential ingredient.

Develops Breath and Center. Your practice is a special time in your day to develop breath and center, and so it stands to reason that this is the first essential element of a good course in Body-Learning. We've seen how meditative activities develop our breath and center, as we learn to breathe deeply into our center and set the *hara* on every exhale. The same attentiveness to breath and center that we bring to sitting or walking meditation we can bring to other activities, such as gardening or cooking. If we are able to focus on breath and center as we go about one of our daily activities, we have an ideal candidate for one element of our practice.

Aerobic activities can also develop our breath and center, but from a different set of demands. When we jog or run, for example, we learn to relax our breathing so we don't "run out of breath." Steady aerobic activities, such as rapid walking, running, bicycling or swimming, tend to develop our breath more steadily than do activities with start-stop patterns of exertion, such as baseball or waterskiing. Aerobic activities develop our breath through exertion. They also develop our center by training us to make it the center of our motion.

If we are open to aerobic activities and have the discipline to focus on breath and center in meditative activities, we have the widest spectrum of choices in designing our BodyLearning practice.

Develops Awareness. Without exception, a good course in BodyLearning requires and further develops our awareness. Awareness develops through our senses. Meditative activities develop our awareness as we consciously focus through our senses.

> Monk: "What is the one road of Ummon?"
> Ummon: "Personal experience!"
> Monk: "What is the Way?"
> Ummon: "Go!"
> Monk: "What is the road? Where is the way?"
> Ummon: "Begin walking it!"

Other BodyLearning activities develop our awareness by demanding it—giving us much that we have to pay attention to. By paying attention to what the body is sensing and doing, the thinking mind comes into the present moment.

Unifies the Body—The More, the Better. The hallmark trait of a solid path for BodyLearning is that it requires us to use our body and unifies us while we do it. Activities in which we focus our conscious attention on what the body is doing allow us to practice being whole. They both require and develop a combined mental-physical awareness. At least for the period of our practice, we are one being. We are of one mind-body, concentrating on doing one thing, being in one place.

We have a large say in the extent to which an activity unifies us. The only way we experience wholeness is to practice whole-heartedly; that is, to commit our entire being to our practice. Activities that are good for BodyLearning give us something clear to do—the more of our mind and body involved, the better. Not only do we focus the thinking mind on what the body is doing, but we also enlist the consciousness of all parts of our body in the activity. By extending our intention and energy into what we're doing, our practice takes on a new quality. We don't just go through the motions. We are fully present; every fiber of our being reports in to the present moment.

It's important that we "follow our bliss" in designing a Body-Learning program, because we will more fully commit to activities we enjoy. If we enjoy the outdoors, we might choose outdoor activities. If we love music, we might make music a part of our practice through dance or playing a musical instrument. Many activities, when we commit to them fully, can be rich sources of BodyLearning. Yoga, photography, crafts and fine arts, walking, driving, even cleaning the house in full awareness can become the foundation of our practice. If we can't find something that we sincerely enjoy, at least we can find activities that we dislike the least. These are places where our resistance will be the lowest and our chance for progress the greatest.

Has Standards of Excellence. By seeing our condition fed back to us in the quality of our practice, we can see whether we're on track and adjust our practice accordingly. As such, the fourth characteristic of a solid path in BodyLearning is that it has objective standards of performance. Such standards give us an honest basis for assessing our development. In aligning our practice toward excellence, such standards keep us from trailing off on eccentric tangents. They keep us honest.

Feedback can come in the form of tests, contests, scores, recitals, shows, races, demonstrations or progression through levels. The feedback can come from our own observation of the measurables. Or, better yet, it can come from teachers, coaches or teammates whose judgment we trust. Most outward, active forms of Body-Learning have many such measures of performance. But even in the more meditative forms, guidance and feedback are possible and will help our development enormously. Teachers can guide our training in a practiced form of meditation, such as Zen or Yoga. If our passion is music or art, we can find teachers to guide us or groups in which we can participate. We can enter shows or recitals with our work. If gardening is our practice, we can occasionally enter shows or be part of a community of gardeners, which includes some seasoned experts who can teach us.

The point is not to exaggerate a competitive or judgmental element in our practice, but rather, to align ourselves toward increasing excellence in some of what we do. We need a way of getting feedback. In devoting ourselves to excellence, we organize ourselves internally along a path of progress. To the extent we commit ourselves wholeheartedly to a development goal, we give that goal the power to align us.

Teachers along the Way

In many forms of BodyLearning our drive toward excellence will require that we find a teacher. We will be able to go only so far on our own initiative. If we consider Olympic gymnasts, college basketball players or professional football players, we know that top-caliber athletes reach their peak form only with teachers and trainers along the way. Generally the best martial artists are students of the best martial artists. While we may be able to cover significant ground on our own, to go further we need teachers.

And we need good ones. The same essential ingredients we look for in good BodyLearning activities can guide us toward good teachers. The teachers from whom we can learn the most have found ways to integrate breathing and centeredness into the activities they teach. They have developed an awareness and appreciation of their practice that goes beyond the routine. They deeply enjoy what they teach and take to it wholeheartedly. They respect the standards of excellence of their practice and are honest in giving us feedback on our progress. Our most valued mentors will be people we respect. They are people with whom we feel a resonance—a sense that they have gotten to a place where we want to go. They are people who respect us and help us develop in directions appropriate to us.

Not all of our teachers need to be a permanent presence in our lives. Some of the teachers in my life have guided me for years and some of them have been present in my life for only a few days. Most of my teachers I see only now and then, and it is up to me to maintain my practice between such times.

As we come to work with teachers, we will learn the most from them if we are willing to empty our cup of preconceptions. This image comes from a story that is told about a university professor who visited Zen master Nan-in to learn more about Zen.[1] Nan-in served tea, filling his visitor's cup to overflowing. The professor watched the tea flow over the cup until he could restrain himself no more. "It is overflowing," he said. "No more will go in." "Like this cup," Nan-in replied, "you are full of your own opinions and speculations. How can I show you Zen unless you first empty your cup?"

In the spirit of an empty cup, we gain the most from our teachers. We leap to new learning only when we're willing to let go of the old. At the point of letting go, it feels as if the old knowledge may be lost to us forever. Yet, in my experience, this is rarely the case. More likely it becomes integrated and transformed into a fuller, richer body of knowledge.

We vary in how much we seek and need teachers in our development. One of the factors we'll consider in customizing a program in BodyLearning is our preference for guidance from outside teachers versus following our "inner teacher." A strong, clear inner teacher opens up a wider range of BodyLearning practices, where we can still make progress by ourselves. Even if we have a strong sense of internal direction, finding a good teacher for at least one of our activities has inestimable value. Someone who can point to true north.

A Menu of Choices

BodyLearning is possible through a wide variety of activities that develop our breath and center, build our awareness, unify our body-mind-spirit, and align us on a path toward excellence, often with teachers along the way. Numerous activities meet most or all these criteria.

The Activity Checklist that follows lists dozens of activities that can be rich sources of BodyLearning. This list is not meant to be exhaustive but representative of the kinds of activities available to adults that meet at least three of the BodyLearning criteria. If activities that interest you are not on the list, try to associate them with a similar item that is on the list. If they're not similar to anything on the list, but they still meet at least three of the criteria of being a good source of BodyLearning, feel free to add them at the bottom.

Appendix B includes an extra copy of this checklist, as well as all the instruments and work sheets you need for designing a practice. I'd suggest you tear these sheets out as you use them and add them to your notebook for a complete view of your journey into BodyLearning.

Consider each item on the Activity Checklist as a potential candidate for your practice. Which ones are already in your life? Which ones appeal to you? Which ones are out of the question? By going through the list and characterizing your reaction to each

ACTIVITY CHECKLIST

- For each activity, note how much you DO it and how much you LIKE doing it.
- If you've never done the activity, guess whether you'd enjoy it.
- Where multiple activities are listed, answer for your favorite of the group.

Activity	How Much You Do This				How Much You Like This				
	Almost Daily	Now & Then	Rarely	Never	Not at All	Dislike	Neutral	Enjoy	Love
Driving									
Housecleaning									
Drawing, Painting, Calligraphy (*Shodo*)									
Crafts, Sculpture, Ceramics									
Needlework, Weaving, Sewing									
Woodwork, Mechanical Work									
Meditation, *Zazen*									
Fishing									
Photography									
Breathing Exercises									
Stretching Exercises									
Flower Arranging (e.g., *Ikebana*)									
Gardening									

(continued)

ACTIVITY CHECKLIST (continued)

Activity	How Much You Do This				How Much You Like This				
	Almost Daily	Now & Then	Rarely	Never	Not at All	Dislike	Neutral	Enjoy	Love
Walking									
Yoga									
Golf									
Singing or Playing Musical Instrument with Others									
Singing or Playing Musical Instrument Solo									
Cooking									
Tai Chi									
Archery									
Cross-Country Ski Machine									
Hunting									
Target Practice									
Bowling									
Horseback Riding									
Sailing									
Flying (as Pilot)									
Martial Arts									
Jogging, Running									
Aerobic Exercise with Group or Music									

(continued)

ACTIVITY CHECKLIST (continued)

Activity	How Much You Do This				How Much You Like This				
	Almost Daily	Now & Then	Rarely	Never	Not at All	Dislike	Neutral	Enjoy	Love
Aerobic Exercise Solo, without Music									
Weight Lifting, Power Lifting									
Skiing (Downhill, Cross Country, Water)									
Crew, Canoeing									
Bicycling, Wheelchair Racing									
Football, Soccer, Hockey									
Baseball									
Bird-watching									
Power Walking, Racewalking									
Basketball, Volleyball									
Dance									
Tennis, Racquetball/ Squash									
Skating, Rollerblading									
Stationary Bicycle									

(continued)

ACTIVITY CHECKLIST (continued)

Activity	How Much You Do This				How Much You Like This				
	Almost Daily	Now & Then	Rarely	Never	Not at All	Dislike	Neutral	Enjoy	Love
Swimming									
Scuba Diving, Snorkeling									
Kayaking									
Hiking									
Rock/Mountain Climbing									
Sailboarding, Surfing									
(write-in)									
(write-in)									

activity, you can develop a profile of your current body practices and interests. Characterize each activity in two ways: (1) the extent to which it is currently in your life and (2) the extent to which you enjoy it or might enjoy it. If you don't know what the activity is, skip over it. If you do know what the activity is but have never done it, it's fine to guess whether you think you'd enjoy it. Be as honest as possible in assessing each activity.

The Four Activity Areas

To characterize your interests and eventually design a well-rounded practice, it's useful to consider four general categories of Body-Learning activities. In particular, it is useful to characterize activities in terms of whether they make you break a sweat and how quickly they change.

We'll use the terms *meditative* and *aerobic* to describe the sweat scale, shown vertically in Figure 7-1. This is not so much a measure of whether an activity can be a form of meditation—a number of aerobic activities could be forms of moving meditation. Rather, it's a measure of whether the activity drives your heart rate into an aerobic range.[2] We classify aerobic activities in the top two areas and nonaerobic activities in the bottom two.

From left to right is the scale of how quickly the activity throws change your way. We'll use the words *static* and *dynamic* to describe this scale. This is not so much a measure of whether you're moving but of how quickly your movement changes, depending on external events to which you have to respond. On this scale, *static* does not mean completely still but only that the rate of change is relatively slow. For example, jogging would be considered a static activity, even though you're moving, because you don't have to change your motion a great deal. You can get into a groove and more or less stay there. Fishing, on the other hand, would be considered a dynamic activity, even though it requires very little motion most of the time. When a fish bites, you have to react instantly. Dynamic activities present you with rapidly changing events that develop agility in your response.

Figure 7-2 maps all of the activities on the checklist into one of these four areas. Some amount of subjective judgment goes into assigning an activity to a given area. Many activities could be more or less aerobic, depending on how they're done. Sailing, for

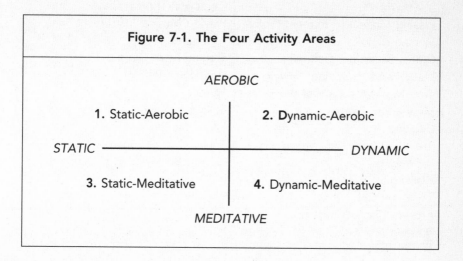

Figure 7-1. The Four Activity Areas

AEROBIC

1. Static-Aerobic   2. **D**ynamic-Aerobic

STATIC ——————————————— DYNAMIC

3. Static-Meditative   4. Dynamic-Meditative

MEDITATIVE

Figure 7-2. Activities Mapped Into Four Areas

STATIC-AEROBIC	DYNAMIC-AEROBIC
Jogging	Martial Arts
Running, Wheelchair Racing	Aerobic Exercise (with Group or Music)
Aerobic Exercise (Solo, Not to Music)	Skiing (Downhill, Cross Country, Water)
Weight Lifting, Power Lifting	Football, Soccer, Hockey
Skating, Rollerblading	Baseball
Swimming	Basketball, Volleyball
Kayaking	Dance
Power Walking, Racewalking	Tennis, Racquetball, Squash
Stairmaster	Crew, Canoeing
Rowing Machine	Rock/Mountain Climbing, Vigorous Hiking
Stationary Bicycling	Sailboarding, Surfing
Cross-Country Ski Machine	Bicycling

STATIC-MEDITATIVE	DYNAMIC-MEDITATIVE
Housecleaning	Driving
Gardening, Flower Arranging, *Ikebana*	Fishing
Drawing, Painting, Calligraphy (*Shodo*)	Photography
Playing Musical Instrument (Solo)	Golf
Singing (Solo)	Ceramics (Thrown Clay)
Crafts, Sculpture, Ceramics	Playing Musical Instrument (with Others)
Needlework, Weaving, Sewing	Singing (with Others)
Woodwork, Mechanical Work	Horseback Riding
Meditation, *Zazen*	Hunting
Cooking	Sailing
Breathing Exercises, Stretching Exercises	Flying (as Pilot)
Walking	Scuba Diving, Snorkeling
Yoga, Tai Chi	Hiking, Bird-watching
Archery, Target Practice	
Bowling	

example, could be a fairly relaxed play with the wind or it could be a sweat-breaking race, requiring Olympic-caliber performance. An activity could also vary in the extent to which it challenges us with changing events. For example, canoeing down a quiet river would be a fairly slowly changing activity, whereas canoeing through rapids would be much more dynamic. If the generalizations in this table don't apply in your case, feel free to move an activity into the area that matches your primary experience of it. If you've added any write-ins to the Activity Checklist when you filled it out, try to map them into one of these four areas as well.

Organizing Your Interests

We now want to look at how the activities you do—and especially those you like to do—stack up against the activity areas. By analyzing your interests with respect to the four activity areas, you'll see which area is most emphasized by your current patterns. Recording your answers on the Activity Work Sheet, you can profile your activity preferences through the following stepwise process. An additional work sheet is included in Appendix B that you may wish to tear out and add to your notebook.

Step 1. Look for the activities on your checklist that you do almost daily (far-left column on DOING) and that you love to do (far-right column on LIKING). If you find any, circle these on your Activity Work Sheet; these are strong candidates for including in your program of BodyLearning. If you don't have any of these activities, go on to the next step.

Step 2. Look for activities on your checklist that you do almost daily or now and then AND that you enjoy or love to do. Underline these on your work sheet. These are also good candidates.

Step 3. Cross out activities on your work sheet that you do not enjoy at all (far-left column on LIKING).

Step 4. Cross out activities on your work sheet that you do rarely or never AND that you dislike doing. Don't cross out activities that meet only one of these criteria, but only those that meet both.

ACTIVITY WORK SHEET

STATIC-AEROBIC	DYNAMIC-AEROBIC
1. Jogging 2. Running, Wheelchair Racing 3. Aerobic Exercise (Solo, Not to Music) 4. Weight Lifting, Power Lifting 5. Skating, Rollerblading 6. Swimming 7. Kayaking 8. Power Walking, Racewalking 9. Stairmaster 10. Rowing Machine 11. Stationary Bicycling 12. Cross-Country Ski Machine 13. Write-ins:	1. Martial arts (Aikido, Karate, Kendo, etc.) 2. Aerobic Exercise (with Group or Music) 3. Skiing (Downhill, Cross Country, Water) 4. Football, Soccer, Hockey 5. Baseball 6. Basketball, Volleyball 7. Dance 8. Tennis, Racquetball, Squash 9. Crew, Canoeing 10. Rock/Mountain Climbing, Vigorous Hiking 11. Sailboarding, Surfing 12. Bicycling 13. Write-ins:
Check ☐ if favorite area	Check ☐ if favorite area

STATIC-MEDITATIVE	DYNAMIC-MEDITATIVE
1. Housecleaning, Cooking 2. Gardening, Flower Arranging, *Ikebana* 3. Drawing, Painting, Calligraphy (*Shodo*) 4. Singing or Playing Musical Instrument (Solo) 5. Crafts, Sculpture, Ceramics 6. Needlework, Weaving, Sewing 7. Woodwork, Mechanical Work 8. Meditation, *Zazen* 9. Breathing Exercises, Stretching Exercises 10. Yoga, Tai Chi 11. Walking 12. Archery, Target Practice, Bowling 13. Write-ins:	1. Driving 2. Fishing 3. Photography 4. Golf 5. Singing or Playing Musical Instrument (with Others) 6. Ceramics (Thrown Clay) 7. Horseback Riding 8. Hunting 9. Sailing 10. Flying (as Pilot) 11. Scuba Diving, Snorkeling 12. Hiking, Bird-watching 13. Write-ins:
Check ☐ if favorite area	Check ☐ if favorite area

Step 5. In each area, count the number of lines where you have circled or underlined an activity. Count each line once, even if it contains more than one mark (including something else in that line crossed out). Note the area having the highest total count. If two or more areas score the same, pick one that feels closer to your top preference. An activity in this favorite area is probably your best choice for including in your BodyLearning program.

or

Alternate Step 5. If you don't have any circled or underlined activities in any area, just count the number of lines containing activities you haven't crossed out. Using the same process as above, select the area with the highest total count of remaining activities as your relative favorite.

Step 6. Look at the activities in the area opposite (diagonally) to your favorite area. Place a star by the activities in this area that you do rarely or never but you feel you would enjoy or love doing. (If you'd enjoy no new activities in this area, look at the two adjacent areas and see if there is such an activity in each of them.) One (or two) of these activities could be a good complement to your favorite existing activity in a balanced BodyLearning program. Keep these activities in mind as you do the next assessment of patterns and needs.

Looking at your activity work sheet, you might ask yourself these questions: "How balanced or lopsided are my activity interests?" "Am I ignoring any of the four areas in my current set of interests?" As we'll see later in this chapter, different activities develop us differently, and each activity area has a special development emphasis. You may find that an area you're ignoring is one where you have strong development needs. In the next section you'll have a chance to find out, as you assess your patterns and needs.

Assessing Your Patterns and Needs

We want to play to our interests in the design of our practice, but it's best if we also consider What do we need to work on? What would make the most positive difference in our life? We're not all working on the same challenges or goals. Some of us are changing how we manage; others are struggling to manage change. Some of us are trying to control our temper; others are trying to temper the need for control. Our practice will be all the more beneficial when it caters to our needs. Understanding where our goals and needs are the strongest, we can identify activities that emphasize these areas. In this exercise you'll be able to assess your patterns and needs for any area you would do well to reinforce in your practice.

Perhaps you've already identified a specific development goal; in that case, take a moment to jot it down in your notebook. The following assessment and analysis may reveal a new area to develop or a way to work on an area you've already identified. In this self-test, you'll consider aspects of your well-being that can be directly improved through BodyLearning. You'll then map your responses into the four activity areas identified earlier to see if there's a new area you might want to emphasize in your practice. You'll also use this assessment to gain insight into your preference for guidance and the extent to which you should select activities where teachers are readily available.

An additional copy of this self-test is in Appendix B. You may wish to complete that copy and add it to your notebook. For each question, mark the box that describes you best.

PATTERNS AND NEEDS CHECKLIST

Part 1. Indicate the extent to which the following statements describe you by placing an "X" in the appropriate box. Use the following scale:

- *Not At All*: This statement doesn't apply at all to me; indeed, it may be opposite to what I know of myself.
- *Rarely*: On rare occasions, this statement applies to me, but it's not typical of me.
- *Now and Then*: This statement applies to me now and then.
- *Typical*: This statement is fairly typical of me; it applies to me most of the time.
- *Definitely*: This statement is me all over; it's one of my defining traits.

Personal Patterns	Not at all	Rarely	Now & Then	Typical of Me	Definitely
1. I'm in excellent health.					
2. I'm an honest person.					
3. I always follow instructions.					
4. I'm generally sluggish.					
5. I'm a strong person.					
6. I take time to unwind or "smell the flowers."					
7. I have plenty of endurance.					
8. My life has a good deal of stress.					
9. I often reflect on my experience and figure out where I need to improve.					
10. I get along well with people.					
11. I don't hold up well under pressure.					
12. I'm often lost in thought or daydreams.					
13. I'm willing to look at the truth, even when it casts me in an unfavorable light.					
14. I know myself well.					
15. I don't see things very clearly; I'm easily confused.					

(continued)

Personal Patterns	Not at all	Rarely	Now & Then	Typical of Me	Definitely
16. I get very angry.					
17. I seem to be a "day late and a dollar short."					
18. My life has too many ups and downs.					
19. I find it easy to accept good news but hard to accept bad news.					
20. I am strongly self-motivated.					
21. It's hard for me to shift my attention from one thing to another.					
22. I'm a good listener.					
23. There are many things I don't like.					
24. I can't wait for things to happen; I need to make them happen.					
25. My attention tends to drift off.					
26. I wish I understood myself better.					
27. Sometimes my life does not seem worthwhile.					
28. I'm uncoordinated.					
29. I'm sure of myself.					
30. I find it difficult to take a large task and break it down into approachable steps.					

(continued)

Personal Patterns	Not at All	Rarely	Now & Then	Typical of Me	Definitely
31. I'm aware of my thoughts and feelings.					
32. I know when it's appropriate to put in my "two bits."					
33. I have a good sense of balance.					
34. I tend to be impatient.					
35. I don't notice many things that go on around me.					
36. I prefer having my work or tasks laid out for me.					
37. I'm a nervous person.					
38. When I'm outside, it's easy for me to feel in tune with nature.					
39. I generally know where other people are coming from.					
40. I have difficulty breathing.					

Part 2. Complete the following two sentences.
　　　Mark as many (or as few) of the answers as apply to you.

"My life would be much better if only I had—"

more energy	
deeper insight	
more patience	
more of a sense of purpose	
better health	
a better attitude	
more endurance	
more guidance	
more strength	
better relationships	
more money	
more of nothing; my life is fine as it is	

"If I were my own doctor, I would tell myself to—"

lose weight	
quit smoking	
take it easy, relax more	
take care of my heart	
get a hobby	
get some exercise	
not let things get to me	
get some rest	
keep doing whatever I'm doing because I'm doing fine	

Organizing Your Answers

Copy or highlight your answers onto the following score sheets (additional score sheets are in Appendix B). Some of the boxes where you marked an answer will be blank; others will have one or more numbers in them. Ignore the boxes you marked that are blank. Tally the number of 1's, 2's, 3's, 4's and 5's that are in the same boxes as your answers. If you've marked a box where a number appears twice, count it twice. If you've marked a box with more than one number in it, add to the tally for each number that appears. Note the totals at the bottom of each page.

PATTERNS AND NEEDS SCORE SHEET

Part 1. Copy or highlight your answers below. Ignore boxes that have no
number in them. Tally the number of 1's, 2's, 3's, 4's and 5's in
the boxes where you've marked an answer.

Personal Patterns	Not at All	Rarely	Now & Then	Typical of Me	Definitely
1. I'm in excellent health.	3	3	1 2		
2. I'm an honest person.	3	3	3		
3. I always follow instructions.				5	5
4. I'm generally sluggish.			1 2	1 2	1 2
5. I'm a strong person.	3	1 2 3	1 2		
6. I take time to unwind or "smell the flowers."	3 4	3 4			
7. I have plenty of endurance.	1 2	1 2	1 2		
8. My life has a good deal of stress.			1 2	1 2 3	1 2 3
9. I often reflect on my experience and figure out where I need to improve.	5 5	5 5	5		
10. I get along well with people.	2	2	2		
11. I don't hold up well under pressure.			3	3	3
12. I'm often lost in thought or daydreams.			2 4	2 4	2 4
13. I'm willing to look at the truth, even when it casts me in an unfavorable light.	3	3	3	3	

Page Totals of: 1's ☐ 2's ☐ 3's ☐ 4's ☐ 5's ☐

(continued)

Personal Patterns	Not at All	Rarely	Now & Then	Typical of Me	Definitely
14. I know myself well.	3 5	3 5	3 5		
15. I don't see things very clearly; I'm easily confused.			1 3	1 3	1 3
16. I get very angry.			1 2	1 2	1 2
17. I seem to be a "day late and a dollar short."			2 4	2 4	2 4
18. My life has too many ups and downs.			1	1	1
19. I find it easy to accept good news but hard to accept bad news.			2 4	2 4	2 4
20. I am strongly self-motivated.	5 5	5 5	5		
21. It's hard for me to shift my attention from one thing to another.			2	2	2
22. I'm a good listener.	4	4	4		
23. There are many things I don't like.			3	3	1 2 3
24. I can't wait for things to happen; I need to make them happen.				4	4
25. My attention tends to drift off.			2 4	2 4	2 3 4
26. I wish I understood myself better.			3 5	3 5	3 5

Page Totals of: 1's ☐ 2's ☐ 3's ☐ 4's ☐ 5's ☐

(continued)

Personal Patterns	Not at All	Rarely	Now & Then	Typical of Me	Definitely
27. Sometimes my life does not seem worthwhile.		3	3	3	3
28. I'm uncoordinated.			2 3	2 3	2 3
29. I'm sure of myself.	3 5	2	2		
30. I find it difficult to take a large task and break it down into approachable steps.				5	5 5
31. I'm aware of my thoughts and feelings.	3 5 5	3 5	3 5		
32. I know when it's appropriate to put in my "two bits."	2	2	2		
33. I have a good sense of balance.	3	2 3	2		
34. I tend to be impatient.			3 4	3 4	3 4
35. I don't notice many things that go on around me.			2 4	2 4	2 4
36. I prefer having my work or tasks laid out for me.				5	5 5
37. I'm a nervous person.			3	3	3
38. When I'm outside, it's easy for me to feel in tune with nature.	4	4	4		

Page Totals of: 1's ☐   2's ☐   3's ☐   4's ☐   5's ☐

(continued)

Personal Patterns	Not at All	Rarely	Now & Then	Typical of Me	Definitely
39. I generally know where other people are coming from.	2	2	2		
40. I have difficulty breathing.		1 2	1 2 3	3	3
Page Totals of : 1's ☐ 2's ☐ 3's ☐ 4's ☐ 5's ☐					
Part 1 Totals (sum of page totals) of : 1's ☐ 2's ☐ 3's ☐ 4's ☐ 5's ☐					

Part 2. Copy or highlight your answers below. Ignore boxes that have no number in them. Tally the number of 1's, 2's, 3's, 4's and 5's in the boxes where you've marked an answer.

"My life would be much better if only I had—"

more energy	1 2
deeper insight	3
more patience	3 4
more of a sense of purpose	3
better health	1 2 3
a better attitude	1 2 3 4
more endurance	1
more guidance	5 5
more strength	1 2
better relationships	2
more money	
more of nothing; my life is fine as it is	

"If I were my own doctor, I would tell myself to—"

lose weight	1 2
quit smoking	1 2 3
take it easy, relax more	3 4
take care of my heart	1 2
get a hobby	3 4
get some exercise	1 2 3 4
not let things get to me	1 2
get some rest	3
keep doing whatever I'm doing because I'm doing fine	

Part 2 Totals of: 1's ☐ 2's ☐ 3's ☐ 4's ☐ 5's ☐

Development Strengths of the Four Areas

What do the scores mean? To have a framework for interpreting our answers, we need to revisit the four activity areas we defined earlier. Each area was defined in terms of two qualities: static versus dynamic and aerobic versus meditative. We now want to consider further the particular development strengths of each area. In an earlier chapter you may have done the exercise "What are you already learning from your body?" based on one of your current practices. The same thought process that distilled those lessons down to one or two words can now be used to describe the lessons learnable for different activity areas.

First, considering the two extremes of static-meditative activities versus dynamic-aerobic activities, we easily see differences in their development emphasis. They place very different demands on us, and consequently, we learn different lessons from them. The development characteristics of these extremes are shown in Figure 7-3.

Static-meditative activities develop our strength and energy from within—like the molten center of the earth, or like a pot cooking. This is the sense we develop in sitting meditation, of "cooking" from our center and letting our energy and awareness build and permeate our entire being, eventually radiating out from our center in all directions. Meditative activities build our inner strength by dropping our resistance. In learning to relax, we release the dams cutting off the flow of energy. When we allow more *ki* to flow in us and through us, our energy level comes up. Meditative practices raise our baseline energy to a new level of aliveness that corresponds to our increased awareness.

Dynamic-aerobic activities build our strength in the world. They develop our peak energy by demanding more energy and giving us a focus for it. When we're doing an aerobic exercise, our whole body kicks into a higher gear. We take in more oxygen, our blood pumps faster, we metabolize more energy from our environment. All of this added energy flows into us, through us and from us. Moreover, energetic activities give us a physical outlet for blowing off steam that can free pockets of energy that had been trapped inside. It is as if we get access to more of our energy when we have a way of directing it.

Figure 7-3. Development Strengths of
Static-Meditative vs. Dynamic-Aerobic Activities

$\longleftarrow$ ——————— **Activity Spectrum** ——————— $\longrightarrow$

STATIC-MEDITATIVE	DYNAMIC-AEROBIC
Inner Strength	Outward Strength
Building Steam	Blowing Off Steam
Resting Energy	Peak Energy
Patience	Timing
Listening Skills	Speaking Skills
Concentration	Dynamic Focus
Stick-to-it-iveness	Endurance
Long-Term Awareness	Dynamic Awareness
Foundational Stability	Active Stability
Conditioning	Aerobic Fitness
Being Present	Being Active
Emphasis on Being	Emphasis on Doing

Static-meditative activities can be very good for developing our patience. By giving us a rest from asserting ourselves, they give us a chance to pay more attention to what is going on around us. We hone our ability to listen and sense the natural timing of situations. Dynamic-aerobic activities can develop our sense of timing in a very different way. We learn the timing of hitting a baseball. We learn the timing of responding to an attack with an Aikido throw. We learn to change what we're doing quickly, as the situation calls for it. We develop a sense for the instant when it is appropriate to act.

Our mental focus develops a little differently at the two ends of the spectrum. Static-meditative activities tend to develop a sense of endurance in our mental capabilities, such as concentration, stick-to-itiveness and the ability to see broad and long-term consequences. Highly energetic activities tend to hone our awareness sharply and quickly through their rapidly changing conditions. We learn to focus and refocus our attention quickly as the situation demands.

Stability develops slowly and solidly through static-meditative activities. We build a stable foundation through meditative practices that supports balance and extension into more dynamic activities. Dynamic activities can further develop our balance by challenging us with rapidly changing conditions that require mental and physical agility.

Our general body conditioning is improved through static-meditative activities. As we learn to relax and breathe more fully, our body is more nourished. All our systems get more of "a breath of fresh air" as our circulation improves. Dynamic-aerobic activities, on the other hand, develop peak fitness. They adapt our body to a condition of high performance, which tends to increase our strength, improve our health and control our weight.

Overall, our static-meditative training allows us to focus on being present in the present moment. Dynamic-aerobic activities also invite us into the present moment, but it is a moment of action. The slower time scale of meditative practices supports an emphasis on *being*. The faster time scale of dynamic-aerobic activities places more focus on *doing*.

As we regard the different emphases in these areas, it is important to realize that we need both aspects in our development. We may need one more than the other, and our interests may heavily favor one area over another. But as we tend to our development, like a potter turning clay, we are more likely to get the shape we want when we work both from inside out as well as from outside in. Static-meditative activities tend to work us from inside out. Dynamic-aerobic activities work from outside in. By participating in activities that hone our abilities in different time ranges and from different directions, we learn to find ways around all our barriers and bad habits.

Each of the four activity areas draws traits from these development endpoints. In addition, each has a particular development emphasis, listed in Figure 7-4 and summarized below.

Area 1: Static-Aerobic. In addition to aerobic fitness, these activities particularly develop our endurance and steadiness. They tune our internal rhythms to a higher level of performance and give us a chance to blow off steam.

Area 2: Dynamic-Aerobic. These activities develop our aerobic fitness amidst the challenges of a dynamic setting, where we are constantly and quickly responding to new inputs. A volley to return, music to merge with: these activities force us to listen to our senses and hone our sense of timing. Most of these activities also involve other people or teams and give us a chance to develop stronger interpersonal skills.

Area 3: Static-Meditative. More than any other area, this area emphasizes the development of inner strength and clarity. These activities most easily lend themselves to developing slow, deep breathing and, as such, are excellent for relaxation. By eliminating inner tension, they build our resting energy level. They are excellent for developing quiet concentration and patience.

A subset of these activities can be taken to a level where they become an art, such as cooking, painting, sculpting or woodworking. As such, they can provide an enduring outward expression of our inner condition. They can be an invaluable aspect of our practice because they provide a way of seeing our progress.

Area 4: Dynamic-Meditative. The unique character of these activities is their invitation to listen to nature's timing. They tend to open our senses and invite us into harmony with what is. They develop our willingness to work with the natural timing of situations. Rather than dissipate ourselves, "pushing on a wave," we learn to let the wave break with its own timing.

Figure 7-4 summarizes—with some simplification and generalization—where various development traits are served in the largest portions. Not all lessons are equally emphasized in all activities of a given area. How we do the activity is certainly an important factor in whether our experience absorbs some or all of its lessons. For example, dynamic-aerobic activities generally give us an opportunity to practice our interpersonal skills, since they tend to involve other people. But rock climbing, while it's in this area, is not going to teach us much about interpersonal interactions if we go it alone. On the other hand, if we're part of a rock-climbing group and someone's holding our harness, we're going to learn something about interpersonal trust. We need to use our judgment and be honest with ourselves as we do these activities to discern how many of the traits that they could develop are really part of our experience.

We can also adjust the ways we do activities so as to pick up

Figure 7-4. Development Strengths of the Four Activity Areas

STATIC-AEROBIC	DYNAMIC-AEROBIC
aerobic fitness	aerobic fitness
strength	strength
endurance	managing anger
steadiness	managing stress
managing anger	dynamic balance
managing stress	timing
overall energy level	confidence
clarity	interpersonal interactions, teamwork
performance breathing	dynamic focus
active self-awareness	overall energy level
	openness
	coordination
	assertiveness
	endurance
	alertness
	performance breathing
	external awareness

STATIC-MEDITATIVE	DYNAMIC-MEDITATIVE
foundational stability, ballast	listening
balance	patience
inner strength	sense of natural rhythms
self-awareness	resting energy
honesty	openness
patience	timing
calm	resting breathing
relaxation, reduction of resistance	harmony
resting energy	external awareness
larger framework of meaning	
concentration	
clarity	
resting breathing	
insight into condition of inner state	

more than the traits assigned to their general class. For example, we can practice a dynamic-meditative activity, such as photography, in such a way that it picks up some of the additional benefits of static-meditative activities, such as relaxation or concentration.

Mapping Your Patterns and Needs

You're now able to look at the relationship between your own patterns and needs and the four areas that BodyLearning activities develop. To do this, transfer your total scores onto the Development Area Work Sheet. (An additional work sheet is included in Appendix B.) Note that several of the numbers get doubled as they're added. Copy the new totals from the top part of the work sheet to the corresponding area in the bottom part (e.g., write the total number of 1's in area 1 and so on; 5's are entered at the bottom). Put a checkmark in the area having the highest relative score. Also put a checkmark in any area in which you scored more than 10.

The higher your score in a given area, the more your patterns and needs suggest you would benefit from practice in that area. Please remember, this is your assessment of your situation. These are the messages you're giving yourself. All that I provide is a framework on which to hang your messages so that you can see some patterns.

> "The unexamined life is not worth living."
> —Plato

For example, if your patterns indicate you have a lot of anger in your life, you tend to have strained interpersonal relationships, or your timing seems to be off, you would have a high score in Area 1, dynamic-aerobic activities. These activities would give you the most direct practice in managing anger, interacting with people and developing your sense of timing. If your high score is in Area 2, static-aerobic activities, your patterns suggest that developing aerobic fitness, building your endurance and/or giving yourself an outlet for managing stress would be positive additions to your life. A high score in Area 3, static-meditative activities, would indicate a need for more relaxation, centering, and greater clarity. As this area

DEVELOPMENT AREA WORK SHEET

	1's	2's	3's	4's	5's
Part 1	*			*	
Part 2				*	
Total (Parts 1 and 2)					

*Multiply your score in this area by 2.

Transfer the totals to the appropriate area below:

STATIC-AEROBIC	DYNAMIC-AEROBIC

1

Total 1's _____

Check ☐ if you scored **10** or more

Check ☐ if highest relative score

2

Total 2's _____

Check ☐ if you scored **10** or more

Check ☐ if highest relative score

STATIC-MEDITATIVE	DYNAMIC-MEDITATIVE

3

Total 3's _____

Check ☐ if you scored **10** or more

Check ☐ if highest relative score

4

Total 4's _____

Check ☐ if you scored **10** or more

Check ☐ if highest relative score

Total number of 5's: _____ (guidance preference)

develops stability, it is fundamental to our development in other areas as well. Area 4, dynamic-meditative activities, would score highly if you have a need for more patience, better listening, or greater awareness or acceptance of the world and its timing.

"What counts as a high score?" I'm always asked in seminars. That question has two answers. The first answer, and I think the most important, is relative to your own experience. In whatever area you scored the highest, you'll find the greatest potential payoff. On a more absolute scale, any area in which you scored more than ten points is asking for more practice. If all your area scores are below ten and there's not much difference among them (a one- or two-point spread), your current activities are already tending to your development needs in a balanced way.

A final factor we want to consider in designing a BodyLearning program is our preference for guidance.

Assessing Your Preference for Guidance

If you're serious about reaching the top of your game in virtually any activity, you need to find a teacher, mentor or coach to guide you. Even if your guidance preference is low, it's best to include a guide for at least one of the activities along your path. But with a low need for guidance, you'll be able to make considerable progress in activities where teachers are not always or immediately available. If your guidance preference is high, it's best to stick with activities where teachers are steadily available. There's no right and wrong preference for guidance; what's important is that you honestly know where you are and work with that knowledge in developing a BodyLearning program that works for you.

On your Development Area Work Sheet, look at the total number of 5's. If your score is 5 or more, you have a strong preference for guidance. You would do well to seek out a teacher with whom you can interact frequently in the principal activity you select for BodyLearning. You may want to migrate toward activities that are amenable to instruction, such as martial arts or music. If your score is 2 or less, your preference for guidance is low. You may still want to find teachers or mentors for one of your activities, but you can probably go for extended periods without them. A wider range of activities is open to you, where instruction is not readily available. If your score is 3 or 4, you have a moderate preference for guidance. You will tend to make more progress in areas where you have a teacher or a mentor, but you'll also be able to derive benefit from activities where instruction is not available.

Taking Stock

The essential characteristics of solid BodyLearning activities are that they (1) develop your breath and center, (2) build your awareness, (3) give you something physical to do and unify your body-mind as you do it, and (4) have external standards of excellence by which you can judge your progress. Many activities can be done in a way that meets most or all of these criteria, covering a range of static-meditative activities as well as dynamic-aerobic activities. Assessing your interests, you've had a chance to profile how your preferences stack up against four activity areas. You've also assessed your own patterns and development needs. Perhaps this assessment confirmed your earlier sense of what you needed to work on; perhaps it offered some fresh insights. Either way, you come to this point with greater clarity on where your practice could have the most payoff. Now you have a chance to turn insight into action.

Looking at your Development Area Work Sheet, identify the area where you scored the highest (or pick one if your scores tied). Looking at

> "There is no end to the opening up that is possible for a human being."
> —Charlotte Joko Beck

Figure 7-2, which lists activities that develop each area, pick one that you can commit to doing for at least twenty minutes. In the next chapter, we'll look at designing an enduring practice, but for now you don't have to commit to this activity for the long run; just try it once. You might use this opportunity to check out an activity you're considering for your practice. All the better if this activity is relatively new to you; sometimes it's easier to bring new awareness to new activities.

For these twenty minutes, focus on your breath, your center and being completely in the moment. If the activity you select is meditative, you can apply the same breathing and setting of the *hara* as practiced earlier in sitting meditation. If you select an aerobic activity, your breathing will be faster. Make an effort, however, to pay attention to your breathing and to move from your center, as practiced in walking meditation. Open your senses and pay attention to all that is going on around you. This time of practice is special time. Commit to it totally, and it will be of inestimable value.

8

⚜

Total Fitness: Designing a Practice That's Right for You

"Integral practices reorder elements of body and mind as if they were artistic materials, into new forms of power and beauty."
—Michael Murphy

Beyond Body Beautiful

"What does total fitness mean to you?" I asked at a recent Body-Learning seminar. "Having a body beautiful," one of the participants answered instantly. But then a discussion ensued on whether a beautiful body is always a healthy body. "How about having a body that's beautiful to live in?" another participant suggested.

I like this definition better because it's a truer guide. Beauty trends come and go, but a body that's beautiful to live in goes beyond style to an essential harmony of body, mind and spirit. A body that's beautiful to live in moves in a relaxed and natural way. It's a centered, grounded body, flowing with energy. This is what we build in BodyLearning. This is what you'll have a chance to build through the practice you design in this chapter.

BodyLearning improves our health. While it's no cure for the common cold, the more we relax and energize our body through practice, the less we create openings for illness to strike. Moreover, the more we listen to our body through our practice, the less it has to resort to drastic measures to get our attention—such as collapsing in illness after we've been piling on too much stress.

This was Jill's pattern for years, starting in college. She always managed to scrape herself together through final-exam week, but then she'd be sick for the week or so of vacation that followed. "I never remember a Christmas or a spring break when I wasn't down with something," she said in one of my seminars. "I always thought of it as my body rebelling. It never occurred to me that my body was something to listen to." Jill didn't start working out with the goal to have healthy holidays. Yet her health has most assuredly improved through her practice in aerobic dance. "I didn't notice it at first," she said. "And then one Christmas I thought, 'Gee, it's Christmas and I'm not sick. What's going on?' But when you start doing physical things, you have to listen to the body. And once you're listening, it doesn't have to shout."

As we move toward total fitness by opening the channel between body and mind, "I" becomes more than our conscious thoughts. "I" becomes our entire, integrated body-mind-spirit. Our body assumes a better fit with our mind, and our mind with our body. At the same time, the energy or spirit that runs through our physical body connects us to everything else.

> "I am large. I contain multitudes."
> —Walt Whitman

Total fitness is a body that totally fits our life and enables us to live our life totally. Without resistance. Without betraying us or failing us in the clutch moment. A body that's beautiful to live in is not torn by constant conflict with a mind that goes in different directions. Ordinary exercise may build a body beautiful. However, only by listening and learning through the body, by connecting to the energy that runs through us, do we develop the essential harmony of body, mind and spirit that is total fitness.

Total fitness develops by habit. We reinforce this habit each day that we practice sincerely: developing breath and center, building energy and awareness, enabling alignment of conscious mind and body wisdom.

Total fitness grows out of a well-rounded practice that matches your needs and interests. In the last chapter you had a chance to take a personal inventory of your needs and interests, as well as your preference for guidance. In this chapter, you'll have a chance to use that information to customize a practice.

Figure 8-1 summarizes the four areas of BodyLearning activities and the development strengths of each. A well-rounded practice combines activities from diagonal areas (e.g., static-meditative and dynamic-aerobic), so that you develop from more than one angle. In a balanced program you have more than one way of developing breath and center. You develop one kind of breathing under aerobic pressure and another kind when you breathe deeply and slowly. In a balanced program you have more than one way of developing awareness, engaging in activities that rapidly demand it as well as those where you have learned to consciously focus. You have more than one way of building energy, both through aerobic activities that require it as well as through meditative activities that relax your body, thereby allowing the energy to flow.

Figure 8-1. Summary of Four Areas with Sample Activities and Development Strengths	
STATIC-AEROBIC	**DYNAMIC-AEROBIC**
Examples: jogging, swimming, weight lifting, most health club machines *Development emphasis:* performance breathing, steadiness, endurance, peak energy, stress release, active self-awareness	*Examples:* dance, tennis, martial arts, most team sports *Development emphasis:* performance breathing, dynamic awareness, peak energy, centeredness through motion, stress release, interpersonal skills
STATIC-MEDITATIVE	**DYNAMIC-MEDITATIVE**
Examples: gardening, yoga, arts and crafts, meditation *Development emphasis:* deep centered breathing, inner strength, relaxation, focused awareness, outward expression of inner condition (arts)	*Examples:* driving, photography, golf, sailing *Development emphasis:* deep centered breathing, external awareness, patience, harmony

The beauty of a balanced program is that one activity can help you get around the barriers you confront in another. Moreover, each activity bootstraps the other(s) to a higher level. Tim, for example, studied Aikido for many years. But after he started Zen training, his Aikido kicked into a higher gear. The solidity he built through meditation made him virtually unstoppable on the Aikido mat. Conversely, Tim found the intensity of Aikido allowed him to practice *Zazen* with more vitality and for longer periods. In similar ways you'll begin to notice the quality of your meditative practice revealed in the more dynamic and aerobic things you do. Going the other way, the more dynamic-aerobic parts of your practice will bring new strength and intensity to the quieter activities.

Putting It All Together

Through this step-by-step process, you'll be able to identify two to four activities that would make a particularly good BodyLearning practice for you. Adapting the old rhyme, we'll look for a program with *something old, something new, something balanced and something true.* The "old" component of your program is, at best, a favorite activity already in your life. The "new" component ideally addresses the area of your greatest development needs or a specific development interest. You'll also want to make sure your practice is balanced with respect to the four areas, possibly adding an activity to achieve a better balance. Finally, it's best if at least one element of your practice has a true direction (i.e., external standards of excellence) and a teacher to guide you.

> "Listen to what you know through your body."
> —*Francis Payne Adler*

The steps that follow are suggestions—an order in which it's easy to organize personal inventory data and sort out practice possibilities. If one of the steps doesn't make sense for your situation, skip over it. In the end you'll want to identify two to four activities that, in your best judgment, make up your best practice. As you go through this process, write down possible activities as candidates on your Personalized Program Work Sheet (see page 174). (An extra copy of this work sheet is in Appendix B.)

Step 1—Look at Your Patterns and Needs and Compare Them with Your Interests. Consider your patterns and needs profile. If all areas are within one point of one another and all are less than ten, your patterns and needs are not a discriminator for selecting BodyLearning candidates. Rather, you should work from your interests (go to Step 2). On the other hand, if your patterns and needs show more than a one-point spread, identify the area with your highest relative score. Look back to your Activity Work Sheet for favored activities in this area. If two development areas scored equally, try to identify a good candidate activity from each area. Identify a candidate activity in any area where you scored more than ten points on your patterns and needs. Write down all candidate activities on your work sheet.

Step 2—Look at Your Interests and Compare Them with Your Patterns and Needs. Look at your Activity Work Sheet and consider the activities in your favorite area, as well as any activity you starred. Activities that you currently enjoy and do often are good candidates for *something old* in your practice. Starred activities (i.e., those you enjoy but don't currently do very often) are good candidates for *something new*, especially as they address high-need areas. Write down the candidates that emerge from your interests.

Step 3—Factor In Your Preference for Guidance. If you scored 5 or more on the guidance assessment (total number of 5's), make sure you've identified at least one candidate activity that could be done under the guidance of a teacher. If you don't have one yet, add your best option. Note this activity as one of your strongest candidates. Even if you don't have a strong preference for guidance, you would do well to include one activity with a teacher, coach or mentor in your final selection.

Step 4—Consider Including Meditation and Breathing Exercises. Meditation and breathing exercises may not show up as an already familiar habit, but they merit special consideration in your program. In chapter 6 you had a chance to select the type of meditation program that was a best match for you. Consider whether you can retain elements of that program at least several days a week. If you're able to carve out twenty minutes a day for this kind of practice, you will develop awareness and stability that filters through everything else you do.

Step 5—Consider Special-Purpose Development Areas. If you have a specific development goal that's not covered in the general

PERSONALIZED PROGRAM WORK SHEET	
STATIC-AEROBIC	**DYNAMIC-AEROBIC**
Candidates: Selections: 1. 2.	Candidates: Selections: 1. 2.
STATIC-MEDITATIVE	**DYNAMIC-MEDITATIVE**
Candidates: Selections: 1. 2.	Candidates: Selections: 1. 2.

development areas, scan the table of Specialized Development Areas. Identify the physical activities that would most directly support your goal, adding these as candidates to your program.

Specialized Development Areas

As suggested in Step 5, you might have a more specific development goal than what emerged in the patterns and needs assessment. Virtually any attribute or behavior has a physical component that can be practiced, thereby strengthening that attribute or behavior. Give some thought to what activities might strengthen a pattern that you want to develop.

The table of Specialized Development Areas (Figure 8-2) might help. In addition to the traits generally developed in each of the

Figure 8-2. Specialized Development Areas

STATIC-AEROBIC	DYNAMIC-AEROBIC
Jogging, Power Walking, Racewalking: determination Running, Wheelchair Racing: determination, peak performance Aerobic Exercise (not to music): body conditioning Weight Lifting, Power Lifting: body conditioning, peak performance, concentration Skating, Rollerblading: sense of rhythm, balance in motion Swimming, Kayaking: harmony, sense of rhythm Stairmaster: breath endurance, determination Rowing Machine: sense of rhythm, breath-body coordination Stationary Bicycling: endurance, determination Cross-Country Ski Machine: sense of rhythm, balance	Martial Arts (general): self-defense, self-realization Aikido: conflict resolution, leadership, adaptability Kendo: instantaneous timing, cutting through (self-delusion) Karate, Tae Kwon Do: competition, victory over self Judo, Jujitsu: sense of leverage, balance, timing Aerobic Exercise (to music): sense of rhythm Downhill Skiing: risk taking, dynamic harmony Skiing (cross country, water): harmony and balance Football: strategy, sense of dynamic patterns Hockey, Soccer, Basketball, Volleyball: strategy, sense of dynamic patterns, nonstop performance Baseball: coordination, instantaneous timing Dance: sense of rhythm, balance, harmony Tennis, Racquetball, Squash: dynamic interaction, instantaneous timing Crew, Canoeing: harmony, sense of rhythm Rock/Mountain Climbing, Vigorous Hiking: risk taking, planning, harmony (with terrain) Sailboarding, Surfing: dynamic harmony, sense of rhythm Bicycling: balance in motion, burst performance

(continued)

Figure 8-2. Specialized Development Areas (continued)

STATIC-MEDITATIVE	DYNAMIC-MEDITATIVE
Housecleaning: integration of practice into daily life Cooking: nutritional awareness, sense of culinary balance and timing, integration into daily life Gardening, Flower Arranging, *Ikebana*: Sense of natural balance, beauty Drawing, Painting, Calligraphy (*Shodo*): develops the eye, expressiveness, creativity Singing, Playing Musical Instrument (solo): develops the ear, expressiveness, breathing (wind instrument) Crafts, Sculpture, Ceramics: expressiveness, creativity, timing (if material changes over time) Needlework, Weaving, Sewing, Woodworking (with patterns): attention to detail, care Needlework, Weaving, Sewing, Woodworking (without patterns): creativity, attention to detail, care, expressiveness Mechanical Work: attention to detail, making things work Meditation, *Zazen*: alignment, self-realization Breathing Exercises: health, deeper and more relaxed condition, integration into daily life Stretching Exercises: flexibility Yoga: flexibility, health, more relaxed condition Tai Chi: deep power, focused energy, coordination Walking: health, integration of practice into daily life Bowling: coordination, moving from center Target Practice, Archery (Western): develops the eye, coordination Archery (*Kyudo*): self-realization, natural motion	Driving: integration of practice into daily life Fishing, Hunting: sense of timing, patterns Photography: develops the eye, sense of nature's balance Golf: coordination, goal orientation, natural motion, can also have benefits of walking Singing, Playing Musical Instrument (with group): develops the ear, expressiveness, breathing (wind instruments) Ceramics (thrown clay): centering, timing and rhythm of working with changing material Horseback Riding: sense of rhythm, oneness Sailing: dynamic sense of rhythm, working with momentum, planning Flying (as pilot): concentration, risk taking, sense of freedom, planning Scuba Diving, Snorkeling: concentration, planning, inquisitiveness Hiking: harmony (with terrain), inquisitiveness Bird-watching: inquisitiveness, appreciation

four areas, each BodyLearning activity has something unique to offer. These specialized development areas are listed in Figure 8-2. Admittedly, this table contains subjective judgments that will not be true in every case. But perhaps it can provide a source of insight for your deliberations from the collective wisdom it represents. You may find an additional activity that gets right at the heart of a matter you want to work on. If so, add it to your personalized program.

A few of the activities in the Specialized Development Areas table are noteworthy for their ability to help us integrate our practice of awareness into everyday life. These are activities that we tend to do frequently and have to do anyway, such as driving, cooking, walking, housecleaning—or certainly breathing. If you've had a hard time integrating change into your life in the past, or if you have experienced the difficulty of "walking a new talk," you might want to include one of these activities in your practice. Since they have so many hooks and inroads into our everyday lives, once these activities are done with new awareness, that awareness surfaces elsewhere in our lives.

If you know of a specific pattern you'd like to practice that you don't find in the table, try to identify the more general development area or activities to which it's related. As an example, imagine you've read Stephen Covey's book on *7 Habits of Highly Effective People*,[1] and decided to work on developing the effective habit of "beginning with the end in mind." You could do that by relating it to traits that BodyLearning develops, as in the following exercise:

1. Imagine someone who excels in the trait you want to develop. Make a list of the attributes this person would exhibit that demonstrate excellence in this trait. How would they be? What would they do?

2. Select the attribute(s) on your list that you particularly want to develop.

3. Look through the list of activities in the Specialized Development Areas table for the best match. For attributes that are fairly general (e.g., patience, endurance) consult the Development Strengths table (Figure 7-4, p. 163) to determine which of the four areas would emphasize them the most. Pick your favorite activity in that area.

To work the example of "beginning with the end in mind," here's my list of several attributes I'd associate with someone who does this exceptionally well:

- is confident
- has clear intent and is flexible in tactics
- can dynamically replan when the situation calls for it
- acts in a focused, not spurious, way
- knows how to aim and fire

In the second step you select the attributes that are most important to you. You have to decide, for example, if your weak link is dynamic planning skills, confidence, or learning how to aim and hit your mark. Once you focus on a particular attribute, you can select activities that would strengthen it. For example, if you decide you want to emphasize dynamic planning skills, activities such as sailing, flying or rock climbing would give you plenty of practice. On the other hand, if you want to practice aiming and hitting a goal, archery, bowling or golf could all be excellent practices. If you prefer activities that are not sports, you might consider sculpture or woodworking, where each shape or cut is made with a clear end in mind.

Through this simple process, you can identify activities that will strengthen the traits that are most important to you. Add to your list of candidates any additional activities that emerge from your reflection on specific development areas.

Winnow and Balance

Having assembled a list of candidate activities, you are now ready to take the last step in customizing a practice. As you whittle down your list of candidates, note your final selections on the Personalized Program Work Sheet. Remember, just because you don't select a candidate activity doesn't mean you can't do it. It just means you're not making it part of your practice at this time. Neither does it mean the activity will never be part of your practice. You can always add and subtract activities as you go. This is for getting started. This is for Now.

Step 6—Winnow and Balance. Trim your candidates down to two to four activities, at least one of which you can do every day. Ideally, your final selections should include *something old, something new, something balanced and something true.*

If you've gotten to the last step and don't have at least two candidate activities, I recommend starting with one of the meditation programs outlined in chapter 6. Basic breathing and meditation exercises are excellent for building awareness and inner energy that will likely lead you into other activities.

It is more likely that you have more than two to four candidate activities. In this case, it's wise to whittle them down to a realistic program that meets your needs and interests but doesn't overcommit you. If you're not able to do some of your candidate activities very often (for example, downhill skiing when you live in Florida), they're not good selections for your day-to-day practice. It would be terrific if, when you do get a chance to do them, you maintain your practice mindset. But they're not the best activities to design a practice around now. Rather, you should choose a small set of activities, at least one of which you can do almost every day. As you whittle down your list, you should keep balance in mind. If you select only two activities, for example, they should be from diagonally opposite areas (e.g., static-meditative and dynamic-aerobic).

Another balance to keep in mind as you design a practice is your time constraints. It's pointless to design a practice that is so time-consuming you can't possibly maintain it. If your schedule is already under serious pressure, all the more reason to include *something old* in your practice. By making part of your practice something you're already doing (but can now do with new awareness), you don't have to find new time for it.

You will also find it valuable to balance your practice with respect to your patterns and needs. The best place to add *something new* to your practice is in an area where your development needs are the strongest. Consider activities in this area that you enjoy (or think you'd enjoy) but don't currently do very often. A new activity addressing an area we sincerely want to develop has the greatest potential payoff in our practice. Moreover, while *something old* is easier to integrate into our schedule, most people find that *something new* is easier for practicing a new level of awareness. Designing a well-balanced practice, we take a little of each.

A final balancing consideration is to include at least one activity that has external standards of excellence. (If you have a strong guidance preference, this is probably the same activity for which you're seeking a teacher, mentor or coach.) Keeping *something true* in your program gives you an important objective mirror in which you can see yourself and see your progress. Since each activity will influence the other(s), seeing your progress in even one activity will give you valuable feedback on your entire practice.

Six Steps in Designing a Practice

1. **Consider your patterns and needs.** Select candidate activities from areas where you scored the highest or more than 10.
2. **Consider your interests.** Select candidate activities in your favorite area or those you don't currently do but might enjoy.
3. **Consider your guidance preference.** If it's high (5 or more), select activities with teachers. Even if it's low, try to pick one activity with external standards and a teacher to (at least occasionally) guide you.
4. **Consider meditation and breathing exercises.** If you've already started a meditative practice from earlier chapters, try to include it several days a week. It will make a huge difference in other things you do.
5. **Consider special development needs.** If you've identified a particular goal or area you'd like to work on that's not already covered, select a specific activity to address it.
6. **Winnow and balance.** Trim your candidate list down to two to four balanced selections, at least one of which you can do almost every day.

Practice Made Perfect

For some people, designing a practice is a very systematic process and they'll follow each of the six steps I've outlined. For others, it's a more intuitive process. Whether we arrive by reason or inspiration, we generally know when we've hit pay dirt—that is, when we've hit on a practice that develops us the way we need to grow.

Charlotte was the last person you'd think needed another activity in her life when she attended my BodyLearning seminar. Strong and fast, she had already learned a great deal through her years of jogging, weight training, kayaking and basketball. By any medical definition she was totally fit. Charlotte's personal inventory showed that her interests were numerous and heavily favored fast, aerobic activities. Her patterns and needs, however, revealed an area causing her trouble. "I have no patience, it's true," she said, looking over her high need scores in the meditative areas. "I always feel like I'm pushing on a rope, trying to make things happen. It's very frustrating." "Is it frustrating enough?" I asked her. "Just as your current activities help you develop speed and initiative, quieter activities could help you build patience and a sense of nature's timing. If you've had enough frustration, practice patience."

Charlotte finally designed a practice that combined her old interest in basketball with the new activity of ceramics. In addition to developing the patience of learning a new skill, Charlotte would learn to work with the natural timing in which ceramics shape and set. Moreover, she knew of a ceramics class she could join where she could get guidance from a teacher. Even playing her familiar basketball, she could develop new awareness of the timing at which each play developed, moving with it rather than forcing it. Her practice was perfectly designed for what she needed to work on.

Helen wouldn't have met anyone's definition of being totally fit when she attended my class. She was almost apologetic about her personal inventory. "I used to do so many things," she said. "But since my back started hurting, there's less and less I can do. Now, I don't do anything. And I have no energy. I've got to get back into shape, but everything seems to hurt." She had been to doctors and chiropractors. While she got temporary relief from their drugs or treatment, nothing had a lasting effect. They also could not find something wrong enough to fix. Helen was concerned that she wasn't in good enough shape to start a practice. "Just the opposite," I told her. "You've got to start with exactly the shape you're in. And you probably have more motivation to practice than most people because you're suffering enormously."

What I recommend to people like Helen is to start with breathing exercises and meditation: sitting, walking or lying down, whatever they can do. And to practice these diligently until the body's energy and awareness build to the point where other activities are possible. If you're like Helen, as soon as possible in your practice you should find an activity in which you can work with a good teacher who can discern whether your inevitable pains are par for the course or indicating a problem.

Jim's dilemma in designing a practice was that too much was possible. He had plenty of interests but only enough time for a couple of them. His personal inventory didn't single out any area as a strong development need, though all his areas scored around 10, and he definitely felt the need for changes in his life. "But I can't decide what would be the best practice. I'm not sure if I can maintain awareness and develop my breathing doing a lot of the things on the [activity] list. And I'm not just looking for something else to do." For people like Jim who have trouble narrowing down a practice, I suggest the following exercise:

After you've lined up all your candidate activities, pick five, each of which you can do (once) over the next five days. Include all the candidates you're seriously considering (if that's more than five, take more days). Go through the week, doing each of the activities and evaluating it for your practice. Notice which activities you didn't do at all by the week's end. Forget those for your practice. Notice which activities were easiest for maintaining your concentration and breath awareness. Those are good candidates. Notice which activity took you furthest out of your comfort zone. That's a good candidate, too (provided that it's not so far out of your comfort zone that you won't do it). At the end of the week, throw out two (or so) of the activities and continue with the rest.

As you whittle down your list of candidates to a few final selections, it's not necessary to cast the other activities out of your life forever. Certainly keep as many activities in your life as feel comfortable. Not all of them have to be part of your practice. Over time, as you move toward wholeness and total fitness, you will almost certainly modify your practice. Experiment. Discover which activities best develop your energy and awareness. As new goals take shape in your life, some of the activities you cross out today will become just the right things to do at a later date. Keep your practice work sheet in your notebook. Even more important, keep your sense of inquiry into what belongs in your practice. Far from being a one-shot survey, customizing a practice that tends to your personal development is an ongoing process, informed by your increasing awareness. Periodically, reassess where you are and where you want to be in terms of your practice.

Developing a practice that develops you is the greatest gift you can give yourself and, at the same time, your most fundamental responsibility.

> "Nothing happens without personal transformation."
> —W. Edwards Deming

Maybe you think being a good parent is your greatest responsibility. Or being a good employee, friend, or contributor to society. These are all important responsibilities. But the quality with which we do any of these things is grounded in who we are. And the quality of who we are is honed through practice. It's *that* important.

And Now to Practice

Total fitness is more than a body beautiful. It's a body that's beautiful to live in, expressing an essential harmony of body-mind-spirit. Total fitness grows out of a well-rounded BodyLearning practice that meets our needs and interests. If you've gone through this design process, you now have a balanced practice that enables your development toward total fitness. Perhaps you've already settled on the exact set of activities constituting your practice. Perhaps you have to try out a few activities before you finish winnowing your list of candidates. But in either case, you know the next step.

Before reading further, please give yourself twenty or thirty minutes to enjoy an element of the practice you've just designed. The whole point of this book is not just to read it but to move toward your own total fitness through your own practice. Select an activity that you can do now—best if it addresses the area of your highest need. As you practice, make this time come alive: be aware of your breath, and all that your senses present. Be aware of this vital present moment. Be aware that this activity is answering a voice within you that rejoices in being heard.

9

Commitment: Developing
Staying Power

"Stay with something because that's how you deepen your life;
otherwise you are always on the surface."
—*Natalie Goldberg*

Commitment to Practice Is Practicing Commitment

"Getting my black belt is the most important thing to me right now," Greg said after his first Aikido class. "My wife wants me to get in shape, I need this for my job, and I'm really dedicated." My uneasiness with his vocal enthusiasm was confirmed a few weeks later when he caught the flu, missed a couple of classes, and then found one reason after another that kept him off the mat.

I don't think Greg was lying to me when he said getting his black belt was the most important thing to him. I think in that particular moment he meant what he said. As with any thought or emotion, however, enthusiasm has a limited life. As long as Greg kept up his physical practice, his enthusiasm had a chance to be recharged. But as soon as he caught the flu and quit coming to class, the batteries of enthusiasm ran down, and he forgot all about this "most important" thing. Next, Greg will go on to some other "most important" thing for a few weeks.

Greg's pattern is familiar to many of us. So often we tear into activities or relationships and then proceed to back out. Sometimes backing out is appropriate, but if it's a principal pattern of our life, we're cheating ourselves out of the depth that comes only with commitment. Moreover, we lose credibility with ourselves when we casually drop activities that are "most important" to us. At some level we know that if we can't stick with what's most important, we can't stick with anything. And if we can't stick with anything, life is very limited.

It's limited to the surface—superficial relationships, thin under-standing—nothing deep enough to sustain us, much less transform us. We might liken it to the level at which we, as children in ele-mentary school, learned of world cultures and religions: an Epcot Center of main foods, costumes, and a count of religious holidays and deities. If we've since penetrated any one of those cultures or religions, we know there's much more to it than would fit into an Epcot Center display or an eight-year-old's textbook. But if we've never developed much depth in anything, we don't know the differ-ence. Epcot Center looks like the real world. Veneer looks like solid wood. And we're left with a sense that life is shallow. We think the shallowness is out there, rather than in us, as we ask, "Is this all there is?"

It's a good question to ask. And if it burns hotly enough, we do something about answering it. Many of us turn to traditional religions. Others look elsewhere for answers, fueling what has be-come the human potential movement in the latter part of the twen-tieth century. From a host of mind-body practices and therapies to a recurring romance with angels, spirits and paranormal phenom-ena, and a bounty of books promising food for the soul—we have a wide buffet from which to choose mental, physical and spiritual nourishment. The irony is that the wide array of choices is part of what keeps us hopping from one thing to the next. So long as we keep hopping, we never go deep.

As a Zen and Aikido instructor, I have met many students hopping through the practices I teach. On the one hand, Aikido and Zen are not for everyone. And it is appropriate for people to move on to something else if the training doesn't feel right for them. As we've emphasized in designing a program in BodyLearning, it's easier to practice wholeheartedly when you love what you do. That connection may not happen on the first try. On the other hand, some people move on because they feel they need to hit the whole human potential buffet. Aikido for three weeks. Aromatherapy for three weeks. Rolfing for three weeks. Next.

"Clarity and perseverance are difficult in American society," writer Natalie Goldberg observes, "because the basis of capitalism is greed and dissatisfaction. There's always a better stereo system, television, car, and shoe."[1] There's always this season's mental, physical and spiritual fad. Why stick with the boring practice we did last week when this week we could find something new?

The reason is depth. So long as we operate on the surface with a lack of commitment in the moment and a lack of commitment over time, it almost doesn't matter how fine a teaching we encounter. We'll hardly notice it. No matter how perfectly designed our practice, if we lack commitment, it will amount to nothing in our life. Conversely, if we fully commit to our practice in the moment and sustain our commitment over time, the particulars of our practice are secondary. We will deepen. And we will grow.

We learn commitment through our body—and no other way. Even though commitment may start out as an intellectual concept, such as a

> "If you go deeply in one thing, you know everything else."
> —Natalie Goldberg

New Year's resolution or a religious belief, in order to stay with us, it must take shape in a change of physical habit. The new habit, changing our very body, eventually embodies our commitment.

And so it is that our physical practice not only benefits from commitment but is also the most effective way to build commitment. By learning how to stick with our practice, we learn how to stick with what's most important in our life—for longer than three weeks! By learning to deepen our practice, we learn to deepen our life. Since so much rides on the matter of commitment, we turn next to some practical considerations to help clear the way for commitment to our practice.

Making Space for Practice

You've already had a chance to design a best practice for you. In this exercise you have a chance to design the best chance for your practice to survive amid the demands of daily life. By sculpting time for your practice within your day and week, you make room for the commitment that allows practice to go deep. And with it, your life.

In the first step of this exercise, you survey your week for possible time slots for practice, noting them on a weekly calendar. An example from one of my students is shown below.

SUN	MON	TUE	WED	THURS	FRI	SAT
A.M. open	A.M. 6:30–7:30	A.M. 6:30–7:30	A.M. 6:30–7:30	A.M. 6:30–7:30	A.M. 6:30–7:30	A.M. 9–12
P.M. open	P.M. 12–1 7–10	P.M. 12–1	P.M. 12–1 7–10	P.M. 12–1	P.M.	P.M.

These were the openings Ellen could find in her weekly schedule. She didn't plan to fill all of them with practice, but these were times that at least had the possibility for practice. While "spare time" was a contradiction in Ellen's life, she figured she could allocate some time before breakfast, during most lunch hours, and a couple of evenings.

Now get your notebook and give yourself about fifteen minutes to design your own time for practice.

Step 1—Consider Your Schedule. In your notebook draw a sample calendar week running from Sunday to Saturday, such as the one below:

SUN	MON	TUE	WED	THURS	FRI	SAT
A.M.	A.M.	A.M.	A.M.	A.M.	A.M.	A.M.
P.M.	P.M.	P.M.	P.M.	P.M.	P.M.	P.M.

For each day of a typical week, fill in time slots that would be available for practice. You don't have to commit to using all these times; indeed, it would not be wise to fill all your spare time with practice. But identify those times when you're not already scheduled to do something else and some element of practice might be possible.

Consider the following questions, especially if your time is highly constrained and you don't see any openings in a number of days.

1. Could I get up twenty to thirty minutes earlier on any mornings for practice? If so, which ones?
2. Could any lunch hours be freed up for practice? If so, how many?
3. Could I practice in the half hour before dinner sometime during the week? If so, which evenings?
4. Could I carve out some time for practice after dinner? If so, which nights?

Fill in any candidate times on your sample calendar as you think of them. Remember, an interval has to be only twenty to thirty minutes long to be useful for practice. Of course, depending on what you do, you may need additional time for transportation, showering or whatever. In the next step, you'll consider the realistic time demands of each element of your practice.

In my experience it's useful to associate practice with meals, such as practicing right before breakfast, lunch or dinner, because meals are already a confirmed habit in our life. We borrow a bit of their structure in tagging our practice to them. My habit is to sit before breakfast and do something aerobic before lunch. It has allowed me to quit asking whether I feel like sitting or working out today (which is basically irrelevant—nothing more than a pleasant coincidence if the feeling of wanting to practice happens to coincide with the time to do it). Whether I feel like it or not, I practice before I eat. And not surprisingly, I never forget to eat.

Of course, you have to find what works for you. But the truth is, commitment to practice eventually requires you to practice on a day— maybe many days—when you don't feel like it. Even if you enjoy your practice most days, on some days when it's time for practice, everything in you will say, "Oh gee, not today." In my experience, the best way around the internal whining is Don't Ask. That's the value of having a routine time of practice in your day: it moves you beyond the question of whether-you-want-to to knowing-you-will.

In the next steps, you have a chance to consider the time requirements of each part of your practice and map those activities to specific time slots. To continue Ellen's example, she developed a schedule for her practice consisting of (1) aerobic dance, (2) sitting meditation and (3) painting. She wanted to do aerobic dance at least three times a week, sitting five times a week and painting once a week. She also wanted a day off. Here's what she came up with:

SUN	MON	TUE	WED	THURS	FRI	SAT
open	A.M. 6:30–7:00 sitting P.M. 12–1 aerobic dance	A.M. 6:30–7:00 sitting P.M. 12–1 aerobic dance	A.M. 6:30–7:00 sitting P.M. 7–10 option for painting class	A.M. 6:30–7:00 sitting P.M. 12–1 aerobic dance	A.M. 6:30–7:00 sitting P.M.	9–12 noon option for painting class P.M.

Ellen's example shows a solid practice of at least thirty minutes a day, six days a week. Yet it takes up less than half of the free time she had identified and still leaves Sunday open. Ellen's schedule is realistic. Not overcommitted. We can build commitment only through an enduring practice. And our practice will have endurance only if it's realistic.

Step 2—Consider Your Practice. Look over the set of activities you've selected as the best practice for you. Assign a time interval to each activity that realistically represents how much time you'd need to set aside to do this. Include any time for transportation, setup or cleanup afterwards—whatever the activity requires.

Next, estimate for each activity how many times during a typical week you'd like to do this. Some activities you'll be able to do only on the weekends or when a particular class is offered. Other activities you can do on your own every day. For some activities you might find it useful to estimate a range of no-less-than X times a week and up to Y times a week. At this step in the process, don't be too concerned with time constraints—we'll reconcile those next. First, get an idea of what you want. Try to identify enough intervals of practice that some activity can fit almost every day (i.e., six or more intervals).

Step 3—Match Your Practice to Your Week. Look over the calendar of intervals available for practice and the time requirements and "desirements" of each activity. Redraw your weekly calendar to show the intervals and activities where you think they fit best. If you don't know exactly where an activity fits (e.g., you plan to take a class and don't yet know when it's offered), take a best guess or show it optionally in a couple of places. You may have to reshuffle pieces of your practice later. But it's always easier to reschedule a class or a practice session than it is to find new time for it. Design your typical practice week now in a way that looks workable, ideally allocating some activity to six of the seven days.

When we match our available time slots to the amount of practice we want to do, it's best not to use up more than half of our free time. We need to leave a little slack in our schedule. Then when we encounter a non-negotiable demand on Tuesday, maybe we can pick up that aerobics class on Wednesday and still make three sessions during the week. We want to avoid being so overcommitted that as soon as reality knocks (as it will), we're giving up on our practice altogether. We can change the plan, but we don't want to lose it. My friend Janet has a saying: "It's good to have a plan so you know when you need to change it." Take your best shot at a realistic schedule now and stick to it until it's clear you need to change it.

Making space for practice is drawing a line of realistic commitment in our day-to-day life. Not too little and not too much. Too little and we're missing too many days to develop deep habits and learning. Too much and we're not able to maintain our practice for the long run. We need to find the balance in our schedule—and then honor it.

Clearing the Obstacles to Practice

As a management consultant well steeped in the theories and practice of managing change, I've learned that one of the ways to make a change stick is to get rid of the reasons for it not to. We can apply this same reasoning to incorporating a BodyLearning practice into our week. I've emphasized the real benefits of BodyLearning, from increased energy to commitment. At times the positive pull forward will be enough to keep us practicing. But sometimes the most effective way to secure a positive change in our life is to reduce the things that work against it.

"My biggest obstacle is time," Jim said at a recent BodyLearning seminar when asked what stands between him and practice. "Some weeks I can manage to get to the gym regularly, but then I get sent on travel for my job, or my wife has to go out of town and I need to be at home with the kids at night. I tell you, it's just not workable week after week."

While the specifics of Jim's situation don't apply to everyone, almost everyone I ask in seminars who either works full-time or has young children at home (or both) reports time as a major obstacle to practice. We certainly can't manufacture more time. How then can we reduce the obstacle posed by time constraints?

The first thing we need to realize is that time in general is never a problem. All we have is time—twenty-four hours a day of it. And every day, with varying degrees of awareness and freshness of choice, we allocate those hours to the things that are most important to us. While time in general cannot be a problem, the specific way we allocate our time can become a problem for us. The problem we call "time" is always a mask for an internal disagreement about what's important. We feel the time pinch when new things become important to us and fight for air time in a schedule that refuses to budge. We feel the pinch when the normal time demands in our life start expanding. We tend to regard the demands on our time as coming from "out there"—a job wanting us to work overtime, a family wanting us somewhere else, and so on. It's useful to remember that the decision to honor the demands is always "in here." "In here," within each of us, we can decide to honor the demands differently.

In effect this is what we did in the previous exercise. We mined our current schedule for time slots we could reallocate to practice, trying to be realistic and not overcommit all our free time. This is a necessary starting point for committing to a practice, but for some people it's not sufficient. I watch some people in seminars struggle with the calendar exercise, looking almost as though they're going to burst with anxiety. On the one hand, they want to make a positive change in their life and see a BodyLearning practice as a way to do that. On the other hand, they've been down this self-improvement road before. They know they can make a commitment to practice in the comfort of a seminar setting (which you might liken to your relatively comfortable setting of reading a book). But as soon as they rejoin a crazy work setting or a hectic household, their good intentions go out the window. They feel stuck—dissatisfied with where they are and unable to change.

Jim was one of these people. "I can fill out the make-believe calendar," he said. "And on a good week, I can stick with it. But as soon as I'm sent out of town, it's all over." I told him it was over only if he wanted it to be over. "I also travel a great deal for my work," I said. "And it's true my practice changes when I'm on the road, but I can always do something. Even if it's twenty minutes of breathing exercises in my hotel room." He gave me a look that communicated hell would freeze over before he'd do breathing exercises in his hotel room, so I suggested he look over the Body-Learning Activity Checklist and put a mark by all the activities he could take on the road with him. "If travel is one of your obstacles to practice," I told him, "design a portable backup practice."

"I also travel for my work," said Ellen, the seminar participant whose schedule and practice we saw as the example in the calendar exercise. "And that's one of the reasons I've put off taking a painting class for so long. I'd like to learn watercolor, and I know I have to take a class to do it. Yet when I've started classes before, I've missed too many sessions and eventually dropped them. Between travel, my son's basketball games, the report for work that has to be ready first thing in the morning or what have you, I can't seem to work a steady class into my schedule."

Classes can pose a challenge when our schedule isn't used to accommodating them. Yet we can do many things to lower the obstacles to practice, even when it involves inflexible class schedules. I put Ellen's dilemma to the group of seminar participants and asked them to brainstorm ways Ellen could clear the path to make a painting class more possible. Here are a few of the suggestions they came up with:

Reducing the obstacles of work and travel:
- Find a class time of least travel conflict; weekends are probably better than weekdays.
- Try to arrange with a co-worker to cover for you during class times.

- Tell your boss and others at work that you're not available during class time.

Reducing the obstacles of home and family demands:
- Make sure your family understands this class is important to you, and you don't want to miss it for routine matters.
- [If you're married with children] Arrange with your spouse to handle "kid matters" during class time and arrange a backup (baby-sitter, neighbor) for times when your spouse can't do it.
- Look at ways to rearrange the household schedule to support your class; e.g., order out dinner, rent movies for the night, look for activities for your children that meet at the same time.

When all else fails:
- If you do miss a class, commit to practicing whatever you can do on your own.
- Find someone in the class you can meet with afterwards to learn what was covered.
- Plan up front to take the class a couple of times, figuring you may get some of the material twice but most of it at least once.

More important than the specific suggestions to help Ellen in her practice is the mindset that finds a way around every obstacle. This is the mindset that makes practice possible for the long run. This is the mindset that learns commitment and develops depth. In the following exercise, you're invited to explore this same mindset as you reflect on the specific obstacles to your own practice. For this exercise, you'll need your notebook and about fifteen minutes.

Step 1—Consider Your Obstacles. Look over the weekly schedule you've designed for your practice and consider for a few moments all the things that are likely to get in the way of it. Be more specific than "time constraints" or "lack of motivation." What is most likely to constrain your time? What is most likely to de-motivate you? Write down a few of the biggest, most likely obstacles you can think of.

Step 2—Consider Ways to Reduce Your Obstacles. Pick one of your big and likely obstacles and brainstorm for a few moments all the ways you could reduce its effect or eliminate it altogether. Can it be delegated, counteracted, rearranged, ignored, substituted, rewarded, defused, planned for in advance or placated afterwards? If all else fails and the obstacle remains, can you do something else? Jot down as many ideas as you can think of.

After you're done with one obstacle, go on to the next. Develop a brainstorm list around each of the obstacles that seriously concern you.

Step 3—Select Your Best Options. Go back over your list for each obstacle and mark each idea that sounds promising enough to put into practice. The more ways to reduce an obstacle, the better, but only mark those ideas that you're willing to implement. Then do it.

It's good to have a number of ways to handle each obstacle, and even a backup plan if all the ways fail. In Ellen's case with her painting class, it was actually the suggestion that she plan to take the class twice that lit up her face with the new sense of "Why didn't I think of that?" possibility. If some of your obstacles involve the schedules or expectations of family members, you might involve them in this exercise, asking them to brainstorm with you on possible solutions. You might also do this exercise with a friend and brainstorm with each other, just to get a different perspective on your obstacles.

In the end, where there's a will, there's a way. This exercise and the calendar we did earlier are only tools to help our will find a way to make practice possible. If there's not a will to practice, it's only a matter of time before the way is obstructed. If that's the case, we must be happy enough with our life. We're not suffering enough to make a change in what drives us or in which time demands we honor. Put another way, if we cannot clear the path for what we've designed as the best practice for our life at present, our life will have to get worse before we'll be amply motivated to make it better.

Breaking the Start-Stop Habit

Perhaps we've never thought much about the relationship between our level of suffering and our motivation toward change. But this is one of the factors behind the start-stop pattern that many people fall into when they try to make improvements in their life. By gaining some insight into this relationship, we have a better chance of clearing even this barrier to an enduring practice.

"I start out with a bang," as Mary put it in one of my seminars, "and then after a while—maybe weeks or months—I start to feel a little better, and I lose my motivation." Mary was describing a Tai Chi class that she had started and stopped several times. "It's kind of a vicious cycle. It's as though things have to be really bad in order for me to do something good for myself."

The fact that Mary even had insight into her situation was a promising sign. Many people fall into this start-stop habit without recognizing it. As long as we require things to get really bad in our life before we make changes for the better, our life will tend to keep getting really bad. If, as soon as things start getting a little better, we abandon our practice, we severely limit how good things can get.

I have seen two approaches work effectively to break this start-stop pattern of practice. One way is to keep raising the bar. Recognizing that the difference between where we are and where we want to be is a significant motivator for us, we can raise our sights on what's possible even as we improve our current condition. As things get a little better, we set a higher goal. We might think of this as maintaining a healthy dissatisfaction, so whenever we start internally debating whether to go to tonight's Tai Chi class (or whatever our practice is), our fatigue or laziness finds a counterbalancing drive.

The second approach to ending the start-stop pattern is not to stop. We can settle the internal debate about attending tonight's Tai Chi class by not holding it. We simply go. We don't let our feelings in the moment be a factor in maintaining our long-term commitment. We quit entertaining the question of whether we feel like practicing in favor of just doing it. In this way, we free ourselves from having to run on the fuel of dissatisfaction or despair or any particular emotional state, which may or may not be present at a given time.

This second method clearly works best for the long run. It's the Don't Ask approach we talked about earlier in connection with structuring a schedule for our practice. While it may seem like a tall order, most of us have several examples in our life of where we've moved "beyond the question" in significant, enduring relationships.

For example, if we're married or otherwise committed to a partner, we probably passed through some time early in our relationship when we asked ourselves whether we wanted to be involved with this person. But at some point we answered "Yes" in a big way. And quit asking the question. We don't wake up every morning wondering if we still want to stay married. If we're having a bad day or we're angry with our partner, we don't break off the relationship as a first measure. Likewise, if we've developed some commitment to our work, we don't wake up every morning asking ourselves if we still want to do it.

And so it is with our relationship to practice. We enable our commitment to practice by moving beyond the question on a day-to-day basis. That doesn't mean we should never change our practice. We will change it as we change. Just as we change our work or people relationships over time. But we base the change on something more than a mood swing.

It is a fact of our physiology that our thoughts and emotions change frequently, certainly far more frequently than it takes to develop depth in anything. We aren't always going to "feel like it" when it comes time to practice. If we can simply acknowledge this fact—know that we won't always feel like practicing, but that it doesn't really matter what we're feeling—and practice anyway, we can break the start-stop habit. We can break the vicious cycle in which conditions never get very much better in our life. We can break the habit that otherwise confines us to life at the surface.

How to Practice: Absorbing the Full Benefits of BodyLearning

What you practice is important, which is why you've been given the opportunity to put some effort into designing a practice that meets your needs and interests. *That* you practice is paramount, which is why you've had a chance to make space for your practice and overcome its obstacles. But *how* you practice is also critical in determining how much you get out of it. Your practice can be a profound path for growth or a waste of time, depending on how you do it. As my Zen teacher Hosokawa Roshi puts it, "When we train incorrectly, we're just warming cushions."

From Zen training—done correctly—we can distill six essential qualities that make practice worthwhile and apply them to the specific activities we've chosen for our BodyLearning.

Be Whole(hearted)

The more we put into our practice, the more we get out of it, and the more our commitment grows. We want to practice as one whole being. Wholeheartedly. "I really put my heart into it," we say of efforts engaging our total commitment. When we act wholeheartedly, we move beyond sending mixed signals. We express clarity and unity of intention. By contrast, when we act in doubt or insincerity, we label our attempts "halfhearted." More than a metaphor, this imagery reflects our lack of internal alignment. When we do something with our whole heart, we become more integrated: we muster all our resources and concentrate them on the goal at hand. This is the pattern we want to develop and reinforce through our practice.

> *"I shall become a master in this art only after a great deal of practice."*
> —Erich Fromm

How can we be wholehearted in our practice on those days when we don't even feel like practicing? While it may seem like a contradiction, what I've experienced over and over is that knowing my practice requires 100 percent of me is part of what pulls me out of the doldrums of a bad attitude. If I give myself fully to the practice, nothing is left over to carry on the debate about whether I feel like practicing. To feel whiny about not wanting to practice, some part of me has to be standing apart from the practice itself. Once I totally plunge into what I'm doing, that part disappears.

By paying full attention to our breath and body, and being in the present moment, we derive the full benefit of our practice. In this sense BodyLearning differs from the way many of us approach recreation, where we might be drinking or partying with friends and not paying attention to the condition of our body—much less our breath.

This way of practice is also different from the way many people approach their workouts. When traveling, I often go to health clubs, joining the ranks of people trotting on treadmills or climbing stairs to nowhere. I think many of these clubs were designed to help people forget they're exercising. Plastered along the wall, within clear view of every workout station, are enough television sets to watch all major networks and half the cable channels at once. And watch is what most people do, letting their mind wander off elsewhere while their body sweats on automatic. Some people may be able to watch television with less distraction than I can, but it's virtually impossible for me to concentrate on my breathing and body motion when I'm watching a television program.

"That's the whole point," explained Mark, a friend of mine, in response to my complaints about the distracting televisions at the health club. "The TVs are supposed to distract us. We want to be distracted. People basically hate exercise." I understand the problem, but I would submit that the cure of splitting ourselves up is worse than the illness. We might be getting a decent aerobic workout, but we're reinforcing a pattern of mind and body in separate spheres.

Other people prefer the method of working out with friends and using conversation to draw their attention away from the exercise at hand. But again, it's much harder for us to concentrate on our breath and body when we're caught up in a stream of conversation. Eventually, as our concentration develops, it may be possible to maintain awareness and conversation at the same time. But it's not a good way to get started. Early on, our awareness will not be very strong. When we make it compete with television or conversation, our awareness will lose out, and we'll draw less than full benefit from our practice. Our hearts may still appreciate the good aerobic workout. But we've missed a good chance to unify our mind and body through our practice.

If we think of our body as an orchestra, the first step to getting all our instruments on the same page of music is to get their attention. Then we can tune and train them together. How do we get their attention? We call for it with our heart, which we experience as "putting everything into it." Sometimes in life we're called upon to do things that we cannot approach wholeheartedly. So be it. But in our precious time of practice, in activities of our choosing, we don't want to reinforce halfhearted attitudes. Halfhearted attitudes

are self-defeating. Sometimes we try to protect ourselves from dis-
appointment or criticism (especially our own) by lightly dabbling
in our avocations. Forget dabbling. Having designed a practice that
matches you best, jump in wholeheartedly. Anything less is too
weak to make us strong.

Being whole is being connected: mind, body and spirit. When
the mind is paying attention to what the body is doing, it is better
able to learn from the body. It more fully absorbs and informs our
thoughts with the physical lessons of our practice, such as stability,
timing and appropriate spontaneity. When the mind and spirit are
fully engaged in our physical practice, they gain concrete expression
through our body's activity. In other words, the clear intentions of
our mind and the larger life that comes through us enter the world
through our wholehearted practice.

Being whole is fully connecting our mind to our body through
our breath, and our body to the present moment through our
senses. This condition of mind takes some doing, and (unless we're
extraordinary individuals) we won't be able to maintain it twenty-
four hours a day. But we can maintain this condition—or at least
maintain our commitment to return to it once we've lost it—during
the precious twenty minutes of our practice.

Be Aware

Awareness is our conduit between living and learning. Breath is
our conduit to awareness. Awareness of our breath is our most
valuable tool for unifying body-mind-spirit and fully being in the
present moment. Whatever you have chosen for your practice, you
will get the most out of it when you maintain breath awareness.

> "You are always a slave to what you're
> not aware of."
> —Anthony deMello

Breath awareness devel-
ops gradually, as does our
ability to breathe deeply to
and from our center. Don't be
discouraged if initially your
breath is too high or your mind wanders away from following it.
Just keep coming back. Your awareness will grow if you tend to
it. Once you can be aware *that* you're breathing, pay attention to
the way you're breathing. Tension in the body causes the breath

to rise up into the chest, sometimes even into the throat area. As you begin your practice, let your awareness survey your body, inviting the tension to drop and the breath to sink more deeply. The breath drops physically lower in the body, not by force, but by relaxing what otherwise keeps it from dropping, namely tight muscles in the upper body.

As you continue either your aerobic or meditative activity, maintain awareness of your breath as much as the activity allows. Static activities are easier for maintaining breath awareness. Highly dynamic activities will tend to pull your awareness into the fast and furious action of the moment. But they'll still afford many opportunities to come back to your breath awareness, such as between volleyball serves or Judo throws. Eventually your moments of breath awareness will become more frequent and connected until you don't need any break in the action to be aware of your breath and body.

Your rate of breathing will vary, depending on whether you're doing aerobic or meditative activities. Over time, for a given activity, your breath should slow down as each breath becomes more deep and nourishing in the body. You can't force this process, but it's good to be aware of the proper trend and enable it through your gradual relaxation.

For meditative activities, work toward allowing the breath to sink into your center. Set the *hara* at the start of each exhale, and allow the center to "cook" during a long, slow outbreath. Relax on the inhale. Make your exhale two to three times longer than your inhale.

Some meditative activities involve little motion. Others are dynamic with timing demands of their own. But

> *"Let the nothingness into yer shots."*
> —*Golf in the Kingdom*

wherever possible, weave this breath cycle into any body motion involved in your activity. When your activity involves exacting motions, such as swinging a golf club, cutting a piece of wood or releasing a bowling ball, exhale during those moments. Let your inhale be a moment of recovery. If you're painting, put brush to paper on the exhale and replenish the brush with paint on the inhale. Sometimes the way the breath merges with the activity will be fairly automatic, such as in singing or yoga. Other times it may be up to you to find a rhythm that works. For example, if you're pulling weeds in a garden, you might gather them on the exhale and dispose of them on the inhale. By developing a rhythm in breath and body, whether it's strictly required by the activity or not, your mind will stay better focused.

For aerobic activities the breath will initially be led by the demands of the body. Let it be. Simply be aware of what's going on. Over time, begin to develop a rhythm between breath and body. If your activity involves moments of high exertion, such as swinging a bat or pulling yourself up a rock, weave your exhale into those moments. If your activity is steadily aerobic, such as jogging or bicycling, develop a rhythm that lengthens your exhale and allows your breath to drop closer to your center.

A secondary type of awareness you may wish to bring to your BodyLearning activities is an overarching awareness of what you're working on. This is not in conflict with (or a replacement for) being aware of your breath or paying attention to what you're doing. Rather, it's a background awareness that sets the stage for your moment-to-moment activity. This awareness is the conscious mind's message to the body of the larger picture into which this practice fits.

For example, if you want to use your game of golf to practice the specific pattern of "beginning with the end in mind,"[2] you can bring this awareness to each game, to each hole. This very awareness will begin to refine and direct each body motion. As you reflect on your game, you can ask whether you were able to keep the end in mind, or whether some of your shots were rushed or haphazard. In this way, the pattern you want to practice is further reinforced.

It's worth stressing that this kind of intellectual awareness is no replacement for basic breath awareness and being in the moment. If you're in the midst of practice, and your mind has slipped off elsewhere, simply bring it back. Come back to your breath. Come back to the present moment. The whole point of having a practice is that, left to its own habits, our mind *will* drift off. We break that habit and come alive in the present moment only through the discipline of returning to breath awareness. We may not be able to do this forever. But we can certainly manage it for twenty minutes.

Be Centered

Related to our sense of wholeness and awareness is a fundamental centeredness we build through our practice. Physically we build this centeredness by making the physical center of our body the source of our motion and breathing.

In meditative activities that have little or no movement, we develop our center purely by using our breath and setting our *hara* with each exhale. In most BodyLearning activities involving movement, we further develop our center by putting it squarely in the center of what we do. What does it mean to move to from our center? It means we make the center of our body the master control center for all our motion. We move as if every intention to move arises and emanates from our center (not from our head). If we're walking or running, for example, we might imagine a rope connected to our center, pulling us evenly forward. If we're dancing, we want to find that point of balance that makes our motions light and balanced.

Even if our efforts to be centered start out as metaphors of master control centers or images of ropes connected to our center, the experience and signs of centeredness eventually become very real. When we shape a ceramic pot by moving from our center, the pot turns out centered and balanced. When we move from our center in martial arts, our motions become more powerful and co-ordinated. In BodyLearning activities such as fine arts and martial arts, we can readily see our condition of centeredness fed back to us in the quality of our practice. Even when the feedback is not so obvious, a discerning eye will be able to detect increased stability in our posture. And on the inside we'll experience increased emotional stability and less mind chatter.

Handing over the controls, as it were, from head to center is not the normal pattern of the thinking mind. Yet once we get used to connecting our mind to our center—breathing into the center, focusing on the center and moving from the center—we discover our most effective action and our most balanced condition. Practicing centeredness, twenty minutes at a time, we discover our most capable self.

Be Experimental

Last year I decided it would be good for me to learn to take more risk. I didn't want to go out and do something stupid, but I thought if I could stretch myself a little toward risk taking, it would give me a little more courage. Last winter I had an opportunity to go snow skiing several times. Normally, I'm a steady flatland cross-country skier. But last winter I was in Colorado, and so I thought I'd experiment. I took steeper hills. I made sharper turns. I hung up my cross-country skis and tried downhill skiing for a couple of days. I didn't head for the advanced, black diamond slopes. But I did make a point to lean out over the hill, to face the hold-back fear that I surely felt. In an environment that was not particularly dangerous, I found ways to take some risk.

Be experimental. Try things. Look at ways in which your practice can help you grow. You can even do activities that are familiar favorites in new ways that help build new patterns. For example, if you normally do needlework to patterns, but you'd like to further develop your creativity, try designing your own patterns. If you normally do aerobic exercise on a stationary bike, but you'd like to develop more external awareness, try doing aerobic dance with a group. If you love to hike and you'd like to work more on your planning skills, you might plan a long hike that takes provisions and contingencies into account. By considering variations to our practice, we can gently stretch ourselves into important areas of growth.

Another way to be experimental is with timing. For example, let's say you've designed jogging into your practice as a way to manage anger and stress in your life. You might try jogging in the morning to see if that makes your day less stressful. You might try jogging in the evening to see if that helps you sleep and makes you feel better rested for the next day. You might try jogging as soon as possible after someone or something has riled you to see if that helps you settle down. By experimenting with when and how often you do activities, you can see under what conditions the practice has the most payoff. It's always good to start with a plan. But as my friend Janet would add, "Know when to change it." If something's not working well, try variations until you find what works better.

By being experimental we commit ourselves to listening to our own practice, listening to our growing awareness and finding ways around any barriers that confront us. If one way doesn't work, we try another way. If we get injured doing one thing, we try something else. If we get bored with one thing, we look for ways to spice it up or trade it in for a new activity. If we're discouraged and on the verge of giving up, we find ways to enliven or scale back our practice to something we'll stick to. If we're experiencing new or old injuries in something we're doing, we might augment our practice with a healing bodytherapy. If we hit a brick wall in our progress in a dynamic aerobic activity, we might try a meditative activity to tunnel underneath it.

> *"Our body is a source of truth."*
> —*Albert Pesso*

It is our nature to grow and change. By being experimental and creatively persistent in our practice, we align our conscious mind with our deepest nature to evolve. As our awareness develops and clarifies, it naturally leads us toward filling in our own gaps. Our experiments become guided by a growing wisdom.

Be Realistic

Several years ago I read a wonderful book that talked about being alive and mindful in the present moment.[3] It struck me as a great idea. "From now on," I promised myself, "I'm going to be alive in the present moment." Well, a few moments later I was off thinking about work. I pulled myself back to the present moment. A few moments later I was remembering a telephone conversation I'd had earlier. I pulled myself back. Then I was remembering last night's dream. And then I was noodling over a problem at work. And then the phone rang, and I was pulled into a lengthy conversation. By the end of it, I'd forgotten all about the present moment and my promise. Later when I thought of it, I felt embarrassed for how quickly I had lost my mindfulness and didn't want to think about it again.

This is what happens when we're not realistic. We set up conditions we can't possibly meet. It was no more possible for my jump-around mind to permanently stay in the present moment than it would be for a bee to fly in place. Now, years later, it's much more possible for me to be in the present moment. I'm still not here all the time, but whatever settling into the present I've done has come through small, realistic steps. One practice session at a time.

Be realistic in what you ask of yourself. Be patient in your practice and in your expectations of progress. Some of the patterns that you're working to change are stored in your muscles and skeleton; they will not change overnight. Some of the patterns are in your heart, in your blood pressure and in the openness of your veins and arteries. These can and will change but they don't change instantly. It is our nature to store progress invisibly for long periods of time, leading up to a sudden leap of growth. It is easy to grow discouraged when progress is not apparent. But if you can be realistic in your expectations, knowing the pump takes a while to prime, it will be easier for you to continue your practice to the point where its payoff begins to flow.

Another aspect of being realistic is not to overcommit. We don't want to set ourselves up for failure. That's why we select only a few activities in which to practice the breath-awareness and presence of BodyLearning. That's why we choose activities that we already like to do or may have to do anyway and initially limit our practice to fairly short intervals. As our awareness develops, we'll be able to extend our practice with ease. But if we ask too much of ourselves initially, we may abandon our practice before we get anywhere.

With this in mind, initially limit your practice to one or two twenty-minute intervals a day in which you can maintain your commitment to returning to awareness, if not the awareness itself. For example, if you select driving as part of your BodyLearning program, you might start with picking a specific commute, such as to and from work. Later on you can add more driving opportunities to your practice. But if you drive often, it's not realistic to start with all of it.

If golf is one of your activities for BodyLearning, you might want to start your practice with just the first three holes. Eventually, if you can maintain awareness beyond three holes, you can grow your practice. But it's not realistic to start out trying to play every hole on every game in full awareness. If gardening is your practice, perhaps a specific bed or time of day is the starting point for growing your awareness. Understand yourself and your limits.

It's fine to push limits, but it's useless to push yourself right out of practice. If you're tiring of your practice, you may be trying to do too much.

The other side of being realistic is Don't Do Too Little. Maintain your commitment to your time of practice. If you do not set this time aside and guard it jealously, it will evaporate. And yet without this time to practice, you will almost certainly struggle unnecessarily, operating at less than full strength. Stephen Covey relates the following story behind his highly effective habit of "sharpening the saw."[4] A person struggling to cut down a tree with a dull blade is asked, "Why don't you sharpen your saw?" He responds with "I don't have time to sharpen my saw; I have to cut down this tree." When we get sucked into the endless demands of our day one of the first things to go is the very perspective that would let us get on top of matters. This perspective is our awareness. When we don't give it time to cook, we cannot enjoy its nourishment.

If you do not protect your time of practice and stick to it, it will evaporate. If you allow it to evaporate, telling yourself you'll just always stay in the present moment (as I tried to) you'll quickly tire of the whole exercise. It is more realistic to do a little each day than to kid yourself into thinking you can do it all at once. It is only through practice that our hopes for growth—whether that's more energy, awareness, focus, alignment or depth in our life— become realistic.

Be Now

The way to get started in a program of BodyLearning is to start. How to practice is to practice now, in this day. The way to continue practice is to know that each day is this day.

You now have all the tools for practice: you know what to practice, when to practice and how to practice. The *what* is based on activities that are most important to you. The *when* is based on times that are most realistic for you. And the *how* is rooted in 2,500 years of Zen experience in what it means to live fully.

The second step of BodyLearning is complete. Before going on to the third step, I invite you to select the element of your practice in which you think the awareness of breath and being in the present

How to Practice BodyLearning
Six watchwords to guide your practice

During Your Time of Practice:

1. **Be Whole(hearted).** Commit 100 percent of yourself to your time of practice.
2. **Be Aware.** Maintain breath awareness and being in the present moment. When your mind drifts, bring it back.
3. **Be Centered.** Let your center be the source of your breathing and/ or motion.

Shaping Your Practice over Time:

4. **Be Experimental.** Try variations to work around obstacles or stretch in new directions.
5. **Be Realistic.** Be patient in your practice and expectations of progress; don't try to do too much or too little.
6. **Be Now.** Don't procrastinate. Start now.

moment will most easily develop, and do it for twenty minutes. Reflect on these elements of how to practice. The first three elements—wholeness, awareness and centeredness—should be part of your actual time of practice. The last three elements—being experimental, realistic and not procrastinating—shape your practice over time. See if you can, during these twenty minutes, experience wholeness, awareness and centeredness through your body. More than any words I say, it is the truth of your own experience that will ultimately fuel your commitment to practice.

STEP 3

GROWING
THE PRACTICE

10

❧

Peace: Resolving Stress and Conflict

"If we are peaceful, if we are happy, we can blossom like a flower and everyone in our family, our entire society, will benefit from our peace."
—Thich Nhat Hanh

Peace Starts Within

Thich Nhat Hanh, the wonderful Vietnamese Buddhist teacher, tells the story of a talk he gave in the U.S. in 1966, calling for a cease-fire in Vietnam.[1] An angry young peace activist jumped up and challenged Nhat Hanh for being in the United States, rather than conducting warlike counteroffensives in Vietnam. The young man shouted, "[You] go back to your country and defeat the American aggressors!" Practiced in such matters, Thich Nhat Hanh took a long, deep breath before answering. When he did answer, he was able to answer calmly, dissipating the toxic anger the young man had thrown into the room. Peace starts within.

The peace we would wish for in war-torn regions of our world, in our cities, on our streets, in our homes and in our hearts begins within. It starts with each of us. Yet if our peace of mind is nothing more than an intellectual concept—a nice image we have of ourselves as being peace loving—it won't hold up under pressure. As soon as we're in a situation in which it's more important to us to give someone a piece of our mind rather than keep our peace of mind, we're embroiled in conflict.

A deeper, genuine peace of mind can be learned only through the body. The fruits of our practice—energy, awareness, focus and alignment—increasingly develop a deep and enduring sense of peace within us. As we become more energized and alive in our body, we have less need of the blind energy of anger that subconsciously fuels our need to pick a fight or keep one going. By developing awareness, we more clearly see what's going on with people and situations. We're less driven to anger because we're more able to act from a position of understanding. By learning to focus broadly, with a mind that keeps moving in the present moment, we become less stuck in narrow opinions. Finally, as we become more aligned within, we quit fighting ourselves. Our condition becomes more peaceful because we're more in one piece. It's easier to declare an internal cease-fire when all parts of us are on the same side.

So if greater peace is a natural result of our practice and does not require a special effort of its own, why do we give it special attention now? Because peace is an important link. It is one of the most visible ways our inner condition shows up in our everyday life. As such, it is a great motivator for the third step of BodyLearning: growing our practice. While the results of our practice will naturally begin to seep into the rest of our day, when we consciously give our practice room to grow, we enable the process all the more. By growing our practice, we grow all the more through it. And nowhere will we be more motivated or rewarded for growing our practice than by applying it to those points in our day that cause us the most trouble.

"All the arts we practice are apprenticeship. The big art is our life."
—M. C. Richards

We can grow our practice in any of three ways, applied in any order, any number of times: (1) We can increase the intensity of what we do. (2) We can expand the range of activities we include in our practice. (3) We can apply the awareness and centeredness of our practice to other points in our day. It is this last way of growing our practice that is of particular interest to us now. We'll consider the other ways of growing our practice later. But first we consider growing our practice by applying it, and specifically by applying it to the stress and conflict in our life.

Imagine you've just answered your tenth phone call in what

seems like as many minutes, each one wanting you to do something different, each one with its own sense of urgency. You're starting to feel pulled apart and frazzled by all the demands. Can you, in this moment, find your breath? Can you let out a smooth, long exhale and find your center? If you can, you'll find the essential groundedness and stability that keeps you from flying apart. This is the moment to apply your practice.

Or imagine you're in a business meeting and tempers are starting to flare. It's tempting, on the one hand, to flare along with everyone else. But can you, in this moment, weigh in with something more than just another heated opinion? If you can connect to your breath, relax into your center, and bring your full awareness into the present moment, you might see the reconciling position others are missing. If you can speak from a condition of centeredness, the words you choose and the energy with which you say them will be more compelling.

Finding our breath and center in difficult moments gives us an enormous advantage. Immediately we gain a perspective from which we see more clearly, as well as a stream of energy to support our patience. We don't have to resort to the blind energy of conflict when we have a more stable source.

As Thich Nhat Hanh has been teaching for the past thirty years, we can bring peace and awareness into our everyday lives in so many ways—

> breathing between telephone calls, walking meditation between business meetings . . . What is the use of practicing meditation if it does not have anything to do with our daily lives?[2]

By having something to do with our daily lives, our practice grows in a visible way as our lives become visibly less conflicted.

The Conflict Within

Joe was an argument waiting to happen. A self-described "old-timer" at NASA, Joe was a smart and capable engineer. But attending a meeting with Joe was like being in a room with a time bomb. A group of us used to place bets on how far into a meeting we could get before Joe was red-faced and sputtering. Fifteen minutes seemed to be about the maximum. "That's the stupidest idea I ever heard," was a typical opening from Joe; "we're not going to try anything newfangled on this design. We know how to build systems like this, we've been doing it for twenty-five years, and we're going to build this system the same way. Case closed." But of course, Joe's was not the only opinion that mattered, which meant the case could not be closed so easily. And so the fireworks would begin. The veins leading to Joe's bloodshot head would bulge and pulse, and we'd really wonder if he was going to make it through the day, much less the whole design-cycle. In Joe's terms, we were all "jerks and assholes" who stood between him and the way things ought to be.

Elizabeth is at the other extreme. Somewhat older than Joe in years but ever so much younger at heart, Elizabeth brings a peaceful presence into every room she enters. With never an unkind word to anyone, Elizabeth greets life and everyone in it as so much of an adventure. We were playing cards one night, Elizabeth, two others and I. As the game ended, Elizabeth gleefully announced the scores. "You're the first winner," she said to one of us. "And you're the second winner, I'm the third, and you're the fourth winner!"

It's hard to imagine an argument breaking out in Elizabeth's presence and inconceivable that it would involve her. Like the mist-touched Oregon moss around her home, she gives no chance for sparks to ignite. One might almost believe her life had been free of adversity. Yet I've come to learn her doctors terminated her cancer treatment program when it appeared certain she was going to die—some thirty years ago. Elizabeth lives fearlessly. I don't think she's met a "jerk or asshole" in her entire life.

When we see people at the extremes—Joe, a conflict waiting to happen, and Elizabeth with her peaceful, compassionate presence—it's easy to see how we reap what we sow. But at all points between these extremes, where most of us live, it is no less the case that we make our own conflict. Putting ourselves at the center of our own universe, we want things to go our way. The more certain we are of our opinions and the more attached we are to our desires, the more conflict arises when the world fails to accommodate us. Anger and frustration arise in the gap between the way things are and the way we want them to be. Zen Master Sosan said, "Don't seek the Truth, just drop your opinions." The same could be said of seeking peace or resolving conflict. The goal of more peace and less conflict is not "out there" waiting to be discovered. It's "in here," in our willingness to relax our opinions and conditions on life.

Most of us have a number of hot buttons that, when pushed, stir our anger, frustration or belligerence. Like the most contagious virus, we spread our anger through clanging pots, screeching tires and hasty ultimatums. Maybe we succeed in pushing other people's hot buttons, and on and on the virus spreads. What hope is there for peace in the world when our individual actions spread conflict? We cannot stop the madness when we're partly mad ourselves.

Much is written these days about conflict resolution as so much negotiation strategy. People are given pointers—valuable tips to be sure—on ways to develop win-win resolutions to conflict, to see the other person's point of view, rethink assumptions, and treat others with dignity. All well and good, but this advice is second nature to people like Elizabeth. And it's completely unintelligible to people like Joe. We can resolve conflicts in our world (and I'm not talking about a negotiation table in the Middle East; I'm talking about the world we touch with our actions every day of our life) only to the extent that we resolve our own conflicts. Peace must start within, because that's where the obstacle to peace resides.

In *Zen and the Psychology of Transformation*,[3] Dr. Hubert Benoit sheds a great deal of insight on the inner struggle. The struggle begins with the illusion, which we

> *"It is with our capacity of smiling, breathing, and being peace that we can make peace."*
> —*Thich Nhat Hanh*

take as an actual fact, of our self-as-a-distinct-being. It's not surprising we come to this conclusion; that's certainly how things appear. Full of its own thoughts and opinions, the mind cannot help but perceive itself as distinct. Yet as soon as we identify with the little self, we define who and what we're not. It is as if we cut a slice out of the pie of reality and define that as our self, thereby defining the rest of the pie as everything besides our self. At some level we know we're the whole pie, but because we're conscious of being only a small piece of it, the struggle begins: the struggle of self against the world (or self against not-self). Benoit calls this the "great lawsuit," the case we're always trying to win to feel complete, worthwhile and affirmed in our piece of the pie.

As a result of defining our little self separately, each of us operates on a couple of channels. One channel is the "real world" channel, through which we conduct our day-to-day affairs. On that channel, currently, we're reading a book, sitting in a chair, and so forth. At the same time, we're monitoring a second channel, if only subconsciously, that registers how the lawsuit is going for us in the moment. If things are going well, our little self-assessment meter goes up; we feel cheerful, encouraged or some set of positive emotions. If things are not going so well, our meter goes down; we feel frustrated, angry or some set of negative emotions. If not much is going on to threaten or affirm us, our meter is relatively quiet.

Most of us live our days in the grip of this meter, experiencing stress and conflict whenever the meter goes down. Joe, for example, couldn't stand to have his opinions challenged. Knowing he wasn't powerful or persuasive enough to control the outcome of meetings, Joe felt threatened. His meter dropped, his blood pressure rose.

Even if our lawsuit is not as vivid or visible as Joe's, it carries on nonetheless. Someone close to us leaves or dies, and we feel negated (e.g., abandoned or lonely); our meter drops. Someone praises us, and we feel affirmed; our meter rises. Someone cuts us off on the freeway and we feel negated (e.g., powerless, insignificant); our meter drops. We give someone a piece of our mind and we feel affirmed ("I told HIM"); our meter goes up. As long as we're alive and identified with the little self, the lawsuit continues. It's never settled once and for all. How could it be? As long as self is distinct, events will come along to threaten or affirm it.

The good news is that the awareness developed through our practice can make the lawsuit matter less and less. The awareness of breath and center, of being in the present moment, can break the absolute grip of the meter on our life. Awareness interrupts what is otherwise a chain reaction of emotion, impulse and action. Awareness gives us a crucial perspective on our inner condition, meaning that the condition itself loses its absolute rule. Our very ability to watch the meter rise and fall, to know what's going on, diminishes the meter's effect. Moreover, as our centeredness develops, the movement of the meter is met by greater internal stability. We move further away from the extremes of manic-depression toward a more stable middle ground.

Our movement toward a less conflicted life may be resisted by the little self. Our conflicts, after all, are rooted in all that it cherishes—its opinions, desires, values and, above all, its wanting to be at the center of all things. Our little self may prefer to be in the center of conflict rather than to see beyond the narrow opinion that is causing it. But if the conflict in our life has done enough damage—taken enough toll on our health or hurt enough people around us—and we're ready to find a new perspective, we'll find that perspective by applying the awareness we cultivate in practice.

In the moment when tension begins to rise, we can find our breath and allow it to sink to our center. We can watch our own inner condition, even as we watch the outer circumstances that are driving our meter down. If we can accept our discomfort for a moment and continue to watch our breath and watch the situation for what's appropriate, our actions (or restraint) will come from a larger perspective.

The situation is something like being the parent of an infant. When the infant cries (which we can liken to the meter going down), the parent's first impulse is to do whatever it takes to stop the crying. The crying stops; the parent is happy. But the seasoned parent learns that sometimes the crying cannot be stopped and has to be accepted. If every time the baby cries, the parent jumps into action to stop the crying, the crying (like the meter) becomes a tool of blind manipulation. If instead, the parent learns to tell the difference between crying that calls for action and that which doesn't call for action—even if it's uncomfortable—the parent is able to act out of a larger perspective.

This perspective comes through our breath and centeredness. Rather than blindly riding the impulses of our meter, we learn to give each situation what it requires. And we needn't worry about our downturned meter; doing the right thing—like being a good parent—is affirming in its own right. Our meter will rise again.

Understanding What's at Stake

The awareness we need for resolving conflicts is to understand what's at stake for us. What's driving our meter? If nothing's personally at stake, it's easy for us to see all sides of an issue and not get sucked into its drama. Good parents, for example, develop this kind of understanding with their children. I remember listening to my friend Emily referee a dispute between her two young daughters, Rachael and Anne. She patiently helped them see where the other was coming from. "Rachael, how would you feel if Anne did this to you?" It was easy for Emily to stay out of her daughters' drama, since she wasn't trying to get one side to win over the other, nor was she feeling the least bit threatened. Eventually, the whole conflict ran out of juice.

> "When your child is agitated, you don't have to say, 'Go to that room!' You can take his or her hand and walk together into the room for breathing, and sit quietly together. This is the best education for peace."
>
> —Thich Nhat Hanh

Now, if Emily had felt threatened by her daughters' fighting, a very different scene could have ensued. If she had started thinking, "Gee, I'm a failure as a parent if I can't show my kids how to resolve their arguments," then she would have had a hook into the drama herself. Or if the argument had evoked a memory from her own childhood, she might have felt something personally at stake: "I hated it when my sister did that to me, and I refuse to let Rachael act like that." Or if she was just very tired and couldn't stand one more thing to call on her energy, she might have gotten pulled into the dispute.

Lord knows there are enough times when we're not above it. Times when we scream at our kids, screech at our parents, or yell at others who are dear to us. We grit our teeth plenty of times through an angry exchange at work, on the phone, or in the car as four crowded lanes squeeze into two. If we let the drama build too long, it will blast angry adrenaline through our system, washing out awareness and feeding itself into a frenzy. Our awareness works best early in the process. When the first warm blood starts to stir, when our breath shortens, and our words start coming out rushed and chopped—this is where awareness can make a big difference.

What's at stake here? Why am I feeling sucked in? What's making my meter drop? We should focus our awareness on these questions, peeling back the layers of camouflage until we get to the heart of the matter. What's at stake here? "Well, I remember how awful I felt when my sister did that to me and I don't want Rachael acting like that," we might answer if we're the fictitious Emily. And we ask more deeply, Why did I feel awful? "Well, I just felt overwhelmed and powerless." And how did that make me feel? We keep mining for gold. "I couldn't do anything right. I just wasn't good enough." Bingo. We keep peeling until we can't go any further. Until we hit pay dirt. Pay dirt almost always revolves around one (or more) of the following fears negating the self:[4]

- fear of being inadequate, unimportant or wrong
- fear of not having control (over people, situations, emotions, etc.)
- fear of being abandoned or not being loved or included
- fear of pain or death

Most of these fears intertwine (indeed, at some level they're all one fear, that of being negated). For example, the fear of pain can be fueled by the fear of losing control, i.e., of not being able to cope with the painful situation. Our fear of death, which is generally the most camouflaged of our fears, can fuel our need to feel important through wealth or position, and fuel our anguish when the proof of importance proves temporary.

Once we understand what's driving our meter south, we gain a critical perspective on it. We can ask if our fear has a real basis. Many times our awareness will reveal that what we think is at stake is not really at stake at all. For example, If we're getting sucked into a drama because it stirs a childhood memory, our fear doesn't have a basis in present reality. It's being fueled by our imagination. If we can simply "get out of our head," we may get beyond our conflict. Finding our breath and center and reentering the present moment through all of our senses is exactly the way to "get out of our head" and exit the conflicts we imagine.

On the other hand, if our fear does have a basis in the present moment, we can simply acknowledge it with our awareness, without making it worse than it is. We can acknowledge, for example, that when our kids argue, it's going to trigger our fears of inadequacy as parents. So when it happens, we can observe it with our breath. "Sure enough, I'm feeling like a lousy parent again." We can watch our emotions develop. We don't have to completely ride away with them. We can acknowledge the meter is down. Acknowledge it's been a bad day for the lawsuit. So long as we don't dwell on our sadness, it won't last. If we do dwell on it, we can make it last much longer, but then we're operating out of our imagination once again and not living in the present moment.

> *"Worry is interest paid on trouble before it comes due."*
> —*William Ralph Inge*

Without a doubt, the situations we're afraid of will arise now and again in our life (except for death, which we can be reasonably certain will happen only once). We will be wrong, we will be unable to control, we will be left, and we will be hurt. But for every actual time these events arise, we can imagine them a million times. And often we do! It's part of the way our little self keeps its drama going. It may not always make for a happy picture show, but at least we know who's the star.

Even during those times when we are face-to-face with one of the events we fear most, we will be at our best when we are connected mind-to-body, through the breath, fully aware in the present moment. That's the best we can do. And fortunately, that's enough.

Exercise in Awareness: What Are Your Conflict Triggers?

In this exercise you have a chance to understand better the conflict in your life by understanding what kinds of events drive you into it. Similar to discovering what kinds of foods cause you indigestion, understanding your conflict triggers gives you more insight into your discomfort zones. Even when you can't avoid the triggers, being aware of their presence is the start of reducing their impact.

Get your notebook and something to write with. Give yourself fifteen minutes for this exercise.

In your notebook draw a 3 x 4 table like the one opposite for recording your answers.

	A	B	C
1			
2			
3			
4			

Arrange the following groups of four statements in the order in which they apply to you. Assign the number 1 to the answer that is most like you, 4 to the answer that is least like you and 2 and 3 to the answers in between.

A. It's important to me to be—
_____ doing something important.
_____ in charge.
_____ liked by other people.
_____ physically safe.
Write your four answers in column A in your table.

B. Most often I fear—
_____ that I'm not good enough.
_____ that I'll lose control.
_____ that I'm not loved.
_____ for my life or physical safety.
Write your four answers in column B in your table.

C. The actual conflicts in my life most often leave me feeling—
_____ inadequate.
_____ powerless.
_____ unloved.
_____ physically threatened.
Write your four answers in column C in your table.

To identify your most potent conflict trigger(s), cross out each row in your table containing a 4. These are triggers that are either least important, least feared or least likely in your life. Add the scores across each row that remains (if more than one row is left) and write the sum to the side of the table. Each row represents the following conflict triggers—

    Row 1: The need to feel important or adequate.
    Row 2: The need to feel in control or powerful.
    Row 3: The need to feel loved and accepted by others.
    Row 4: The need to feel physically secure.
The lowest score is your most potent conflict trigger.

As an example of the scoring, my table of answers is below:

	A	B	C
1	2	1	1
2	4	3	2
3	3	2	3
4	1	4	4

I'll cross out the second and fourth rows, since they have 4's in them, and add the other rows across.

	A	B	C	
1	2	1	1	4
2	~~4~~	~~3~~	~~2~~	
3	3	2	3	8
4	~~1~~	~~4~~	~~4~~	

My low score is in Row 1, the need to feel important or adequate, which is my primary conflict trigger. Identify your primary conflict trigger and write it in your notebook.

In the next part of the exercise, you're asked to reflect on some of your biggest conflicts and their defining moments. When we tell our conflicts to friends, often we reach a point in the telling where we say something like "And then this part REALLY got me," and we proceed to give the "punch line." We want to look at a few of those defining moments now. By way of example, when I think back over some of my biggest conflicts, a few of the punch lines that come to mind are these:

1) "Our bank is for people who know how to save their money" (spoken by a bank teller refusing my business when I was a graduate student trying to live on $3,900 a year).

2) "I think we should start dating other people" (spoken by my soon-to-be-ex-boyfriend on the first day of what was to have been a fun-filled summer abroad after our first year of college).

3) "We need to get someone with bigger balls running this meeting" (spoken by my boss by way of explaining why a woman couldn't be in charge of the meeting).

You get the idea.

Think back over some of the most potent conflicts you've gotten into and jot down the phrase or event that really set you off. Try to remember three to five punch lines and write them in your notebook.

Punch lines can be laughable after the fact. But we didn't laugh the first time we heard them. And for good reason. In the next step, we track down the reason in terms of our conflict triggers. We'll trace each of our punch lines back to the fundamental fear driving it. We'll also consider whether the same line would still bother us, or whether something has changed.

By way of example, I'll track down my first punch line. This statement made me crazy when I first heard it because I'd been a saver my whole life, but circumstances in graduate school were such that I had no money to save. I didn't need a bank teller to remind me how vulnerable that made me feel. Feeling inadequate and powerless, I felt my meter dropping way down. A repeat of this scenario wouldn't bother me as much now because I don't feel so vulnerable. I also have enough experience with businesses and customer service to know that such a comment is completely out of line, and I'd be far less likely to take it personally.

Look at your first punch line and think back to the conditions of your life when this was said to you. Write your answers to the following questions:

- Why did this punch line send your meter down?
- What did it make you feel?
- What basic fear did it tap?

See if you can trace it back to one of the four fears described earlier. Ask yourself whether this punch line would still drive you into so much conflict. If not, answer what has changed in you between then and now.

Go on to answer the same questions for each of your punch lines.

Looking over your own set of punch lines, consider what basic fears they point to. Does the primary conflict trigger you identified in the first part of the exercise play significantly in your punch lines? In cases where you would be less troubled by the punch line now, can you see where the change is in you—in accumulated life experience, greater understanding, less caring or taking things personally, or whatever the specifics are in your case? In cases where the punch line would still deliver as fierce a blow, can you see what's sending your meter down? When we can simply acknowledge that we have these depressive circuits, they have less power over us.

Know your triggers. You don't have to judge them. You don't have to change them. But by simply being aware of them, we're better able to handle their impact. Raw tomatoes give me indigestion. That's one circuit to manage. Being told I'm worthless makes me feel inadequate. That's just another.

Tools for Trimming Stress and Conflict

Awareness is enormously valuable for exposing our conflict triggers and reducing their effect. But our BodyLearning practice also gives us other tools for reducing or resolving the conflicts in our day. As we've seen throughout this book, some of these tools work in the background, changing the baseline conditions of our life, such as our level of energy, confidence, or inner strength. A BodyLearning practice increases our capacity. It makes us larger, making it easier for us to be bigger than the problems that confront us.

Some of the tools of our practice also work in the moment. For example, the aerobic activities of our practice give us a chance to blow off whatever steam accumulates from the conflicts of our day, so that they don't have to fly out in angry actions. A healthy form of self-control is then possible, where we're not stuffing the emotions that arise from our conflicts. Rather, we're giving them a chance to vent.

Nothing cuts our energy so much as stuffing emotions that we feel unable to express or resolve. When we stuff those emotions into our body, we hold them in place with muscular tension, which in turn cuts our energy. If we carry a great deal of anger, frustration or strong emotions, the aerobic elements of our practice can be just the time to let it vent. Swinging a sword, stepping to music, hammering the ball with a racquet—aerobic activities such as these give us an outlet for the emotions that otherwise divide us. That's one reason why many people feel more energized after a vigorous workout, when simple caloric calculations would suggest they'd be dog tired. The body is more relaxed and flowing.

As you take to your aerobic practice, you might ask yourself if any emotion needs release. Are you angry or frustrated with something at home or work? If so, you might look for ways to release that emotion through your workout. If you're jogging or dancing, you might imagine sweating it out through your pores. If you're rowing a kayak, or even a stationary machine, you can imagine slicing the frustration with every stroke. If hitting a ball is involved in one of your activities, on some days you might want to imagine the ball as the source of your problems and smash the hell out of it.

A number of meditative practices also lend themselves to becoming a physical metaphor for releasing tension. For example, if your practice includes target-oriented activities such as golf, archery or bowling, you can imagine packing your frustration into the ball or the arrow and freely releasing it. You might not play your best game, but you'll probably feel much better. Fine arts and crafts can provide rich media for absorbing your heavy emotions. You can play out your frustration on the keyboard. You can ease the tension from your hands as you mold clay. Sanding a piece of wood, you can imagine grinding away your own conflicts and rough edges. In any meditative activity you can blend your breathing with your stressful thoughts, as you imagine melting your icy stress under the warmth of laser awareness. In many ways you can apply your practice to freeing the emotional barriers that otherwise cut your energy.

Another tool we can apply from our practice to the moments of conflict is the broad focus of a mind that moves freely. Conflicts escalate when the parties involved get stuck in their narrow points of view. Conversely, they can de-escalate when we free the mind to look for solutions from new perspectives. Part of our background development, through our BodyLearning practice, is this essential quality of a mind that moves freely. During a time of conflict, we can enable this valuable perspective by immediately finding our breath, allowing it to relax in our center and looking 180 degrees. Using our senses in the broadest way possible, we open our mind to think broadly as well. In addition, we can use our awareness to break the iron grip of our little self-assessment meter. We can be aware of the ups and downs of our meter and, at the same time, be aware of the real needs of the situation. This broader awareness frees our mind from blindly acting out of little self-interest and opens it up to act appropriately in the situation.

When we are able to see beyond the narrow needs of our meter, we are able to resolve our conflicts. This point was driven home to me again in a conversation with Tanouye Rotaishi. Tanouye Rotaishi has developed a significant reputation in Hawaii as a conflict mediator. Labor and management leaders have come to his dojo for years as a safe place to talk through their disputes. "What is your method of helping them resolve their difficulties?" I asked him, thinking he was going to spell out some four-point conflict resolution model. "I put them in *samadhi*," Tanouye Rotaishi answered instantly, referring to the meditative state in which the sense of a separate self disappears. "As soon as they're not stuck on their narrow self-interest, they can solve their own problems." *Samadhi*, which is a condition you can develop and deepen through your practice, begins with as simple a gesture as opening your vision to 180 degrees and finding your breath and center.

Exercise in Awareness: Ways Your Practice Can Reduce Stress and Conflict

Take a few minutes to reflect on ways your own practice could reduce the stress and conflict in your life. Get your notebook and give yourself ten minutes for this exercise.

List the set of activities you've designed as your BodyLearning practice. Imagine yourself for a moment doing each of the activities you've listed. Let your mind freely entertain each of the following questions. Write down as many answers as possible, and don't censor yourself.

1. Imagine you're having a stressful day and it's time for practice. List all the ways these activities could reduce your stress, either by what they make you do or how you do them. (Answer for all the activities, even though you'd do only one at a time.)

2. Look at your primary conflict trigger from the earlier exercise. Reflecting on each of the activities of your practice, how might these, over time, lessen your primary fear(s)? List as many ways as you can think of.

3. Think about your typical day or week for just a moment. List some of the typical occurrences that cause you stress. Try to think of at least five items. After you've written your list, review it and put a checkmark by those items where you can commit to applying your practice: finding your breath in center in the moment, looking 180 degrees, watching your reactions in the situation and giving it your best. As those situations arise in the coming days or weeks, grow your practice into those moments to see what difference you experience.

It starts with one moment of tension, dissipated by a smooth exhale, stabilized by a strong center. And then a second moment a few days later. A third moment follows, and a fourth and fifth. Pretty soon, it's becoming a habit: as the tension starts to rise, we immediately settle our breath into our center. In this way, our practice grows, as does our peace of mind and body.

Peace and Power

"I'm worried about keeping my edge," said Brian in one of my seminars after we talked about applying our practice to reducing stress. "In one sense I want to be more peaceful, but my image of peaceful people is that they're not high achievers. I don't want to lose that edge. And I certainly don't want people walking all over me."

Many of us can identify with Brian's concerns. In our achievement-oriented culture, many of us identify with the need to get ahead and the aggressiveness that goes with it. While peace and harmony are nice concepts, sometimes we have to do things that cause others consternation. Moreover, many of us equate peacefulness with a kind of passive person who doesn't achieve much and sometimes gets walked all over. Do we have to conclude that ambition and drive are at odds with a more peaceful life?

Not necessarily. But we do well to shine our awareness on this matter of ambition and understand what's at the heart of it. Blind ambition, like blind anger, can lead us to do things that are inappropriate, not because ambition is bad but because blindness is bad. Whenever we operate blindly, that is, without awareness, we're slaves to the ups and downs of our meter. We're scurrying to affirm ourselves, trying to avoid such feelings as inadequacy, loss of control or rejection.

In other words, our ambition or edge is a response to the very same fears we described earlier as conflict triggers. Behind our drive to DO is some sense that we have to prove or complete ourselves through accomplishment. This is part of the "great lawsuit" we described earlier, founded on the fallacy of how the mind perceives itself as distinct. If we can just get one more promotion or a little bigger house or whatever our edge is edging us toward, then we'll be complete, right? Wrong. Our meter will go up for a bit, but then something else will send it down. A new goal will take shape. And on we'll go with what we urgently need to do next.

If we're like Brian, we love our drive. We think of it as giving us reason to get out of bed in the morning. We don't want to lose that. Moreover, we're generally pleased with all that our drive has accomplished—it has produced some of our best evidence in the lawsuit. The good news is that if drive is a big part of our life now, we don't have to worry about losing it. It's not going away.

But if we can infuse our drive with the growing awareness developed through our practice, it can start serving more than our meter of narrow self-interests. As we become more aware of what's going on around us, and what's going on within us—the lawsuit, the meter, the drive—we find a larger perspective. Charlotte Joko Beck calls this growing into "a Bigger Container."[5] Acting from the interests of the larger self, our drive is then able to do what's appropriate in each situation.

Does that mean we let people walk all over us? Not necessarily. Blind passivity is no more virtuous than blind ambition or blind anger. The point of applying our practice is learning to use our power and energy appropriately. We don't have to give up our power to be peaceful. Indeed, it is only through the power of our presence that we can make a more peaceful difference in the world. Through our awareness and applying our practice, we can learn how to use our power in a way that fits each situation.

Sometimes, when we look deeply at a situation and understand what it's asking of us, we'll realize it's best to acquiesce (even though our meter may be pushing us to get loud or get even). Other times, we'll see it's time to hang tough, and we need the power and presence of mind to do that. Sometimes we need to be a rug; sometimes we need to be a tank. Sometimes we need to be a bridge. The point is to act appropriately to the circumstance. How do we know what's appropriate? The best we can do is connect to our breath, connect to our center, and be fully aware in the present moment. We can be aware of our meter and not let it rule blindly. We can be aware of the situation and open to what it will ask of us.

Peace starts within. And a BodyLearning practice does a great deal to enable greater peace in our life. By increasing our energy, a practice gives us more capacity to handle life's difficulties. We're less driven to anger because we're less in need of the blind energy that anger gives us. As

> "Lay down our body and being to the extreme limit of the situation and the inevitable destruction of Aiuchi (mutual killing) is transcended and becomes Ainuke (mutual passing); in other words, the swordsmanship stage of Se Mu I (Give Fearlessness). We must bring forth this personal experience to the present reality of the world."
> —Omori Sogen Rotaishi

our awareness develops, we have better understanding of ourselves and others, including our conflict triggers. By learning to focus our mind broadly through practice, we learn to apply that broad perspective to finding ways around our difficulties. By becoming more aligned and less fractured through our practice, we create less conflict and brokenness in our life. As we build our inner strength, we are less likely to ignite conflict ourselves, and we grow larger than the conflicts that touch us.

In addition to these powerful ways in which our practice works to improve the background conditions of our life, we can also apply our practice in the moment of conflict. As we feel our conflict triggers get ready to fire, immediately we can find our breath, inviting it to sink through a long, slow exhale. Immediately we can adjust our posture so that we feel more centered. Immediately we can open our senses, looking 180 degrees, and watch the situation

---

Applying Elements of Practice to Stress and Conflict

At the moment when stress starts to build:

1. **Find Your Breath.** Immediately let out a long, slow exhale and invite your breath to sink toward your center.
2. **Find Your Center.** Adjust your posture so you feel more centered. Set your center with each exhale.
3. **Look 180 degrees.** Fully open your senses, experiencing the situation in full awareness. If the situation requires resolution, invite your mind to move freely through possible solutions.

If you're starting your practice already feeling a great deal of stress:

4. **Vent the Tension.** Use the aerobic elements of your practice to release the body's tension. You might also use imagery to smash, release, or throw away imagined objects of your stress as you move.
5. **Restore the Body's Energy.** Use the meditative parts of your practice to relax tense muscles and restore the flow of energy. Breathe into the troubling thoughts, as if melting ice under a laser.

for what's appropriate. We can be aware of our reactions, as well as the reactions of others, without being unduly swayed or carried away by them. Immediately we are in the position to give the situation what it requires, acting from the best within us.

Applying our practice to reducing the stress and conflict in our life is not only a wonderful way to grow our practice but also a wonderful gift from our practice to our life and all who touch it. One breath at a time, we build peace in our world.

11

❦

Resilience: Managing the Pains of Life

"What doesn't kill me makes me stronger."
—Albert Camus

Pain Is Inevitable, Suffering Is Our Choice

I was attending a Zen bodytherapy seminar taught by my friend Tom Nagel. I learned something about pain that weekend. Zen bodytherapy, which I described in the first chapter, works deeply to release stored trauma in the body. And because it works deeply, it's often painful in a good-pain sort of way. Tom wanted to make sure we understood where this pain was coming from.

"I, as the bodyworker, do not cause your pain," Tom explained. "All I do is show you where you're carrying your pain and give you a chance to release it. By the same token, I cannot make you release your pain. Hanging on to your pain is one prerogative nobody can take from you. Many things people can take from you, but your pain is not one of them. I always caution my students never to set themselves up as 'healers.' Because even the most skilled bodyworker cannot make you let go of your pain if you want to hang on to it."

Who would want to hang on to their pain? Evidently, a great many of us to some extent and some of us to a great extent. Dub Leigh (who developed Zen Bodytherapy®) tells the story, for example, of a young man he worked on who had taken a fall at work years earlier and injured his back.[1] After surgery, he could move only with great pain, assisted by a cane. At first when Dub worked on him, the young man could hardly stand to be touched. When he was finished, Dub could put pressure on scarred areas without the man's complaining of pain. It was clear he moved with less distress than when he came in. But when Dub asked him if he felt better, the young man replied, "No, it is just the same as before I was operated on the first time."

Dub learned in conversation with the young man that he was getting insurance checks, had an enjoyable hobby, and was waited on by his family—all vast improvements over the difficulty of his work before the accident. "It was clear to me," Dub concluded, "that he was happier with his pain and hobby than with his hard job and healthy body."

Even when the payoff is not so literal, we are often reluctant to let go of the pains in our life. Some of our pain is primarily mind-induced (even though it manifests physically in the body). Someone we love may leave or die, for example. We may lose our job or feel like a failure. We addressed this kind of pain in the previous chapter, as we experience it as stress and conflict in our life. This pain arises in the gap between the way we want things to be and the way things are. Some amount of this pain is inevitable, for life will not always accord with our preferences. But what we do at that point is a matter of choice on our part. We can ease the pain to the extent that we can let go of our attachment to the way we want things to be and develop more awareness and acceptance of the way things are. The alternative is to suffer greater and longer.

Some of our pain is primarily body-induced, generated by injury or illness. Letting go of our physical pain is letting go of the anger or blame associated with the way the pain got there. It is also letting go of whatever sympathy or attention we garner by being in pain. As children, many of us had the experience of scraping a knee and receiving the cooing sympathy of someone who cared for us. Often we go after that same attention as adults. I know some people who talk about nothing but their poor health. How can they be freed from their pain? They'd lose their entire repertoire of conversation at the same time.

Some people don't stop at focusing on their health problems; they create more. Through self-destructive tendencies or punishment-seeking behavior, it is as if they create a focal point for the pain they cannot localize. Pain is part of what keeps us at the center of attention (if only our own). We experience a certain compensation in feeling sorry for ourselves because at least we're focused on self. As a result, even the normal and healthy among us engage in subtle forms of attaching to pain, making it worse than it is.

Letting go of our pain is taking the healthiest attitude of healing toward our body and mind. Some pain in life is inevitable: people we care about die, things don't happen the way we want them to, and our own health fails us ultimately, if not frequently. But how much we suffer with pain is a matter of choice on our part. The best we can do is eliminate unnecessary pain, accept the rest, and learn to tell the difference. This is exactly what our BodyLearning practice gives us a chance to practice.

> "Worry often gives a small thing a big shadow."
> —Spanish Proverb

Through our body we learn resilience. As our practice engages our body physically, we will occasionally feel aches and pains. This is particularly true as we expand our practice by intensifying what we do or diversifying our activities. Many times when we try something new or do something at a new level of intensity, we'll find muscles we didn't know existed—muscles that announce their presence painfully. While we certainly don't want to push ourselves into injury, we develop resilience by learning how to eliminate unnecessary pains, how to accept what's an inevitable part of our practice, and how to recover quickly. Without fireworks. Without drama.

The Fear of Pain

At the other extreme of hanging on to pain is avoiding it. It's not surprising that we try to avoid pain. On the whole, it's a sound survival strategy. Wired into every organism capable of moving is the reflex to move away from pain. We are no different. Yet trying to avoid all pain at all costs is not only destined to fail, but the cost is enormous.

We pay for avoiding pain by missing life itself. If we're not willing to risk falling over, we won't learn to ride a bicycle. If we won't risk the pain of losing a close relationship, we'll keep all our relationships from getting too close. Although life's inevitable pain will happen only occasionally, we can fear it anytime. If we let our fear rule, soon we're avoiding not only pain but also the potential for pain, which becomes utterly paralyzing.

One of the major hotel chains has a motto that runs something like "We believe when you're comfortable you can do anything." In my experience, the opposite is far closer to the truth: When you're willing to be uncomfortable, you can do anything. When we insist on always being comfortable, we cannot do many things; we do not even attempt them. To do something might be uncomfortable by comparison with putting our head in the sand. Yet our denial leads to greater problems.

I consulted for a company once where everyone was paralyzed by fear of losing their jobs. Their fear had a real basis; already 20 percent of the workforce had been laid off, and the remaining 400 were grossly underperforming. More than anything, they needed an aggressive, energizing effort to get clear about what would keep them in business and align themselves to get on with it. But they were so afraid of pain (and so used to comfort) that they could do nothing more than hunker down and hope that the storm that had claimed 20 percent of their colleagues would miraculously blow over. It didn't, of course. Rather than be present for the constructive pain of facing their predicament (such as moving inept managers out of positions of power and streamlining support processes), they brought on the worse pain of being shut down. Four hundred people—out of jobs.

Another consequence of denial is greater brokenness within. Denying the legitimate pain of a situation, we have to cut ourselves off in some way to keep the denial working. We may escape through drugs or alcohol. We may escape through compulsive patterns of comfort—chocolate, television or shopping sprees. Our pain may not go away, but we notice it less as our attention is drawn to something more agreeable. Like a boat trying to escape its own wake, we think if we can just keep moving, the pain will not catch up with us.

Not only does it usually catch us, but even while we think we're escaping the pain, it's landing its blow at deeper levels. The fact is, we experience pain at a deep level, even when we're not conscious of it.[2] Denying pain only creates a disconnection between what is deeply observed and what is consciously acknowledged. Denying we care about someone who's left us doesn't convince our heart. Denying in our head what our eyes have seen amounts to building a barrier between the two. If we do not resolve these disconnections, they cut our energy and integrity. With less awareness and less energy, our fear of pain grows stronger.

Another price we pay for avoiding pain is that it makes us easy to manipulate—especially by people who know our patterns of escape and use them to their advantage. I know a set of parents who are completely at the whim of their eight-year-old daughter, because they try to placate her temper tantrums. She's become so good at this routine that she only has to threaten to throw a tantrum to get what she wants.

It's easy to feel like victims when we're on the puppet end of manipulative relationships. But we're really victimizing ourselves with our own backing up. Trying to avoid the pain of necessary action or confrontation, we lose integrity and personal power. Those who take advantage of us get hooked on the rich diet of these power plays. Everyone loses when our fear of pain stymies us.

Being Present for Pain

"If they could only figure out how to make exercise painless, I'd do it in a heartbeat," a friend once told me. Many people consider the discomfort of physical training to be the main reason not to do it. In my experience, far from being a downside, learning to manage the body's pain is one of the most important gifts of a BodyLearning practice.

As we've seen, we have a choice when it comes to pain: we can be present for it or we can suffer. Suffering happens when we make pain into more or less than it is. Suffering is worse than pain, as it either rages like a four-alarm fire within us or divides us in denial. Yet in our fear and attachments most of us choose to suffer. Applying our practice, we can learn to break the habit of suffering. We can learn to be present simply for life's legitimate pain, neither wallowing in it nor running away.

How does our practice deliver these goods? We've already seen how awareness and the qualities of aerobic and meditative activities can help us manage the pain of conflict. Indeed, awareness, relaxation and the energy of practice help us manage all forms of pain. But in addition, if our practice includes some rigorous physical activities—whether aerobic or meditative—that stretch us out of our comfort zone and into some discomfort, we gain invaluable experience in handling pain in bite-sized chunks. As we expand our practice by intensifying or diversifying what we do, we learn to stretch without breaking. And we learn that what stretches us makes us stronger.

Learning to handle moderate physical pain is learning to handle pain of all forms. Pain does not limit itself to purely physical or mental categories. Our emotional pain finds expression in our physical body. For example, a stiff neck can just as easily result from a tense day at the office as from physical whiplash. The term "heavy heart" aptly describes the leaden feeling many of us get in our chest when we suffer a deep emotional loss. Conversely, the mind expresses pain from the body, amplifying or even manufacturing the signal. Amputees, for example, often report experiencing pain from their missing limbs.

The relatedness of physical and emotional pain allows us to leverage the body in learning to manage all forms of pain. Moreover, it is far

> "The way to be liberated from suffering is to be quickly absorbed into it."
> —Bukuo

easier to learn to manage physical pain in finite doses than it is to manage intense physical pain or emotional trauma. Preparing on the small stuff, we are better equipped to handle big pain when it descends upon us unexpectedly. Unshakable courage arises in knowing we can be present for pain.

And so the moderated pain of physical training is at the heart of what we gain from the training. Far from being the pit, it's the very nectar of our labor's fruit. As we manage pain, we gain in our ability to manage it. As we gain in our ability to manage pain, we conquer our fear.

Pain with a Gain

Learning to manage pain through a rigorous BodyLearning activity is not about creating useless suffering or focusing on a pain we'll accept in place of other pain we do not name. In learning through our body, we always want to be developing our awareness. Awareness requires that we be fundamentally honest with ourselves. Moreover, we want to build (not break!) ourselves. We learn a great deal in handling what I'll call *good* pain, not the least of which is learning to distinguish it from *bad*.

I am no masochist. I seek out dentists who advertise as "gentle" and avoid the doctor's shot when possible. I don't like my body to hurt. So when I talk about good pain, I'm not suggesting that pain is other than pain. Rather, I'm saying that some pain, in the larger scheme of things, is inevitable, manageable and well worth the effort.

"No pain, no gain." This bit of weight-lifter wisdom reminds us that pain is an inseparable companion to our development and to many things we value. I can't think of an important aspect of my life that hasn't caused me pain at some point, whether physical or psychological. Caring about my family and friends opens me up to pain when they struggle. Putting my heart into my work brings pain when things don't pan out. My physical training has certainly brought a share of pain. But this is what I call good pain. It's an inseparable companion or consequence to things we value in life, such as close personal relationships, meaningful work, a fit body or life itself.

Pain can be a great teacher. I can tell my Aikido students to block incoming attacks until I'm blue in the face, and still a few students will never remember to block. But the first time they're hit, they start to remember to block. I'd like to spare them the pain, but I've discovered that they won't learn some things without it.

This is the same lesson many parents struggle with, wanting to spare their sons and daughters some of the painful knocks they, themselves, learned from. "Bob is just like I was when I was a teenager," a friend of mine says of his son. "Irresponsible, lazy, completely without direction, and on the fringes of serious trouble. I lecture him constantly about needing to change his ways, but I might as well be talking to the wall." "What got you out of your irresponsible, lazy ways?" I asked my friend. "It certainly wasn't my father's lectures," he said with a laugh and proceeded to tell me of his own difficult twenties in which he finally "hit bottom" and started cleaning up his act. While it would be nice if his son could learn deeply from lectures, it's not likely. Almost without exception, the lessons I've learned for a lifetime (the I'll-never-do-that-again caliber of lesson) have been learned through my own painful experience.

Good pain is the inseparable companion or inevitable consequence of actions we choose. Good pain is a teacher. It can propel us to growth and learning not otherwise possible. Good pain is also relative. We can deal with it. It doesn't destroy us. Good pain is well worth our efforts at managing it. By being present for this pain, we are also present for the valuable package of which it's a part.

Suffering or bad pain, on the other hand, goes too far. It is pain that is unnecessarily inflicted or amplified by ourselves or others. Going beyond our ability to handle it, bad pain causes needless damage. We can also learn from bad pain, but the lessons tend to be full of bitterness and denial. How can we keep good pain from becoming bad? Several things we can do, which are supported by our BodyLearning practice, are—

(1) Learning our limits, not exposing ourselves to needless pain or situations that would break us.
(2) Learning through our practice which pains are par for the course, versus those that are excessive; eliminating what's excessive, accepting what's inevitable without amplifying it.
(3) Pushing back the barriers of what we can handle by growing our practice.

Exercise in Awareness: Closing the Shutters

Part of building resilience is learning to make the distinction between pain that helps us grow and pain that needlessly damages us. Regardless of how strong we are, some situations can still overwhelm us. Applying the present moment awareness developed in our practice, we are better able to sense when trouble is brewing. We can watch our reactions, even as they develop, and not be overwhelmed by them. We'll notice the heat before it becomes a four-alarm fire.

If damaging pain is heading our way, we would do well to avoid it. It might be beneficial to ourselves or others if we were strong enough to handle it. But if we're not, so be it. Thich Nhat Hanh likens this to closing our shutters when the wind is too strong. "Our senses are our windows to the outside world, and sometimes the wind blows and disturbs everything within us."[3] Sometimes we need to close down our sense windows and let the strong winds pass or come back to them later. Being aware that we're backing off and avoiding pain that we cannot currently handle is much more clear than simply shutting down all awareness.

We can also apply our awareness to avoiding needless pain. We can shut our sense windows to the pain we don't need to be present for. For example, I grow uncomfortable around people who argue, to say nothing of those who engage in more extreme forms of violence. I've learned to avoid those scenes when they're avoidable. I don't go to violent movies. I don't watch people argue and kill each other on television. I don't listen to radio talk show hosts verbally abuse their adversaries. Who needs it? I don't deny that stuff is out there and I don't take issue with the people who have an appetite for it (since I don't like to argue). But it's not for me. Purely out of personal compassion I've learned to avoid useless pain where my presence would add no value.

In the following exercise you have an oppurtunity to find sources of pain relief in your life. Grab your notebook and give yourself about fifteen minutes for the following reflection.

Spend a few moments considering what kind of pains you have felt recently. Write your responses to the following:

1. List three physically induced pains you have felt recently. (Leave several lines of space after each answer to be filled in with items 3 and 4.) These would be pains due to injury, illness or overexertion. Write down the events that triggered them and where in the body you experienced discomfort.

2. List three mentally or emotionally induced pains you have felt recently. (Leave several lines of space after each answer to be filled in with items 3 and 4.) Write down the event that triggered the pain and where in the body you physically experienced discomfort. If you were

uncomfortable only in your thoughts, write "head." But consider where else in your body your anxiety registered. Did your pulse or circulation change? Did you get indigestion? List as many anxiety sites as you can remember.

3. Go back over each of your six pains and answer: What could you have done to possibly eliminate the cause of the pain, and would you do it if given the chance again? Do you add value by being present for this pain, or could you be excused without hurting yourself or others? Is the pain an inseparable part of a package you willingly choose?

4. Go back over each of the pains you either couldn't or wouldn't eliminate the cause of, and answer: What could you do to reduce the symptoms of the pain; i.e., ease the ache where it showed up in your body? Include in your considerations whether any element of your practice could help ease a painful symptom.

When I do this exercise, I always find a pain or two I can choose to avoid or reduce. Often, I find an element of my practice is just the key to reducing the symptoms of a pain I need to accept. For example, sometimes deadlines and commitments pile up to make my day feel very frantic. When this happens, my heart beats too fast and I don't think very clearly. Sitting for a few moments and following my breath helps enormously to settle me down. Perhaps you can also find elements of your practice that bring relief to your pain.

Giving Pain No Room to Grow

The second leg in moving beyond suffering is learning not to amplify pain to be worse than it is. Pain (physical or mental) grows as we attach to it. Our pain may be triggered by events or conditions around us, in the same way an allergen or virus may trigger our immune system. But just as we've learned that it's our immune system going into overkill (rather than the germ itself) that gives us the symptoms of flu or allergies, so our nervous system is quick to turn molehill pains into mountainous reactions. We get stuck in a traffic jam and we're instantly rehearsing the chain of calamity that will befall us if we're held up much longer—we'll miss our appointment, no one will know what to do without us, the whole project will fall apart, and it will all be our fault.

> "There is nothing either good or bad but thinking makes it so."
> —William Shakespeare

Experienced meditators are able to break this so-called normal stress response.[4] They register a stressful stimulus as something of a minor blip, but it doesn't escalate into a nervous system cascade. Likewise, applying the awareness and alignment we develop in BodyLearning, we can keep from allowing the pain we do have to manage to escalate. We can't eliminate all pain. But we can keep the amplifier turned down.

When we're simply present for pain, we're not sucked into the rapids of turbulent emotion. Being present for pain is being able to look at our situation with some detachment. Detachment is not the same as denial. Rather it is a perspective that accepts things as they are. It is a perspective that knows we are nothing special in terms of being exempt from difficulty; we're not always able to make things go our way. Detachment doesn't mean we don't care what is happening. It means that we're aware of our caring, aware of when it doesn't matter, and aware of whatever emotions arise. It is exactly because we're watching them that our emotions cannot completely rule.

How do we do this? By applying the awareness developed in our practice, we can sever the strings of attachment that otherwise fuel our suffering. By following our breath, which stirs our awareness, we can watch what happens when pain enters our day. If we're like most people, almost immediately we'll feel pulled to put the pain in its most dramatic light. For example, if someone tells us we made a mistake, suddenly we feel like a complete failure. Awareness lets us see this pattern; so long as part of us is watching, not all of us can be pulling the trigger.

As illness and ailments descend upon us, a part of us may want to milk them for all they're worth, triggering our desires for sympathy or service. It is especially hard to maintain awareness at these times, since obviously we have something to gain by being unaware. But if we can find our breath and stir our awareness, we will be on our way to better health. "Who is this," we might ask ourselves, "who wants to heal quickly from this twisted knee? And who is this who wants to stay bedridden and have all meals served on a platter?" If we can ask these questions of ourselves, not with harsh judgment but with compassionate awareness, we will come to know ourselves deeply. The more we can expose our internal inconsistencies in the light of our awareness, the less they trip us up in self-defeating patterns.

We can break the cycle of suffering at any point. Our freedom comes in knowing we are the source of our own condition. Pain grows in the cracks of our denial, internal conflict and rigid desires. The awareness, alignment and inner strength learned through our body closes all these cracks, giving pain less room to grow.

Exercise in Awareness: Good and Bad Pain in Physical Practice

Our BodyLearning practice can give us constant practice in eliminating unnecessary pains and not amplifying inevitable pains. We become accustomed to accepting some discomfort without making it a bigger deal than it is. Furthermore, expanding our practice into more intense or diverse activities gives us a chance to push back the boundaries of what we can handle.

I remember running in gym class as a child. It was part of our requirement to try (in my case, in vain) to earn a Presidential Fitness Award. My 50-yard dash had no dash to it. And the 600-yard run walk was a horrible gasping, wheezing, pray-to-God-I-make-it-to-the-finish-line-alive experience. Running was a big deal to me. A big, awful deal. So I was what you might call a hard sell when years later, Richard, a friend of mine who was an avid jogger, encouraged me to become the same.

Over the months that Richard had been running, it was clear to me his energy was growing and his weight was dropping. "I can see jogging is doing great things for you," I told him. "But I don't think I can do it because I run out of breath so quickly."

"Oh, that happens to everyone when they first start," he said with complete authority.

"Everyone?" I asked doubtfully. "I thought it was just me," figuring I had unusually lousy lungs and remembering those 600 yards as if they happened yesterday.

"It's not just you," he assured me. "When I first started running, I thought I was going to die after the first half mile." I assured him I knew the feeling and asked whether he kept going. "Not that day," he said. "But I came back to it the next day and it wasn't quite as bad. And the day after that was easier."

A few weeks later when I ran my first tentative laps around the track at the university field house, Richard's experience was very much with me. I made it only half a lap before I was out of breath, but I knew it was OK since Richard had assured me everyone gets out of breath. I kept running. I made it almost a mile before I was sure I was going to die—but I knew it was all right. This happens to everyone. I knew I was on my way, well past 600 yards. That was good pain.

Now I love to jog. Whether it's the triumph over gym class or the endorphins, I'm not sure. But jogging has become important enough to me that I've learned to distinguish its good pain from its bad pain. For example, I've learned that a little bit of soreness in the legs is OK, but sharp pain in the knee is not. I've learned that if I run hard and fast, I can't run every day. If I want to run every day, I need to take it easy and run just a few miles. I can handle a 10K race, but a marathon would likely overwhelm me.

This learning is not particularly profound. It didn't require any special effort beyond jogging itself. Through our practice, we learn that certain discomfort comes with the territory, and other discomfort is excessive. In jogging and other aerobic activities, for example, we come to accept a certain level of discomfort associated with being slightly out of breath and exerting our muscles. This is good pain. We may want to push ourselves into longer or faster training. As long as our discomfort is general muscle exertion or slight breathlessness, we're stretching ourselves. We're not only improving our training condition, but we're also pushing back the boundaries of what we can handle. But if our joints start hurting or a muscle starts cramping, we're crossing over into bad pain—pain that will cause us unnecessary injury if we continue pressing so hard. For now, we've found the threshold of what we can handle. It's important that we respect that threshold, even as we work to extend it.

One of our objectives in BodyLearning is to be able to keep doing it. We have no opportunity to reach long-term benefits if we push so hard early on that we wipe ourselves out in unnecessary injuries. Another objective of our physical practice is to learn the difference between what we can and cannot handle. For both of these reasons, we want to find and respect the boundary between that which stretches us and that which injures us.

In the following exercise you have a chance to reflect on the good and bad pains of your own practice. What's par for the course, and what should signal you something is wrong? Take a few moments to write down what you know now, but then consult with your teachers, coaches or friends to learn from their experience with these activities.

Draw a line down a full page in your notebook, dividing it into two columns. Label the left column "Good Pain" and the right column "Bad Pain."

1. Starting with one activity of your practice, list the good pains or discomforts that you reasonably expect to come with the territory of doing this activity, especially as you do it harder or longer. Survey your body, from head (i.e., thoughts) to toe for what are the likely, inevitable discomforts of this activity.

The purpose of the good-pain side of the list is to make explicit what pains we're accepting in making this activity part of our practice. When those pains show up, we know it's no big deal. This list will also give some idea of how much our practice gives us a chance to manage mild discomforts. If the list is very short, our practice will not be very useful to us in stretching our comfort zone. That's fine; just the process of bringing our mind out of the thoughts it prefers to get lost in and into the present moment is a type of discomfort that, regardless of the specifics of our practice, we will benefit from practicing. But if we would like our practice to stretch us further in the way of building resilience, we might consider ways to grow our practice by increasing its intensity or adding to what we do.

Jane, for example, expanded her running practice by the mile. She started with two miles a day, then increased to three miles, then five miles. Last year she started training for a marathon. Robert took his photography practice to a new physical level by combining it with long hikes on which he'd carry his equipment. As you fill out the left-hand column, you might consider what good pains would come with expanding your practice.

2. For the same activity, fill in the right column with several examples of pain that should signal you something is wrong. For each good pain item you've listed on the left, what would be the symptoms of its crossing the border into bad pain? Focus on bad pain symptoms that are just over the line (e.g., "chest pains"), rather than extreme cases (e.g., "falling over from a heart attack") or chance events unrelated to the activity itself (e.g., "could get hit by a car").

The purpose of this list is to develop some awareness of the border between good pain and bad, not to fantasize about all possible disasters. You may wish to consult with teachers, coaches, friends or doctors to better understand the bad-pain warning signs. Based on what you know of your condition, fill in the right column with what are the most likely bad pains for you.

3. Repeat the above steps, filling in the left and right columns for each activity of your practice.

From the left-hand column we see a number of ways our practice will give us experience in accepting discomfort, making it no worse than it is. From the right-hand column we see excessive pains that we want to eliminate or avoid in our practice. From the two columns taken together we see ways our practice will give us the ability to distinguish good pain from bad. From the additional pains we are likely to encounter as we intensify our practice, we see ways our practice can push back the boundary of what we can handle. Through all these ways we increase our resilience.

Warning: Too Much Is Dangerous to Your Health

Time for the emphatic warning label: In our enthusiasm, we must be careful not to hurt ourselves. If we have little experience with physical training, our own judgment will be unreliable; it's very important that we seek guidance from teachers, mentors, doctors or trainers as we engage in any form of rigorous training.

First, before we start any rigorous physical practice, we would do well to check with a doctor and understand as much about our condition as possible. Our doctor may have some valuable insights that help us understand the boundary of what we can handle, versus when we'd be overdoing it.

Second, we should learn as much as we can about the physical activity we're doing and what to expect. In doing the previous exercise, if we were uncertain about normal, routine pains versus what should signal us that something is seriously wrong, we should find advisers who know. We can read magazines that carry articles about our activity and learn from others who have done it. We need to be careful with ourselves and not slip into dangerous, masochistic tendencies. This is not about punishment or hurting ourselves to show we can handle the pain. Rather, it is about learning what pain we can eliminate versus that which we can come to accept.

The physical activities that are best suited to stretching ourselves in the way of managing pain are those that have external standards of excellence, which align our training. They are activities for which we can find teachers, mentors or coaches who can guide us in our practice and help us navigate the boundary of good pain and bad. People who have been there understand something about the symptoms and pitfalls of the practice. They can watch how we do things and offer suggestions. They can add to our confidence in discovering what we can handle.

The Five Stages of Handling Pain

Elisabeth Kübler-Ross, in her pioneering studies of people who learned they had terminal illnesses, identified a fairly predictable set of stages through which we pass.[5] This life cycle of emotions not only applies to the way we handle death but also is typical of our reactions to pain. The five stages are denial, anger/blame, bargaining, depression and finally acceptance. Only when we reach acceptance can we be present for pain, without denying it or making it worse. Managing life's difficulties, we differ significantly in how long we take to reach acceptance—or whether we get there at all.

If we don't give up along the way, our physical training allows us to practice the art of reaching acceptance. We will, however, have to work through the forms of denial, anger, bargaining or depression that are likely to visit us first. When we first start working out and feeling the discomfort of exerting ourselves, we're likely to start with denial. We may try to be tough and ignore the pain, feeding ourselves lines like "mind over matter." We may work to distract our mind with television or conversation so that we are less aware of what we're doing or any discomfort that goes with it. If the discomfort is not very great, it may be easy enough to ignore. We may succeed in handling a modest amount of pain, but we haven't really moved beyond the stage of denial.

If we continue our training and perhaps intensify it somewhat, we are likely to reach the point where denying our discomfort no longer works. At this point, we'll likely resort to the extra jolt that anger or indignation gives us. We may get mad at ourselves for not being able to do better. We may blame our weak knees or lousy lungs or whatever we regard as our weak link for not doing its proper part. We may blame someone else for an earlier injury or for discouraging us when we were younger. Sometimes we get very creative in summoning indignation at this point. I know some weight lifters who say they "get mad at the weights" when they really push themselves. Athletes in team sports sometimes taunt those on the other team to stay riled up and fuel their performance.

If we continue our training beyond the stage of anger or blame, we are likely to enter a phase of bargaining. Some of us coax ourselves through a difficult workout, promising ourselves a treat later. Sometimes we think, "If I can just get through this now, I'll treat myself to a hot fudge sundae afterwards." Or perhaps we coax whatever ails us with the encouragement of only a few more reps or a few more laps and then we can rest. There's nothing wrong with this sort of bargaining; indeed, it may spur us on to performance not otherwise possible. But sometimes even the bargaining fails. And that's when we're likely to move into depression.

"I can't believe I'm making so little progress," we may tell ourselves. "I'll never be able to do this; I'm such a failure." We may get snared in depression for quite some time, which discourages us from continuing our efforts. But if our perseverance is stronger than even our depressing suspicion that we're wasting our time, that's when our training hits pay dirt, moving us beyond all these stages, into the realm of quiet acceptance.

In acceptance we're not ignoring our pain. We're not angry about it or blaming ourselves or others for it. We're not promising our-

> *"Exhaust the I."*
> —*Suzuki Shosan, on being asked the nature of spiritual practice*

selves it will soon be over (because we know we're going to do it again). We're not depressed by it. We're simply aware of it. We simply acknowledge our pain in a calm, sort of "so what" way. The only way I know to reach this point is with persistence. If day after day we do some rigorous activity, get a little winded or sore, finish and recover, eventually we become nonchalant about getting winded or sore. We've been here before and we know it's no big deal.

Through our practice we learn to move beyond denial, anger, bargaining, and depression to genuine acceptance of the pain we can't change. Moreover, this is a wise acceptance based on deep understanding. It is not a sheeplike acquiescence to conditions we would do well to challenge. Through our repeated practice we learn what discomfort is unnecessary or injurious and what is par for the course. Perhaps with the guidance of a teacher, mentor or coach, we make refinements, eliminate our errors and distill our practice down to par. By eliminating unnecessary pain, we can be present for whatever remains. A famous prayer asks for this kind of wisdom.[6]

O God, give us serenity to accept what cannot be changed,
courage to change what should be changed,
and the wisdom to distinguish the one from the other.

Through our body's learning to manage pain, we physically practice the pattern of this wisdom over and over. We eliminate what pain we can, we accept what pain remains, and we learn to recognize the difference. Neither seeking pain nor shirking it, we can learn through our bodies simply how to be present for pain.

We find that in being present, we can mine the present moment for the energy and insight to act appropriately. We can act appropriately because we are no longer being sucked into the difficulty, nor are we running away from it. Neither stumbling forward nor backing away, we can learn to give each situation the balanced best within us.

Four Ways the Body Learns Resilience through Practice

1. **Eliminating Excessive Pain.** Learning your limits and not exposing yourself to needless pain or situations that would break you. Learning which pains are excessive in your practice and training correctly so as to avoid or eliminate them.
2. **Accepting Inevitable Pain.** Learning which pains are par for the course and not amplifying them. Moving through denial, anger, bargaining, depression and into acceptance; recovering without drama.
3. **Learning to Tell the Difference.** Learning to distinguish good pain from bad; knowing which pain to accept and which can be eliminated or avoided.
4. **Increasing Your Capacity.** Pushing back the barriers of what you can handle by growing your practice.

A Practice in Managing Pain

Any activity that helps us build awareness and aligns our body and mind in common intent will, over time, help us be present for life's legitimate pain without making it more than it is. However, some activities are better suited than others for learning to manage pain. As we learn to navigate the boundary between good pain and bad, it's best if the consequences of crossing the line are not too severe. On all accounts, the activity I've found to be most powerful in learning to manage pain is sitting meditation.

It may seem ironic that something that can be such a deep source of relaxation is also a powerful tool for managing pain. But in its stillness, meditation lets us see our internal conflicts, which is one reason many people don't like to do it. But if we can do it, we learn a great deal. When we first start sitting, we are almost immediately besieged with the discomfort of wanting to fidget. If we sit longer, a leg may fall asleep or an ankle may get sore. Our tendency may be to get up at that point, shake out our leg and say, "That's enough of *that*." But if we want our practice to deepen, we will instead be aware of our tendency to quit without actually quitting. We will continue sitting and accept whatever discomfort comes our way. Since we're not doing anything particularly dangerous, and no one else is doing anything to us, we are able in this time to sojourn deeply into our own suffering manufacturing plant.

We gain remarkable insights in touring this plant. We learn which pain is due to our lack of experience in sitting, versus which pain is par for the course. We learn how to watch pain with our awareness, versus letting pain carry us away in its rapids. We learn about our patterns of attachment that escalate our pain, versus how to keep the volume turned down. We don't have to learn all these lessons at once. The beauty of meditation is that we can meter out the doses of learning we're ready to digest. For more than ten years I meditated almost daily without experiencing much in the way of pain or its management. Then I attended a Zen *sesshin*, which is a multi-day intensive Zen training session, and learned more about myself in four days than I had in ten years.

Pain is a great teacher. Of course, I also had the benefit of a great teacher in Hosokawa Roshi, who guided the *sesshin*. He taught me that pain in the back was bad pain, owing to problems in my posture, but that some amount of pain in the legs was good, that is, inevitable.

I went through my own version of the Kübler-Ross stages, starting with denying the pain. But fortunately the training was long enough that denial couldn't be maintained. Eventually, it gave way to anger and self-doubt. I was frustrated with myself for my lack of concentration. I was angry at the more senior people for creating such a severe training environment, and I was jealous of their progress, which was so much greater than my own. But I kept sitting. Eventually, a new voice emerged. The bargainer. The one who said, If you can just get through these next few minutes, a nice break is coming up. If you can just make it through this day, tomorrow will be easier. The bargainer worked pretty well for a while, and then I hit a session where the bargain failed. It was a long sit and before I reached the end of it, I had given up on bargains. I felt deeply depressed. I couldn't believe I had been sitting for so many years and had come so little distance. I was a complete failure, and here I was now wasting my time. Then so be it. Out of the denial, fighting, promising and discouragement came a new calm. I had given up all my tools and stumbled into acceptance.

I learned about pain and attachment. An anxious monologue would erupt in the early days of these *sesshins*. "This is nuts, sitting here being in pain. I probably won't be able to walk for a week. In fact, my legs may just fall off. My back hurts; I can't breathe. I feel as if a knife is cutting into my chest." Each of these images would add fuel to the fire. The pain would grow worse. Eventually, awareness entered to quiet this anxious voice.

"This is nuts, sitting here being in pain."
"This is just sitting. Nothing more, nothing less."
"I probably won't be able to walk for a week."
"This soreness is temporary. I feel it now, but I know it fades quickly. It has never stopped me from walking before."
"In fact, my legs may just fall off."
"They have never done that before. Indeed no one in this room, including the Roshi, who has been sitting far longer than I, is missing his or her legs."
"My back hurts; I can't breathe."
"I can relax my back muscles and adjust my posture. This very process will help me learn to breathe more deeply."
"I feel as if a knife is cutting into my chest."
"There is no knife. There is no cutting. Only me."

I also learned something about alignment. Being angry and frustrated while sitting makes it easy to escalate our pain through our own internal tugs-of-war. The ego feels threatened by a practice in which it has no starring role and may go through many gyrations to get us to stop sitting. But I knew I wanted to do this. I remember apologizing to my ankle once after a particularly painful sit. "I'm sorry this is causing you so much pain," I said. "I can't explain to you why this is necessary. I don't fully understand it myself. I just know I need to sit, and I need you to be a part of it. So hang in there with me." This may sound like an odd conversation to have with a part of my own body. But what I experienced was a process of gradual recruitment as more and more of me came onboard with this intent to meditate. My ankles and legs got more flexible, my center developed, my breathing improved, my anxious voice quieted down.

More Than an Exercise

Learning to manage pain through meditation or other activities is not an abstract exercise in masochism. When we're faced with inevitable pain, sometimes it is our only hope. In his television series and book, *Healing and the Mind*, Bill Moyers explored the ways a number of people used meditation to manage severe, chronic pain that was beyond the reach of medication or surgery.[7] These were not easy cases of mild disorders that could have been written off as "all in the mind." These were the toughest cases that had exhausted the catalogue of conventional medical practice. What these people experienced through their meditation practice was the fitful stumble toward acceptance of their pain, with varied passages through denial, anger, bargaining and depression along the way. Through acceptance they could be present for their pain without amplifying it. By not amplifying their pain, they could handle it. Where all other treatments had failed, they found success in the treatment closest to home.

Applying our practice to managing pain is learning to quit fighting ourselves. It is learning to quit amplifying our pain into suffering. We can become a friend to ourselves in the deepest sense as our awareness illuminates our internal conflicts, and our practice gradually resolves them.

As we continue our journey in BodyLearning, particularly as we grow our practice, we will encounter inevitable pains. We need to take care of ourselves. We need to get sufficient guidance to tell the good pain from the bad. But as we recognize the good pains of our practice, we would do well to embrace them. We would do well to remember that pain is inevitable, that suffering is our choice, and that we are learning to know the difference.

12

❦

Wholeness: Experiencing the Connection

"Zen is to transcend life and death (all dualism), to truly realize that the entire universe is the 'True Human Body,' through the discipline of mind and body in oneness . . . Besides this actual realization, there is nothing else."
—Omori Sogen Rotaishi

We Are Ice and Also Water

On a ski trip in Colorado I stopped to admire Boulder Falls. As the winter was not yet deep, the falls were not totally frozen. Along the banks lovely ice sculptures had developed, each distinct and individual. Some were short and stubby; others were tall and sharp as stilettos. Ice covered much of the river, but through its translucent layer and occasional gaps, the flow underneath was unmistakable.

"Exactly like us!" I thought. At the surface, in these temporary conditions we call a lifetime, the flow freezes into separate statues. We can tap on the surface of what appear to be our boundaries. And yet what do we make of the motion underneath? If we watch long enough (and this blessed day at Boulder Falls turned lifetimes into minutes), we see we move ever into and out of the flow. We're distinct, but we're also one. We are ice, but we are also water.

Perhaps we've already come to understand this sense of connection intellectually. It's been around a long time, a part of religious and spiritual traditions for thousands of years: All is one. Beyond the changing forms is an essential unity. From Taoism to modern physics, that message has reverberated through many lifetimes of learning. Despite differences in methods and terminology, the inner task is always the same: realizing and actualizing this oneness within us. Becoming one with God. Becoming one with the Absolute. Becoming one with the flow of life; "according the myriad changes;" that is, to bring our actions into perfect accordance with what is.

Most of us probably have some intellectual grasp of "this oneness thing," as a student of mine put it. However, intellectual understanding is

> "We feel and know that we are eternal."
> —Benedict de Spinoza

not deep enough to accomplish the inner task. Learning purely in our minds, which we likened earlier to hearing a familiar song played on the radio, can be a satisfying level of knowledge. But it's not the same as knowing the song deeply enough to write another one like it. Deeper knowledge can come only through our body and through our own genuine experience. This, then, is the final aim of BodyLearning: the inner connection of body, mind and spirit by which we experience our connection to the Whole.

What we learn through the body enables an inner transformation that is not possible through intellectual processes alone. We cannot think our way whole, because part of what we need to reach down and integrate into our wholeness is our animal nature: our power and our instincts toward survival, toward sex, toward satisfying our hunger. Developing wholeness is not denying whole aspects of our nature and somehow imagining we've risen above them. Rather, it is a process of integrating and aligning all aspects of who we are.

While we undeniably have animal instincts, we also undeniably have higher levels of consciousness, some of which continue to evolve through our lifetime. Psychologists who have studied stages of human development point out, for example, that what we know as the "terrible two's" corresponds with the psychological development of the ego (or little self) and the experience of self-as-a-distinct-being.[1] We then go through a phase when we're so absorbed with our ego's point of view that we're not able to put ourselves in other people's positions or evaluate matters impartially. We may stay in this stage a long time and carry remnants of it well into adulthood.

Another kind of consciousness begins to develop in most of us in which we're capable of abstract reasoning and greater impartiality. Psychologist Hubert Benoit calls this the "independent intelligence."[2] It's the abstract part of us that can see things from others' points of view or conceive of ideas of Truth, Godliness or Oneness and feel drawn toward them. Unfortunately, by the time this independent intelligence develops in us, it arrives alongside years of ego-based partiality. The little self finds an uneasy roommate in this new consciousness that knows, among other things, that there's something more than the little self.

This uneasy arrangement can erupt into conflict and dis-ease throughout our life. First, we run into conflict by trying to be the kind of self we conceive of being. We may have an idealized image of our self in our mind and then be disappointed when the actions of our body fail to live up to it. For example, we may value honesty but then find many times when we're telling lies. We may value being thin but constantly overeat and struggle with our weight. Our self-respect goes up and down with our ability to live in accord with our idealized image of who we are.

BodyLearning can help us with this alignment. It can help us close the gap between our warring factions by giving us time to connect body and mind solidly to each other and to the present moment. We likened this earlier to opening a channel through which alignment of body and mind can proceed. Through this alignment we come to greater peace and less anxiety because we're less self-defeating of our own image of self. But there's more.

A second set of conflicts confronts us, which is not to say they wait until we're done with the first but only that they differ in type. Because no matter how we define our self-as-a-distinct-being and how closely we live in alignment with the self we define, a part of our independent intelligence knows that the self we've defined is illusory. Not wrong, just too small. It knows that All is One, that underlying our distinctions is participation in the Whole. It acknowledges we are ice but knows we are also water.

To the extent that deep down inside we know we're the whole picture, we're never unconditionally satisfied with the piece we define as our self. At some level we feel a lack that we attempt to fill through some combination of worldly accomplishment (e.g., position, wealth, power) and imagination (e.g., fantasizing and all the ceaseless forms of mind chatter). This underlying dissatisfaction breaks through to the surface at such times when we finally reach an important goal, only to wonder why we thought it was so important or "Is this all there is?" Even at times of relative contentment, we fear (and know) the conditions of our contentment can change at any moment. In the flash of a bullet, storm, divorce, death, accident, stock plunge or any number of events, the life we know can be shattered. What often sustains us through the crushing times of our life is a deep-rooted sense that there must be something more.

This deeper sense of lack is answered only when the "something more" that we know within—that we may call God, Absolute, the Whole or in Zen we call the True Self—finally becomes fully realized and actualized through our body and mind. In this way, the abstract Absolute is made real. The "Word made flesh."

What we ultimately learn through the body is this essential convergence. While the words are imperfect, if converging our sense of self-as-a-distinct being is called align-

> "Man has no body distinct from his soul; for that called Body is a portion of soul discerned by the five senses, the chief inlets of soul in this age."
> —William Blake

ment of body and mind, converging our distinct self with the Whole could be called alignment of body, mind and spirit. (The words are imperfect because two or three entities don't really exist separately in need of convergence. All really is One, but we have to drop our illusions of separateness in order to experience the Oneness.) The beauty is that the very process by which we experience the oneness of body and mind lets us experience the oneness of the Whole. What we learn through the body is not only alignment with the little self but also alignment with the True Self. Please don't take my word for it. Through practice, you can experience the connection yourself.

How BodyLearning Lets Us Experience the Connection

How does BodyLearning deliver these goods? Let's consider how some of the gifts of BodyLearning, such as energy, awareness and mind-body alignment, enable us to experience the Whole.

Through a physical practice we gain rich experience and insight into the body's energy. What we learn is that the energy comes *through* us, not just from us. In aerobic activities, for example, even if our workouts tire us at the time, over time we'll find our energy rising. During many workouts we'll experience a second wind; after huffing and puffing part of our way through a session, our body will suddenly shift gears into a new level of performance. Or sometimes we'll start a workout dog tired, with our energy reserves drained. We'll motor through our practice and something will happen—we'll get charged up. We'll feel great. Where does this extra energy come from? What we begin to realize is that the energy is there all the time, and that once we get rid of our surface stress and agitation, we get access to more and more of it.

The meditative parts of our practice also increase our energy and give us a sense of its larger source. Following our breath, finding our center, and relaxing our tense muscles, we experience more energy flowing through us. As we breathe in full awareness, whether we're sitting quietly, shaping a ceramic pot, pruning the garden or cleaning the sink, our tension can be carried away with each breath. The more we relax, the more our energy increases. And it increases quite literally in the measure-it-with-a-thermometer sense. Every time I lead a group through breathing exercises and ask people what they experience, they report similar things: the room feels warmer, their hands get warmer, they feel more relaxed. If we keep having this experience day after day in our practice, we learn very deeply that a connection exists between energy and relaxation. We learn that if we don't tense against the flow, it's ours to be warmed by.

We also notice through our practice that sometimes we're more tense and cut off from the flow than at other times. If we never do anything physical, our body can be tense and we don't even know it. But having a daily physical practice gives us a daily reading of our condition. When our condition is especially tense, our practice will feel more awkward, tiring or difficult.

On such days we're apt to wonder, What's our problem? If we're insightful, we may be able to trace our tension to an argument with so-and-so or this-or-that not going the way we wanted it to. We learn over time that when things don't go the way we want them to, we become tense. When we become tense, our energy is "off" (even if we temporarily shore it up with anger). In this small way, we experience the larger truth that attaching to the little self—our opinions, desires and conditions on the world—cuts us off from the Whole.

The awareness we develop through our practice also contributes to our sense of the larger connection. The practice of bringing our mind into the present moment, something we do over and over even during twenty minutes of practice, is exactly what makes inroads into the thorny brambles of our endless mind chatter. Without a practice we're hardly aware of how quickly our mind jumps from one imagining to the next. We hardly notice that we're not in the present moment because our mind's eye is comfortably occupied—with its own illusory cinema.

As our practice of present-moment awareness vies with our mind chatter, we develop more insight into what our mind is chattering about. A conversation rehearsed over and over, trying to get it right. A love affair more perfect than the one we're in. A failed effort amplified in the voice of our harshest critic. Whether it's shoring up our self-image or tearing it down, our chatter is all about self and our corresponding sense of lack. It has to do with the "great lawsuit" we talked about in an earlier chapter, and how it's going for the little self in this moment.

By contrast, present-moment awareness gives us the experience of stepping into the flow of Now. When we are completely listening to our senses, absorbed in our breathing or in the motions of whatever we're doing, the chatter stops (if only briefly). In the quiet of our present-moment absorption, we experience "something more" than the isolated voice of our little self.

Our BodyLearning practice also teaches us that staying in the present moment is not easy. Without a practice we don't know that it's hard to stay in the present moment because part of our illusion is that we think we're always more or less present. That is, until we try it. Then we see how hard it is. We come to understand that it's hard because we don't like it. The real world is rarely as accommodating to our preferences and opinions as is our personal cinema. Who is this "I," we might ask, who keeps exiting the present moment in favor of its own illusions? And who is the "I" who wants to practice and be here now? By deeply exploring "Who is this 'I'?" we arrive at the True Self.

Sensory awareness is also key to sensing the larger connection. Opening all our senses and using our peripheral vision to see 180 degrees starts us along a path of de-rigidizing the boundaries between self and other. We experience the Whole as the boundaries of a separate self disappear, a condition of mind called *samadhi*. What starts as entering the moment through 180-degree vision deepens and broadens to a transformational experience of being the whole picture. Sitting meditation is, for most people, the most reliable way to cultivate this *samadhi* condition.

Many of the martial arts also cultivate this condition from a very practical perspective: if we become one with the person attacking us, we feel the attack as it forms in his or her mind. We can move spontaneously and effectively because we're not separate from the attack and rushing to react to it. By comparison, when we're not in a *samadhi* condition, we always feel a little late and clumsy in our actions. To master our art, we have to deepen in *samadhi*.

> "Left and right,
> Avoid all cuts and parries,
> Seize your opponents' minds
> And scatter them all!"
> —Morihei Ueshiba

This condition is by no means limited to the martial arts. Many "Ways," both Eastern and Western, emphasize this absorption into the activity. *Samadhi* can exist on the basketball court or baseball field, or in any number of Body-Learning activities. By becoming one with the whole picture, we can move spontaneously and appropriately in the moment. This same condition is cultivated in the fine arts as well. When no separation exists between artist and art, the art becomes more clear. By contrast, when the artist stands apart from the art, the thinking mind makes its clumsy presence felt. A fine eye or ear can tell the difference. Once we've experienced what's possible in a *samadhi* condition, we want to keep coming back to it. And each time we come back to it, we experience the connection.

We've seen how the energy and awareness of a BodyLearning

practice help us experience the connection. How does alignment of body and mind let us experience alignment with the Whole? If we consider how alignment changes us in a physical sense, we gain some insight into the larger transformation at work.

Alignment radically changes the power and effectiveness of our motions. As in *samadhi*, we see such a difference in what we're capable of doing with and without alignment, that we work to achieve it to master our practice. In many sports and martial arts, for example, we pay a great deal of attention to how we move. When we move forward, we want our feet pointing forward, our center pointing forward, our eyes looking forward, and so on. If we think of an Olympic sprinter, for example, every part of him or her is pointing down the track. Only when we're completely aligned on forward do we move forward at full power.

Many activities pull us toward alignment by having targets to aim at or precise cuts or lines that have to be made. They give us no room for wobble or extra flourish. Aligning our grip on the golf club, aligning how we move the saw through the wood, aligning our posture at the potter's wheel so we're as centered as we want our pots to be—every practice with standards of excellence involves some manner of alignment to achieve them.

What is alignment weeding out of our motion? It's weeding out the extra—the extra twist or point of tension that gets in the way of perfect delivery. It's smoothing out the ripples in our mind that otherwise show up as ripples in our movement. If we look deeply, we see that all this extra is our "crap," that is, our extra (positive or negative) flourish that comes from how we define our self-as-a-distinct-being. When we first start a physical practice, we impose this "crap" on our practice. If we think we're great, our actions come out arrogant. If we think we're lousy, our actions come out tentative. If we carry a great deal of tension in our shoulders, and our practice requires us to keep our shoulders relaxed, we'll struggle and feel awkward, and so on. If we're completely rigid in our self-definition, we won't learn anything (as in the Zen story of having an already-full cup of tea). To the extent that we want to master the practice, we allow alignment to soften our boundaries. We become less of an ego imposed on the activity and more of the activity itself. Rather than "I shoot the arrow," our experience becomes "It shoots." We're less of a rigid ego apart *from* and more the whole picture.

When all rigidity disappears, we are completely aligned with whatever the moment requires. When we can do this, not only for one activity but for every activity in our life, we are living the connection, which is the condition of an enlightened person. This is what Zen means when it speaks of "according the myriad changes." By according the demands of an activity having standards beyond the self, we physically induce the softening of our boundaries that moves us toward wholeness.

> *"Enlightenment is the ability to give totally in every second."*
> —*Charlotte Joko Beck*

Exercise in Awareness: Moving toward Wholeness

When Steve first started in Aikido, he was Doubt-in-Motion. Every technique he attempted started off with a movement in one direction, which he quickly undid, tried again, undid, tried a third time, finally settling for some semblance of struggling his partner to the mat. Steve's pattern of speaking was much like his technique: "I'll be in class on Tuesday," he would say. "Unless work keeps me late, which it sometimes does. But I'll try to make it. I might not. We'll see."

Steve learned slowly, in spite of being smart. Only part of him seemed to show up on the mat. His attention and engagement were on-again, off-again. Nothing about Steve was steady, including his progress. But for some reason, he stuck with it. Steve decided Aikido was worth learning, and he worked at it for years.

Of course, the only way he could learn smooth and clear techniques was to become more smooth and clear himself. Steve's techniques are now more beautiful to watch because they express a more stable Steve. He no longer undoes his own efforts. He no longer speaks in contradictions. When he shows up on the mat, he shows up completely.

While Steve didn't start Aikido with a clear understanding of how it would align him toward less doubt and greater wholeness, awareness can be very useful toward enabling the process. In this exercise you have a chance to reflect on an element of your own practice for ways it can soften your boundaries and allow you to experience the connection with "something more." This exercise takes about twenty minutes.

Select an activity of your practice that has external standards of excellence, meaning it can be done in better or worse ways, and you're able to get feedback. (If no element of your practice has external standards, select an activity that you've done in the past that does have such standards. It is best if this is also an activity that you might be willing to expand your practice to include in the future.) Write down the activity you've selected and answer the following questions about it:

1. What would have to be different about your body to master this activity? What parts would have to be larger, smaller, more flexible or move differently? Answer for at least three parts of your body.

2. Where do you carry tension in your body when you do this activity? Think of at least three places that feel too tight or slow compared with what the activity ideally requires.

3. What attitudes or thoughts do you often bring to doing this activity? Write down the main thoughts (or types of thoughts) that cross your mind as you do this activity. Capture both your positive, affirming thoughts as well as those that are not so positive.

Many of us have the tendency, especially given our cultural conditioning toward affirmations and positive mental attitudes, to try to think good thoughts as we do activities, especially those we feel we "should" do. If this is your tendency, you might want to dig a little deeper and ask what negative thoughts are lurking under the positive topsoil.

From the point of view of alignment and oneness with the activity, whether our thoughts are positive or negative is irrelevant—any thought can get in the way. Any time we're stepping out of the activity to think, we're breaking our connection—that is, our absorption in just *being* the activity. That's not to say we can (or should even attempt to) stop our thoughts. That's not possible. When we're learning something new, which may be the case with parts of our practice, we're bound

> *"You can't think and hit at the same time."*
> —*Yogi Berra*

to be thinking all the time. However, the process of mastery will move us toward less thinking and more spontaneous doing or being in the moment.

While no-thought may be the optimal state of mastery, we can gain valuable insight into some of our rigid boundaries and self-imposed limitations by looking for patterns in the thoughts we do, in fact, think.

4. What attitudes, beliefs, values or fears might be behind the thoughts you identified for this activity? Are any of these likely to get in the way of mastering this activity?

5. Overall, assuming you continue to do this activity, what are likely to be your two biggest barriers to mastering it? ("Time" as an answer doesn't count. The question is not whether you'll continue to do this activity or how long it will take you to master it, but rather what physical factors or attitudes will most likely stand in your way?)

Considering barriers and changes, we see a number of our physical and psychological boundaries that the path toward mastering this activity will soften. Allowing ourselves to be changed by our practice is exactly what makes us less rigid and more connected.

We can foster this process all the more when we grow our practice through other supportive activities. We've seen that we can grow our practice by diversifying, intensifying or applying it to other points in our day. Another sense of diversifying our practice is by making other changes in our life, which may or may not be other BodyLearning activities, that are supportive of what our body and mind are trying to learn through our practice.

For example, once Steve became aware that his self-defeating tendency even showed up in his language, he made it a point to catch himself whenever one sentence started coming out of his mouth in contradiction to the previous one. He asked others to help catch him as well. It wasn't long before his language pattern changed, aligning another vector in the direction of his practice.

In the next part of this exercise, you have a chance to consider other activities or changes in your life that would support the direction of your practice.

6. Looking at your answers to question 1, what could you do outside of your practice to foster some of these physical changes?

7. Looking at your answers to question 2, what could you change in your life to reduce or eliminate this tension?

8. Looking at your answers to question 4, what could you do outside of your practice to soften the attitudes, values, beliefs or fears that get in the way of your practice?

9. Looking at your answers to question 5, what could you do outside of your practice to lower the barriers identified?

If you are able to make some of the changes or additions you identified in this exercise, your practice will grow further in your life. And you will grow more toward wholeness through your practice. Even if you don't choose to grow your practice through any of these changes, perhaps you have a better idea of how the awareness and wisdom that develop through a practice point us in the directions we need to go.

The beauty of a practice is that, even if it starts out small, it's self-organizing: it generates the very awareness and wisdom that will lead to its own growth—and ours as well. Of course, we need to be open to that awareness and wisdom for them to be realized in our lives. But that very openness is what softens our rigid boundaries and makes us Whole.

Following the Lead of Practice

The Mississippi River starts in Minnesota, narrow enough to cross in a few steps. By Memphis, it's a huge river. By New Orleans, it's part of the Gulf and, by extension, the ocean.

A good practice grows on us. It can start small enough to "cross in a few steps," small enough to fit into even the busiest life. Twenty minutes a day is enough to get the river started. Twenty minutes of being connected—our breath to our center, our mind to our body, and our mind-body to the present moment. Being here *now*, aware through all our senses. Of course, initially we won't be able to stay connected for twenty minutes. Our mind will be all over the place. But for twenty minutes we make the effort. Over time, the effort is successful over more of the twenty minutes.

That starts the river flowing. All we have to do is keep at it. In my own experience the river started out even more meager than this because I didn't know anything about centeredness or being in the present moment. The only thing I knew about my breath was that I had a hard time catching it. While it wasn't a full BodyLearning practice as I've defined it, I'd trace the start of my practice to when I started college and going to the gym every day.

I didn't know what the heck I was doing. Sit-ups, push-ups, swinging on a metal bar—anything to get the body stronger and develop a little energy. But by the end of my first year in college when I had the opportunity to join a Karate class, I was strong enough to do it.

I still went to the gym every day but now added Karate two or three days a week. The river grew a little wider. For years I learned punches and kicks and katas, but if my early teachers ever mentioned that martial arts were about more than self-defense, I must have missed it.

In any event, I felt something was missing in my training. Enough so that when a friend recommended Aikido, I gave it try. Toyoda Sensei led the Aikido club at the University of Chicago; one of his students, Karl Frogner, taught many of the classes. Here I learned about breathing and centering. I learned about a different kind of power that was as boundless as it was unoppressive. Sitting became part of my practice; Karl refused to teach us how to use the Aikido weapons unless we meditated. "Otherwise, you're just swinging sticks," he said. So I sat.

As Toyoda Sensei became my direct teacher, I learned that he had grown up with the Aikido "greats." He had been a live-in student in the school of Aikido's founder. He had also lived in a Zen monastery and trained rigorously in breathing techniques. More than self-defense, Toyoda Sensei's martial art was about (True) Self-realization. In the early '80's, he invited a Zen master from Hawaii, Tanouye Rotaishi, to his Chicago dojo.

When I first heard Tanouye Rotaishi speak about the selfishness and attachments of the ego, I knew I was hearing the truest words of my life, but I wasn't ready to live them. "Oh please, let me have just this one more ambition," I remember thinking at the time. I was all excited about NASA and the fact that they had called me for an astronaut candidate interview. I wasn't ready to hear that attachments lead to selfish acts and suffering. Even though I knew it was true.

I had to live a little. That's how our practice works. It keeps exposing us to wise teachers and new learning that we gradually assimilate into our life. By now my practice had grown to sitting most mornings, jogging or weight lifting at lunch, and Aikido three times a week. It was taking more than twenty minutes a day, to be sure. But by now, I also knew it was taking me where I needed to go.

I did go to NASA and worked there for a number of years, though not as an astronaut. I married the friend who had introduced me to Aikido, and not long after we moved to Houston, we formed an Aikido club. After several years, the club became a permanent dojo; my practice kept expanding with the class schedule, whether I wanted it to or not. Several of our students expressed an interest in sitting, so I started informal sitting classes. Even though I'd been sitting for many years, I didn't know how to teach it. But it was only when I tried to teach it that I realized how little I knew. Practice is revealing that way. When one of my students said he wanted to go to a weekend Zen *sesshin*, something I had assiduously avoided for more than ten years since hearing Tanouye Rotaishi's lecture, I decided to go with him.

The first *sesshin* was hell; I recounted some of my tale of pain in the last chapter. At the same time it was the deepest, most rewarding training I had ever done. And it was coming at a good time, which is to say, a bad time. My marriage was falling apart, and my job was a mess. Sitting brought a stability that I needed very much in my life. Perhaps sensing this, Toyoda Sensei encouraged me to start regular Zen classes at the Houston dojo and gave me a beautiful wood-carved statue and supplies to get started. Teaching Zen became part of my practice.

As did *sesshin*. Twice a year, Hosokawa Roshi would come from Hawaii to conduct *sesshins* in Chicago. Twice a year I would learn more than I thought possible in a lifetime and discover how little I knew. Eventually I started attending weeklong *sesshins* in Hawaii. Going to Hawaii, where Tanouye Rotaishi still lived and taught, was like coming home to a truth I had not been able to face years earlier.

But practice readies us. By now my practice was widening to more and more of my life. I was drawn to writing to try to express this wondrous process, which further drew me into reading and deepening my training so I'd be able to express it. Moreover, life in a Zen dojo, which I experienced during the *sesshins*, makes no distinction between the time we're sitting on the cushion and anything else we do. "Unlike in football, there are no time-outs in life," Tanouye Rotaishi would tell us. "We need to bring the same condition of our training to everything we do." Whether we're pulling the weeds, cleaning the bathroom, cutting the vegetables or stacking the cushions, we apply the same awareness that we cultivate during sitting. "Why don't I do this all the time?" the question finally occurred to me. "Housecleaning can be part of my practice. Cooking can be part of my practice. Indeed, everything in my life can be part of my practice."

Now we've made it to the Gulf. Which is not to say I live in twenty-four-hour-a-day awareness and being in the present moment. My mind still wanders during many points in my day—sometimes even during sitting. But now I know my practice is life-wide and life-long. I still make specific space for it in my day—sitting in the morning, a workout at lunch, and Aikido or Zen classes at night. But I let it shape my life elsewhere as well. Without a doubt, my practice has led to a different line of work. I drive with less impatience. I take better care of my plants. The meals I cook are less haphazard and thrown together.

This is not to congratulate myself. It has nothing whatsoever to do with my self-as-a-distinct-being. Truly my little self—that part that would happily accept congratulations—wouldn't have done any of this. And many times it has resisted growing my practice in needed directions. But the wonder is that something more powerful comes through the practice. Something universal, learned through the body. It is available to every one of us. And it changes everything.

Exercise in Awareness: Where Does Your Practice Want to Grow?

Practice can grow in several ways. We can *diversify* our practice, either by adding new BodyLearning activities or by making other changes in our life that support improvements in an activity we're already doing. We can *intensify* our practice by doing more of it. We can increase the number of workouts or classes we attend. We can make our practice more challenging. Finally we can grow our practice by *applying* it to other points in our day. We can apply it to ease moments of conflict. We can apply it to cooking dinner. In any and all these ways, the river of our practice gains momentum.

Earlier we talked about becoming one with practice and how that enables us to experience the connection. In this exercise, however, we'll regard our practice as a separate inner teacher: an inner voice or guiding hand that has somehow led us to this point. Perhaps we had a long history of practice before we picked up this book. Perhaps our history is only what we've taken the time to experience through these twelve chapters. Either way, we're going to ask our practice where it wants to go from here. Get your notebook and put a pen in the hand of your inner teacher.

Three Ways to Grow Your Practice

1. **Diversify.** Add new BodyLearning activities to your practice or find other events in your day that you can change to support activities you're already doing.
2. **Intensify.** Increase the challenge of the activities in your practice. Consider practicing longer, harder, faster, less comfortably or more often.
3. **Apply.** Bring the awareness, breathing and centeredness of your practice to extraordinary and ordinary events in your day.

Imagine your practice as the wisest inner teacher you could ever hope for. Ask your practice the following questions and answer as if your practice itself were speaking.

1. When "I" designed "you" (the practice) a few chapters ago, did I leave something out? Do you need me to add another BodyLearning activity?

2. Do you need me to do something else to support the activities we're already doing? What's at the top of your list?

3. Do you need more time than I'm giving you? If so, when and how much?

4. Do I need to let myself be more challenged by you? If so, how?

5. Where else in my life would you like to show up now and then? Where else can you help me?

Maybe your practice wants to grow further right now; maybe it doesn't. Maybe you're ready to grow your practice now; maybe you're not. If you do want to commit to an additional BodyLearning activity suggested by this exercise, go back in your notebook to where you developed a schedule for your practice and schedule this new activity. Likewise, update your schedule if you want to give your practice more time at this point. Updating your practice schedule is important, for that's where the enthusiasm of wanting to do more meets the realism of everything you're already doing. If you're willing to shift your schedule to accommodate the new or expanded activity, it's a positive sign that your enthusiasm is backed by some commitment.

Other areas of growth in our practice, such as supporting it with a new habit or applying it to tense moments at work, don't have to be scheduled. They'll happen as they happen. But you might want to circle in your notebook, and in your mind, those situations you'll especially work on or look for.

Some of your answers for ways to grow your practice may involve religious or spiritual activities. That's fine; if such activities are important to you now, almost certainly they will play a role in the way your practice grows. Some people worry that practice may challenge their religious beliefs. I'm often asked by people curious about Aikido or Zen, "Will this get in the way of my Christianity?"

Or Judaism, or whatever religion they feel close to. Some people regard their religion as an exclusionary citizenship: they can have only one. If they get too many spiritual ideas from elsewhere, it can cause them trouble.

The truth is, there's only one Whole. All really is One, regardless of how we've named it, shaped it, or honored it in various traditions. So in the end there can be no conflict among the paths that let us experience our connection to the Whole. Along the way, we may experience some conflict. Because *we're* conflicted by the attachments and needs of the little self. Old beliefs may be challenged. They may appear to be shaken, then come back to us in a new, deeper synthesis. So be it. Have courage. Breathing, centering and being aware in the present moment can never lead us astray.

The previous exercise in growing your practice might be one you do now, and again in a few years. Practice changes our insights, as well as our readiness to follow them. If we give our practice a voice and follow its insights, it will lead us toward wholeness.

Practice Becomes Our Whole Life

Eventually practice becomes our whole life. "Wait a minute," the little self may protest; "I've already got a life. It's a perfectly good life and I don't want to spend it all practicing. Twenty minutes is enough." That's fine. Wherever we start the river of practice is fine. Saying practice becomes our whole life doesn't mean we eventually do aerobics twenty-four hours a day. It doesn't mean we drop out of our "normal" life and live in a "practice cult." What it means is that eventually we'll see that every moment of our day is an opportunity for practice. Eventually practice becomes our whole life because eventually practice makes our life Whole.

Recognizing that everything in our life is an opportunity to practice is recognizing that the precious awareness and centeredness we develop through our practice belongs in everything we do. In every extraordinary effort. In every routine, mundane, daily chore. Centeredness and awareness will make everything we do take on a higher quality. They'll make every situation easier to face.

Having said that eventually our whole life is our practice, I must strongly caution: This is not where we start. Please don't make the mistake of thinking you can skip the whole part about a

daily practice and just make believe your whole day is your practice. It doesn't work that way. Growing your practice, especially
growing it to the fullness of your life, is the final step of BodyLearning, not the first. Without a finite, well-defined daily practice, we
have no organizing center around which to grow the practice.

Moreover, the true insight for growing our practice has to come
from the practice itself. It must come from the wisdom of the body.
If it's just coming from the voice of the little self mind, it can't be
trusted to lead us anywhere (except toward possible gratification
of the little self). It's important that we understand how practice
grows so that we can be more open to the process, not so that we
can try to short-circuit it. The story I told of my own river of
practice spanned twenty-four years. It has been only within the last
few years that I've been able to put into practice the understanding
that everything is an opportunity for practice. And I still miss
many opportunities.

Don't start with the end-game. Start with the kick-off. Start
with where you are and the practice you've designed. Then stay
tuned to the voice of your practice for further developments.

"But it sounds like it takes such a long time," said one of my
students after I explained the process to her. The truth is, it doesn't
matter how long it takes. Our whole relationship to time is based
on our illusory sense of lack. We always feel we have to *do* something to fill the hole. And the more we feel we have to do, the
busier we are. Only through practice do we tackle the fundamental
problem, which is our sense of lack. Only through practice do we
realize we are, in fact, the Whole. "It doesn't matter how long it
takes," I told her. "Because there's nothing else to do."

Which brings us to the final sense in which practice becomes
our whole life. After we realize everything in life is an opportunity
for practice and begin to live in this way, less and less of our life
remains outside of practice. If we persist in this direction, eventually
nothing exists outside of the present-moment awareness of practice.
In Zen we call this enlightenment. Being the Whole. Omori Sogen
Rotaishi described it as realizing "that the entire universe is the
'True Human Body.' "[3] In the words of Christian mystic Evelyn
Underhill, we become one with the Whole Fact, "which the philosopher calls the Absolute and the religious mystic calls God."[4]

This is not to say the little self becomes God, much as it may want to interpret the game that way. Some danger exists that, as practice increases our energy and power, the little self will soak up the credit. Expect it. And don't be fooled by it. Becoming one with the Whole Fact does not mean the little self becomes more special. Quite the opposite, we become less special and more universal. The true realization is not that our little self is something big but that our True Self embraces all that we appear to be (i.e., little self) plus all that we appear not to be (i.e., everything else).

The more we can stay in the present moment, the more we experience the Whole. Conversely, once we fully experience the Whole, we're able to stay in the present moment because we no longer feel a lack that has to be filled by forced doing or imaginary mind chatter. In this condition we're able to do without doing; that is, without forcing our actions from the needs of the little self. In this condition our mind can move freely with the present moment. It's no longer stuck on the chattering cinema that compensates our needs. When we have no need, we're Whole. Conversely, when we're Whole, we have no need. This is what is meant by ending human suffering, by living heaven on earth, or by transcending dualism. When we have no need, when we live as the Whole, nothing that happens can be a problem. (It may be an inconvenience to the little self, but it cannot be a problem to the Whole.) Even our own death is not a problem because we know we're not confined to the little self. We're the whole picture, constantly changing in the eternal Now.

> "One in All.
> All in One—
> If only this is realized,
> No more worry about your not being perfect."
> —Sosan

Looking Back

It was inevitable in our development that we should come to perceive our self-as-a-distinct-being. That was the evidence in the mirror and, what's more, the mind cannot conceive of itself otherwise. This perception is not wrong; it's just too small. And at some level we know it. This sleeping knowledge leads to a gnawing sense of lack that we attempt to fill through some combination of incessant action and mind chatter.

The self we've defined has many likes and dislikes. Over the course of our life it develops more deeply embedded patterns of tensing and resisting the things it doesn't like. This tension shows up in our body and, among other ill effects, freezes our energy.

Meanwhile, our mind develops a pattern of incessant chatter. Some of that chatter is fueled by our sidebar assessment of how things are going for us in the moment, what we called earlier the "great lawsuit." Some of that chatter is fueled by little self needs: liking this, disliking that, rationalizing one situation or rehearsing another. The presence of the chatter makes us pay scant attention to the present moment. We're here for a moment, then lost in our thoughts. Lacking awareness, we miss much of the present.

The self we define as a distinct being is a needy creature. And the mind that serves its agenda cannot, as a result, stay freely focused in the present moment. Our actions in the world are often inappropriate or too small to the extent that they're based on what *we* need, rather than what the situation needs. Moreover, our actions are often conflicted, since they're based on our needs and our needs conflict. On the one hand we want this; on the other hand, we want that. Lacking alignment, we partly defeat our self in much that we do.

This is how we live. And it can be rather messy and unsatisfying. Fortunately we do learn as we live. For example, if we keep reaching goals we thought were important only to arrive at an empty feeling of "Is this all there is?" we might start developing insight into the "great lawsuit" and our endless efforts to justify the self. Clouding our insight, however, is the little self who just wants to keep its game going (it is, after all, the star of the lawsuit). Rather than penetrating the illusion of the lawsuit, our tendency is to develop winning ways or coping mechanisms to keep it from going too badly. For example, most of us learn what makes us feel comfortable or good about our self and over time we become more proficient at creating those conditions or confining our self to them.

So even though we live and learn, most of us run out of life before we've learned enough. That's why we need another kind of learning to augment the life process. We need a kind of learning that is not an ego-based "head trip," but rather aligns the ego with something more. For this kind of learning we turn to the body. The body is grounded and down to earth; it can be trusted to tell the truth about our condition. The body can taste and feel the truth and shape the knowing of the mind. The body connects us to reality, through all our senses, moment by moment.

We start by connecting the mind to the body through the breath. Allowing our breath to sink into our center, we become more relaxed, energized and stable. Opening our senses and being in the present moment, we become more aware.

We can experience this condition almost instantly through breathing exercises. But to make it a real part of our life, we have to return to it over and over again. To do this, we need a practice. Many activities, if done in breath awareness, centeredness and being in the present moment, allow us to learn deeply through the body. By selecting a few of these activities and designing a daily practice, we make BodyLearning real in our life.

The best practice is one you'll do. Since different activities teach different lessons, you should find a combination that (1) addresses needs you already recognize and (2) enriches your development from a couple of angles. Meditative activities, for example, will give you a chance to develop deep, centered breathing. Aerobic activities will let you blow off steam and learn to move from your center. Activities that change slowly will teach you endurance and patience. Dynamic activities will teach you about timing and spontaneous action. If at least one activity in your practice has external standards of excellence (and possibly a teacher to guide you), you'll have a clear direction for alignment with something more.

From the start of your practice you'll feel more energized. Progressively your practice will restore what the little self has lost in its separateness: energy, awareness, focus and alignment. Without a doubt, this is a more joyous way to

> "So please: give, give, give—and practice, practice, practice. It is the Way."
> —Charlotte Joko Beck

live. Without a doubt, your little self will push back when it senses this energy is changing you.

Being willing to grow your practice and listen to its wisdom, your little self slowly acknowledges its willingness to soften its boundaries. This happens each time you diversify, intensify or apply your practice to daily life. It happens when you give up a habit

Ways to Experience the Connection Through BodyLearning

1. **Through Energy.** You can experience energy moving through you and not just from you. When you're relaxed and more in the flow, you become more energized.
2. **Through Awareness.** By fully opening your senses, especially your 180-degree vision, you fully enter the present moment. In the *Samadhi* condition the distinction between self and not-self disappears, and you experience the whole picture.
3. **Through Focus.** By developing the broad focus of a "mind that moves freely," you're able to move freely with the flow of Now.
4. **Through Alignment.** As you master your practice, you smooth your rough edges, softening the boundaries of self. You become less of an ego imposed on the activity and more the activity itself.

that deadens you, such as excessive drinking or television. It happens when you live the oneness of your practice through compassionate acts.

Ultimately what we learn through the body is the Whole that we are. The matter of the body is but a "frozen" form of the energy that connects us all. Penetrating our nature as ice, we discover we are also water. We are this little self and we are also the Whole. Being willing to grow our practice is the shift by which our life becomes centered in the Whole, rather than in the little self. At last! Free from the "great lawsuit," we move beyond lack. Lacking nothing, we don't have to add anything in our mind. Lacking nothing, we don't have to act out of need, which means we can do whatever it takes to "accord the myriad changes." As we live the Whole, moment by moment, the Absolute Word is made flesh through our very body.

To the body's learning! Go for all of it.

Appendix A
Further Instructions for *Zazen*

❧

Following are more detailed *Instructions for Zazen*, reprinted with permission from Chozen-ji/International Zen Dojo.[1] These figures and instructions provide an excellent reference as your practice matures.

Figure A-1. Placement of Cushions
Select a wide cushion and two or three small ones. Stack the smaller ones under the wide one so they act as a wedge. Sit on the edge with the buttocks off the center of the wedge.

Figure A-2. The Full and Half Lotus Positions

To take the full lotus position as shown on the left, place the right foot near the base of the left thigh, and place the left foot on the right thigh.

To take the half lotus position as shown on the right, simply place the left foot on the right thigh or the right foot on the left thigh.

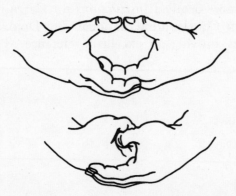

Figure A-3. Positions of the Hands

In the top position place the left hand with palm up and fingers together on the palm of the right hand. The inner sides of the tips of both thumbs touch, creating an ellipse. Viewed from above, the thumbs must be in line with the middle fingers.

In the alternate bottom position grasp the tip of the left thumb between the web of the thumb and the index finger of the right hand. Form a loose fist with the right hand and enclose it with the left.

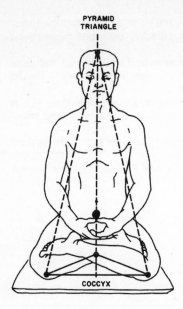

Figure A-4. Stabilizing the Body (front view, Full Lotus Position)

A well-seated and very stable body is in the form of a pyramind. The base is an imaginary triangle formed by the lines connecting the two knees and the coccyx. The diagonal ridge lines extending from the two knees and the coccyx to the top of the head complete the pyramid.

Rock the body from right to left and again from left to right. The amplitude of this oscillation should be large at first and gradually decrease until the body stops moving and becomes stable.

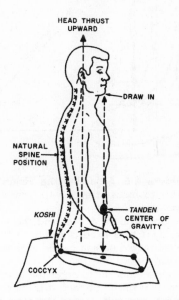

Figure A-5. Stabilizing the Body (side view)

a. Straighten the spine perpendicularly by inclining the upper body forward. Then, push the buttocks backward without moving them while raising the upper body gradually as if to push heaven with the back of the head. This action will straighten the spine into a natural position.

b. Advance the lower abdomen forward to straighten the hips. Raise the upper body until it becomes perpendicular with the neck upright and the lower jaw drawn in. The center of gravity will now coincide with the geometrical center of the plane triangle.

c. Check to see that the lower jaw is drawn in and the back of the neck is straight. If they are in the correct position, the ears and shoulders should fall in the same perpendicular plane.

d. Check also the position of the lower abdomen and the hips. If the lower abdomen is forward and the hip bone is upright, the nose and navel should be aligned.

e. Let the tip of the tongue touch the upper jaw with the teeth in light contact with each other.

f. Sit at ease, heavily and in alert dignity like Mt. Fuji soaring into heaven and overlooking the Eastern Seas.

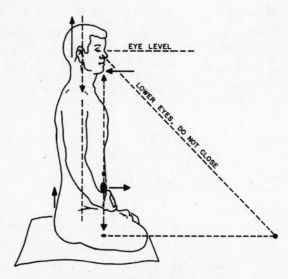

Figure A-6. Adjusting the Vision

Adjusting the vision helps to focus attention to prevent it from being taken up by internal or external stimuli.

a. The eyes should look straight ahead, and the visual field should span 180 degrees. Lower the eyes to a fixed position on the floor approximately three feet ahead. The eyes should be half closed in selfless tranquillity, neither seeing nor not seeing anything.

b. Do not close the eyes. In order to enter the state of Zen concentration and to raise your inner power to the utmost, it is important to keep the eyes open. If one remains quiet with eyes closed like lifeless water, he will never be useful to society. It may seem easier to unify ourselves spiritually by closing the eyes, but then it will be inert *Zazen*. Interpreting it more lightly, keeping the eyes open prevents us from falling asleep in meditation.

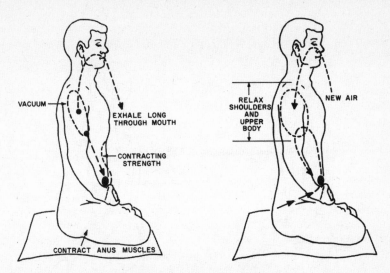

Figure A-7. Initial Deep Breathing

Deep breathing harmonizes the mind and the body.

a. Exhale slowly through the mouth as if to connect the atmosphere with the lower abdomen. Empty all the stale air with the strength created by the contraction of the lower abdomen. At the end of exhalation, relax the lower abdomen.

b. Due to atmospheric pressure, new air will naturally enter through the nose and fill the vacuum in the lungs.

c. After inhaling fully, pause slightly and with the *koshi* (*Koshi* and *hara* both refer to the lower abdomen, hips, lower back and buttocks functioning as a unit. *Koshi* emphasizes the physical body, and *hara* has more spiritual significance.) extended forward, gently push the inhaled air into the lower abdomen in a scooping motion. The key to this is to contract the anus muscle.

d. Start exhaling again just before you feel uncomfortable. Repeat this type of breathing four to ten times.

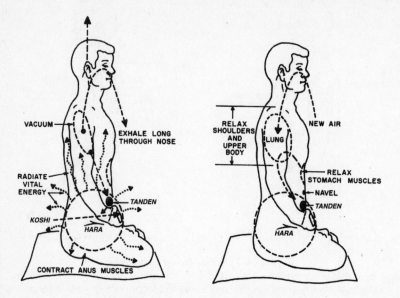

Figure A-8. Breathing in Meditation

a. When the respiration is adjusted, start breathing through the nose with the mouth closed. Inhaling is natural through the nose. Of course the inhaled air comes to the lungs but by relaxing the muscles around the pit of the stomach, you can actually feel the air filling the area below the navel.

b. Exhale through the nose. The breath should be long and directed toward the *tanden* with the power of the abdominal muscles. Contract the muscles around the anus and push the hips upright and slightly forward. The power should feel as if coming out of the area below the navel. In the process of exhaling powerfully, the pressure on the lower abdomen recesses the stomach area. The concentration on the lower extremities of the body should relax the shoulders and the upper body.

c. Inhaling should be left to occur naturally as new air fills the vacuum in the lungs.

d. Beginners should practice breathing with the *tanden* on purpose, but gradually conscious effort will lessen and the frequency of breathing will naturally decrease. In exhaling and inhaling, concentrate energy rather than physical power on the lower abdomen. When the vital power is at the *tanden* and confined in the *hara,* this spiritual strength and vital energy will radiate through the entire body.

e. Count your respirations with all your spiritual powers as if trying to penetrate to the core of the earth. Count the frequency of the exhalation from one to ten. Count in syllables as long as the exhalation. O . . . . ne. T . . . . wo. And so on. Let your mind's eye follow the exhaled air in counting. If you miscount before reaching the count of ten or count beyond ten, start again from one.

f. In order to avoid incongruence between your respiration and the count, it is essential to concentrate your mind on the count rather than on the respiration as such, and feel as if you are breathing in accordance with the count.

The figures and captions are taken from *An Introduction to Zen Discipline*, the unpublished translation of *Sanzen Nyumon*, by Omori Sogen Rotaishi.

Appendix B
Self-Tests and Work Sheets for Designing Your Practice

Following are extra tear-out sheets of the self-tests and work sheets for designing your practice in BodyLearning.

ACTIVITY CHECKLIST

- *For each activity, note how much you DO it and how much you LIKE doing it.*
- *If you've never done the activity, guess whether you'd enjoy it.*
- *Where multiple activities are listed, answer for your favorite of the group.*

Activity	How Much You Do This				How Much You Like This				
	Almost Daily	Now & Then	Rarely	Never	Not at All	Dislike	Neutral	Enjoy	Love
Driving									
Housecleaning									
Drawing, Painting, Calligraphy (*Shodo*)									
Crafts, Sculpture, Ceramics									
Needlework, Weaving, Sewing									
Woodwork, Mechanical Work									
Meditation, *Zazen*									
Fishing									
Photography									
Breathing Exercises									
Stretching Exercises									
Flower Arranging (e.g., *Ikebana*)									
Gardening									

(continued)

ACTIVITY CHECKLIST (continued)

Activity	How Much You Do This				How Much You Like This				
	Almost Daily	Now & Then	Rarely	Never	Not at All	Dislike	Neutral	Enjoy	Love
Walking									
Yoga									
Golf									
Singing or Playing Musical Instrument with Others									
Singing or Playing Musical Instrument Solo									
Cooking									
Tai Chi									
Archery									
Cross-Country Ski Machine									
Hunting									
Target Practice									
Bowling									
Horseback Riding									
Sailing									
Flying (as Pilot)									
Martial Arts									
Jogging, Running									
Aerobic Exercise with Group or Music									

(continued)

ACTIVITY CHECKLIST (continued)

Activity	How Much You Do This				How Much You Like This				
	Almost Daily	Now & Then	Rarely	Never	Not at All	Dislike	Neutral	Enjoy	Love
Aerobic Exercise Solo, without Music									
Weight Lifting, Power Lifting									
Skiing (Downhill, Cross Country, Water)									
Crew, Canoeing									
Bicycling, Wheelchair Racing									
Football, Soccer, Hockey									
Baseball									
Bird-watching									
Power Walking, Racewalking									
Basketball, Volleyball									
Dance									
Tennis, Racquetball/ Squash									
Skating, Rollerblading									
Stationary Bicycle									

(continued)

ACTIVITY CHECKLIST (continued)

Activity	How Much You Do This				How Much You Like This				
	Almost Daily	Now & Then	Rarely	Never	Not at All	Dislike	Neutral	Enjoy	Love
Swimming									
Scuba Diving, Snorkeling									
Kayaking									
Hiking									
Rock/Mountain Climbing									
Sailboarding, Surfing									
(write-in)									
(write-in)									

ACTIVITY WORK SHEET

STATIC-AEROBIC	DYNAMIC-AEROBIC
1. Jogging 2. Running, Wheelchair Racing 3. Aerobic Exercise (Solo, Not to Music) 4. Weight Lifting, Power Lifting 5. Skating, Rollerblading 6. Swimming 7. Kayaking 8. Power Walking, Racewalking 9. Stairmaster 10. Rowing Machine 11. Stationary Bicycling 12. Cross-Country Ski Machine 13. Write-ins:	1. Martial arts (Aikido, Karate, Kendo, etc.) 2. Aerobic Exercise (with Group or Music) 3. Skiing (Downhill, Cross Country, Water) 4. Football, Soccer, Hockey 5. Baseball 6. Basketball, Volleyball 7. Dance 8. Tennis, Racquetball, Squash 9. Crew, Canoeing 10. Rock/Mountain Climbing, Vigorous Hiking 11. Sailboarding, Surfing 12. Bicycling 13. Write-ins:
Check ☑ if favorite area	Check ☐ if favorite area

STATIC-MEDITATIVE	DYNAMIC-MEDITATIVE
1. Housecleaning, Cooking 2. Gardening, Flower Arranging, *Ikebana* 3. Drawing, Painting, Calligraphy (*Shodo*) 4. Singing or Playing Musical Instrument (Solo) 5. Crafts, Sculpture, Ceramics 6. Needlework, Weaving, Sewing 7. Woodwork, Mechanical Work 8. Meditation, *Zazen* 9. Breathing Exercises, Stretching Exercises 10. Yoga, Tai Chi 11. Walking 12. Archery, Target Practice, Bowling 13. Write-ins:	1. Driving 2. Fishing 3. Photography 4. Golf 5. Singing or Playing Musical Instrument (with Others) 6. Ceramics (Thrown Clay) 7. Horseback Riding 8. Hunting 9. Sailing 10. Flying (as Pilot) 11. Scuba Diving, Snorkeling 12. Hiking, Bird-watching 13. Write-ins:
Check ☐ if favorite area	Check ☐ if favorite area

PATTERNS AND NEEDS CHECKLIST

Part 1. Indicate the extent to which the following statements describe you by placing an "X" in the appropriate box. Use the following scale:

- *Not At All*: This statement doesn't apply at all to me; indeed, it may be opposite to what I know of myself.
- *Rarely*: On rare occasions, this statement applies to me, but it's not typical of me.
- *Now and Then*: This statement applies to me now and then.
- *Typical*: This statement is fairly typical of me; it applies to me most of the time.
- *Definitely*: This statement is me all over; it's one of my defining traits.

Personal Patterns	Not at all	Rarely	Now & Then	Typical of Me	Definitely
1. I'm in excellent health.				✓	
2. I'm an honest person.				✓	
3. I always follow instructions.			✓		
4. I'm generally sluggish.		✓			
5. I'm a strong person.				✓	
6. I take time to unwind or "smell the flowers."			✓		
7. I have plenty of endurance.			✓		
8. My life has a good deal of stress.			✓		
9. I often reflect on my experience and figure out where I need to improve.					
10. I get along well with people.					

(continued)

Personal Patterns	Not at all	Rarely	Now & Then	Typical of Me	Definitely
11. I don't hold up well under pressure.					
12. I'm often lost in thought or daydreams.					
13. I'm willing to look at the truth, even when it casts me in an unfavorable light.					
14. I know myself well.					
15. I don't see things very clearly; I'm easily confused.					
16. I get very angry.					
17. I seem to be a "day late and a dollar short."					
18. My life has too many ups and downs.					
19. I find it easy to accept good news but hard to accept bad news.					
20. I am strongly self-motivated.					
21. It's hard for me to shift my attention from one thing to another.					
22. I'm a good listener.					
23. There are many things I don't like.					
24. I can't wait for things to happen; I need to make them happen.					
25. My attention tends to drift off.					

(continued)

Personal Patterns	Not at All	Rarely	Now & Then	Typical of Me	Definitely
26. I wish I understood myself better.					
27. Sometimes my life does not seem worthwhile.					
28. I'm uncoordinated.					
29. I'm sure of myself.					
30. I find it difficult to take a large task and break it down into approachable steps.					
31. I'm aware of my thoughts and feelings.					
32. I know when it's appropriate to put in my "two bits."					
33. I have a good sense of balance.					
34. I tend to be impatient.					
35. I don't notice many things that go on around me.					
36. I prefer having my work or tasks laid out for me.					
37. I'm a nervous person.					
38. When I'm outside, it's easy for me to feel in tune with nature.					
39. I generally know where other people are coming from.					
40. I have difficulty breathing.					

Part 2. Complete the following two sentences.
   Mark as many (or as few) of the answers as apply to you.

"My life would be much better if   "If I were my own doctor, I would
only I had—"   tell myself to—"

more energy	
deeper insight	
more patience	
more of a sense of purpose	
better health	
a better attitude	
more endurance	
more guidance	
more strength	
better relationships	
more money	
more of nothing; my life is fine as it is	

lose weight	
quit smoking	
take it easy, relax more	
take care of my heart	
get a hobby	
get some exercise	
not let things get to me	
get some rest	
keep doing whatever I'm doing because I'm doing fine	

PATTERNS AND NEEDS SCORE SHEET

Part 1. Copy or highlight your answers below. Ignore boxes that have no number in them. Tally the number of 1's, 2's, 3's, 4's and 5's in the boxes where you've marked an answer.

Personal Patterns	Not at All	Rarely	Now & Then	Typical of Me	Definitely
1. I'm in excellent health.	3	3	1 2		
2. I'm an honest person.	3	3	3		
3. I always follow instructions.				5	5
4. I'm generally sluggish.			1 2	1 2	1 2
5. I'm a strong person.	3	1 2 3	1 2		
6. I take time to unwind or "smell the flowers."	3 4	3 4			
7. I have plenty of endurance.	1 2	1 2	1 2		
8. My life has a good deal of stress.			1 2	1 2 3	1 2 3
9. I often reflect on my experience and figure out where I need to improve.	5 5	5 5	5		
10. I get along well with people.	2	2	2		
11. I don't hold up well under pressure.			3	3	3
12. I'm often lost in thought or daydreams.			2 4	2 4	2 4
13. I'm willing to look at the truth, even when it casts me in an unfavorable light.	3	3	3	3	

Page Totals of: 1's ☐ 2's ☐ 3's ☐ 4's ☐ 5's ☐

(continued)

Personal Patterns	Not at All	Rarely	Now & Then	Typical of Me	Definitely
14. I know myself well.	3 5	3 5	3 5		
15. I don't see things very clearly; I'm easily confused.			1 3	1 3	1 3
16. I get very angry.			1 2	1 2	1 2
17. I seem to be a "day late and a dollar short."			2 4	2 4	2 4
18. My life has too many ups and downs.			1	1	1
19. I find it easy to accept good news but hard to accept bad news.			2 4	2 4	2 4
20. I am strongly self-motivated.	5 5	5 5	5		
21. It's hard for me to shift my attention from one thing to another.			2	2	2
22. I'm a good listener.	4	4	4		
23. There are many things I don't like.			3	3	1 2 3
24. I can't wait for things to happen; I need to make them happen.				4	4
25. My attention tends to drift off.			2 4	2 4	2 3 4
26. I wish I understood myself better.			3 5	3 5	3 5

Page Totals of: 1's ☐ 2's ☐ 3's ☐ 4's ☐ 5's ☐

(continued)

Personal Patterns	Not at All	Rarely	Now & Then	Typical of Me	Definitely
27. Sometimes my life does not seem worthwhile.		3	3	3	3
28. I'm uncoordinated.			2 3	2 3	2 3
29. I'm sure of myself.	3 5	2	2		
30. I find it difficult to take a large task and break it down into approachable steps.				5	5 5
31. I'm aware of my thoughts and feelings.	3 5 5	3 5	3 5		
32. I know when it's appropriate to put in my "two bits."	2	2	2		
33. I have a good sense of balance.	3	2 3	2		
34. I tend to be impatient.			3 4	3 4	3 4
35. I don't notice many things that go on around me.			2 4	2 4	2 4
36. I prefer having my work or tasks laid out for me.				5	5 5
37. I'm a nervous person.			3	3	3
38. When I'm outside, it's easy for me to feel in tune with nature.	4	4	4		

Page Totals of: 1's ☐ 2's ☐ 3's ☐ 4's ☐ 5's ☐

(continued)

Personal Patterns	Not at All	Rarely	Now & Then	Typical of Me	Definitely
39. I generally know where other people are coming from.	2	2	2		
40. I have difficulty breathing.		1 2	1 2 3	3	3

Page Totals of : 1's ☐ 2's ☐ 3's ☐ 4's ☐ 5's ☐

Part 1 Totals (sum of page totals) of : 1's ☐ 2's ☐ 3's ☐ 4's ☐ 5's ☐

Part 2. Copy or highlight your answers below. Ignore boxes that have no number in them. Tally the number of 1's, 2's, 3's, 4's and 5's in the boxes where you've marked an answer.

"My life would be much better if only I had—"

more energy	1 2
deeper insight	3
more patience	3 4
more of a sense of purpose	3
better health	1 2 3
a better attitude	1 2 3 4
more endurance	1
more guidance	5 5
more strength	1 2
better relationships	2
more money	
more of nothing; my life is fine as it is	

"If I were my own doctor, I would tell myself to—"

lose weight	1 2
quit smoking	1 2 3
take it easy, relax more	3 4
take care of my heart	1 2
get a hobby	3 4
get some exercise	1 2 3 4
not let things get to me	1 2
get some rest	3
keep doing whatever I'm doing because I'm doing fine	

Part 2 Totals of: 1's ☐ 2's ☐ 3's ☐ 4's ☐ 5's ☐

DEVELOPMENT AREA WORK SHEET

	1's	2's	3's	4's	5's
Part 1	*			*	
Part 2				*	
Total (Parts 1 and 2)					

*Multiply your score in this area by 2.

Transfer the totals to the appropriate area below:

STATIC-AEROBIC	DYNAMIC-AEROBIC

1

Total 1's _____

Check ☐ if you scored **10** or more

Check ☐ if highest relative score

2

Total 2's _____

Check ☐ if you scored **10** or more

Check ☐ if highest relative score

STATIC-MEDITATIVE	DYNAMIC-MEDITATIVE

3

Total 3's _____

Check ☐ if you scored **10** or more

Check ☐ if highest relative score

4

Total 4's _____

Check ☐ if you scored **10** or more

Check ☐ if highest relative score

Total number of 5's: _____ (guidance preference)

PERSONALIZED PROGRAM WORK SHEET	
STATIC-AEROBIC	**DYNAMIC-AEROBIC**
Candidates: Selections: 1. 2.	Candidates: Selections: 1. 2.
STATIC-MEDITATIVE	**DYNAMIC-MEDITATIVE**
Candidates: Selections: 1. 2.	Candidates: Selections: 1. 2.

References

Beck, Charlotte Joko. *Everyday Zen*. San Francisco: HarperCollins, 1989.
————. *Nothing Special*. San Francisco: HarperCollins, 1993.
Benoit, Hubert. *Zen and the Psychology of Transformation*. Rochester, Vt.: Inner Traditions International, 2d. ed., 1990.
Braverman, Arthur. *Warrior of Zen: The Diamond Hard Wisdom Mind of Suzuki Shosan*. New York: Kodansha International, 1994.
Cameron, Julia. *The Artist's Way*. New York: Tarcher/Putnam, 1992.
Capra, Fritjof. *The Tao of Physics*. New York: Bantam, 1975.
————. *The Web of Life*. New York: Doubleday, 1996.
Covey, Stephen. *7 Effective Habits of Highly Successful People*. New York: Simon & Schuster, 1989.
deMello, Anthony. *Awareness*. New York: Doubleday, 1990.
Dürckheim, Karlfried Graf. *Hara: The Vital Center of Man*. London: Mandala, 1962.
Ferguson, Marilyn. *The Aquarian Conspiracy*. Los Angeles: Tarcher, 1980.
Goldberg, Natalie. *Wild Mind*. New York: Bantam, 1990.
Hara Development Exercises. Honolulu: Daihonzan Chozen Ji/International Zen Dojo, 1991.
Knaster, Mirka. *Exploring the Body's Wisdom*. New York: Bantam, 1996.

Kübler-Ross, Elisabeth. *On Death and Dying.* New York: Macmillan, 1969.

Kurtz, Ron, and Hector, Prestera. *The Body Reveals.* San Francisco: HarperCollins, 1976.

Leigh, William S. *Bodytherapy.* Honolulu: International Zentherapy Institute, 3d ed., 1994.

Loy, David. "Avoiding the Void: The Lack of Self in Psychotherapy and Buddhism." *The Journal of Transpersonal Psychology* 24 (1992): 151–79.

Moyers, Bill. *Healing and the Mind.* New York: Doubleday, 1993.

Murphy, Michael. *The Future of the Body.* Los Angeles: Tarcher, 1992.

Nhat Hanh, Thich. *Being Peace.* Berkeley, Calif.: Parallax Press, 1987.

———. *A Guide to Walking Meditation.* New Haven, Conn.: Eastern Press, 1985.

———. *The Miracle of Mindfulness.* Boston: Beacon Press, 1975.

———. *Peace Is Every Step.* New York: Bantam, 1991.

———. *The Sun My Heart.* Berkeley, Calif.: Parallax Press, 1988.

Peck, M. Scott. *The Road Less Traveled.* New York: Simon & Schuster, 1978.

———. *Further Along The Road Less Traveled.* New York: Simon & Schuster, 1993.

Pelletier, Kenneth. *Mind as Healer, Mind as Slayer.* New York: Bantam, 1977.

Pribram, Karl. *Languages of the Brain.* Englewood Cliffs, N.J.: Prentice-Hall, 1971.

Reps, Paul, ed. *Zen Flesh, Zen Bones.* Rutland, Vt.: Charles Tuttle, 1957.

Sayama, Mike. *Samadhi.* New York: State University of New York Press, 1986.

Schutz, Will. *The Truth Option.* Berkeley, Calif.: Ten Speed Press, 1984.

Shibayama, Zenkei. *A Flower Does Not Talk.* Rutland,Vt.: Charles Tuttle, 1970.

Sogen, Omori. *An Introduction to Zen Training.* London: Kegan Paul International, 1996.

———. *Zen and Budo.* Honolulu: Daihonzan Chozen-ji/International Zen Dojo, 1989.

Soho Takuan, tr. by Tenshin Tanouye Rotaishi. *Fudochi Shimmyo Roku.* Honolulu: Daihonzan Chozen-ji/International Zen Dojo, 1989.

Soho, Takuan, tr. by William Scott Wilson. *The Unfettered Mind.* New York: Kodansha International, 1986.

Suzuki, D. T. *Manual of Zen Buddhism.* New York: Grove Weidenfeld, 1960.

Suzuki, Shunryu. *Zen Mind, Beginner's Mind.* New York: Weatherhill, 1970.

Underhill, Evelyn. *Practical Mysticism.* Guildford, Great Britain: Eagle, 1991.

Other Resources

For information on BodyLearning seminars or applications to management or organization development, please see our web site at **www.bodylearning.com,** or contact the author at:

Focus Consulting
118 Ashford Parkway
Atlanta, GA 30338
phone: 770/396-4121   fax: 770/396-6718
e-mail: gwhitelaw@bodylearning.com

For information on publications from the Daihonzan Chozen-ji/International Zen Dojo, contact:

Institute of Zen Studies
3565 Kalihi St.
Honolulu, HI 96819-3036
phone: 808/848-0390   fax: 808/848-0387   e-mail: izs@izs.org

The mission of the Institute of Zen Studies is to make Zen more accessible to modern society and to foster a more peaceful world by developing true compassion and right understanding. For information about programs or membership, contact the Institute: Arthur Koga, president.

For information about Zen training and training centers (*dojo*) on the U.S. mainland, contact:

International Zen Dojo Sogenkai
1016 W. Belmont
Chicago, IL 60657
phone: 773/935-2243   fax: 773/525-5916

For information about Aikido training and *dojo* in your area, contact:

Aikido Association of America/Aikido Association International
1016 W. Belmont
Chicago, IL 60657
phone: 773/525-3141   fax: 773/525-5916
e-mail:aikidoamer@aol.com

Notes

Chapter 1

1. "Roshi" is the honorific title for a Zen master. "Rotaishi" indicates a senior Zen master.
2. See, for example, Mirka Knaster's excellent guide to new and old bodytherapies in *Discovering the Body's Wisdom* (New York: Bantam, 1996).
3. Dub Leigh, *Bodytherapy* (Honolulu: International Zentherapy Institute, 3d. ed., 1994).

Chapter 2

1. I thank my grandmother, Mary Whitelaw, for this exercise.
2. See M. Ferguson, *The Aquarian Conspiracy* (Los Angeles: Tarcher, 1980), and F. Capra, *The Web of Life* (New York: Doubleday, 1996), for excellent discussions of how Prigogine and others have shed light on the evolution of order in complex systems.
3. *Further Along the Road Less Traveled* (New York: Simon and Schuster, 1993), pp. 58–59.
4. See W. Schutz, *The Truth Option* (Berkeley, Calif.: Ten Speed Press, 1984) and R. Kurtz and H. Prestera, *The Body Reveals* (San Francisco: HarperCollins, 1976) for further explanation and examples of the connection between health and patterns of holding.
5. I thank Tanouye Rotaishi for this exercise.

Chapter 3

1. Thich Nhat Hanh, *The Miracle of Mindfulness* (Berkeley, Calif.: Parallax Press, 1988), pp. 2–3.

2. Thich Nhat Hanh, *A Guide to Walking Meditation* (New Haven: Eastern Press, 1985).
3. Anthony deMello, *Awareness* (New York: Doubleday, 1990), p. 56.

Chapter 4
1. *The Aquarian Conspiracy* (Los Angeles: Tarcher, 1980).
2. See, for example, Michael Murphy's excellent compilation of research in *The Future of the Body* (Los Angeles: Tarcher, 1992).
3. *Ibid.*, p. 419.
4. *Ibid.*, p. 527.

Chapter 5
1. *The Body Reveals* (San Francisco: HarperCollins, 1976), p. 67.
2. *Ibid.*
3. The formal *Hojo* walk is taught as part of *hara* development training at Daihonzan Chozen-ji/International Zen Dojo in Hawaii and is documented in their publication *Hara Development Exercises* (Honolulu: Institute of Zen Studies, 1991).

Chapter 6
1. From Omori Sogen, *Introduction to Zen Training* (London: Kegan Paul, 1996), Ch. 3.

Chapter 7
1. *Zen Flesh, Zen Bones,* compiled by Paul Reps (Rutland, Vt.: Charles Tuttle, 1957), p. 19.
2. A formula that many exercise physiologists use for defining the low end of the aerobic range for heart rates is: (220 minus your age minus your resting pulse) x (60%) + your resting pulse. For a thirty-five-year-old person with a resting pulse of 70, the aerobic range starts at 139 beats per minute.

Chapter 8
1. (New York: Simon & Schuster, 1989).

Chapter 9
1. *Wild Mind* (New York: Bantam, 1990), p. 155.
2. *7 Habits of Highly Effective People* (New York: Simon and Schuster, 1989), p. 287.
3. Thich Nhat Hanh, *The Miracle of Mindfulness* (Boston: Beacon Press, 1975).
4. *op. cit.*

Chapter 10
1. *Peace Is Every Step* (New York: Bantam, 1991), p. 114.
2. *Being Peace* (Berkeley, Calif.: Parallax Press, 1987), p. 113.
3. (Rochester, Vt.: Inner Traditions International, 2d. ed., 1990).

4. Derived from the set of fundamental behaviors identified by Will Schutz in *The Truth Option* (Berkeley, Calif.: Ten Speed Press, 1984).
5. *Everyday Zen* (San Francisco: HarperCollins, 1989), p. 50.

Chapter 11

1. *Bodytherapy* (Honolulu: International Zentherapy Institute, 3d. ed., 1994), pp. 75–76.
2. M. Ferguson, *The Aquarian Conspiracy* (Los Angeles: Tarcher, 1980), pp. 75–76. Ferguson reports on the research of Ernest Hilgard on hypnotized subjects. In one experiment a woman's hand was immersed in ice water. In her hypnotized state, she reported feeling no pain on a scale of zero to ten. But her other hand, with access to a pencil and paper, reported a painful increase: "0 . . . 2 . . . 4 . . . 7. . . ." This aspect of consciousness, what Hilgard called "The Hidden Observer," is always present, always fully experiencing.
3. *The Sun My Heart* (Berkeley, Calif.: Parallax Press, 1988), p. 35.
4. Kenneth Pelletier, *Mind as Healer, Mind as Slayer* (New York: Bantam, 1977) and Michael Murphy, *The Future of the Body* (Los Angeles: Tarcher, 1992).
5. *On Death and Dying* (New York: Macmillan, 1969).
6. From a sermon by Reinhold Niebuhr, 1934.
7. (New York: Doubleday, 1993).

Chapter 12

1. See, for example, Hubert Benoit, *Zen and the Psychology of Transformation* (Rochester, Vt.: Inner Traditions International, 2d. ed., 1990), for an excellent discussion of these developmental stages.
2. *Ibid.*, p. 34.
3. From the Canon of Chozen-ji/International Zen Dojo, by Omori Sogen Rotaishi (Honolulu: Institute of Zen Studies, 1979).
4. *Practical Mysticism* (Guildford, Great Britain: Eagle, 1991), p. 29.

Appendix A

1. © 1987 Daihonzan Chozen-ji/International Zen Dojo, excerpted from Omori Sogen, *An Introduction to Zen Training* (London: Kegan Paul International, 1996), Ch. 3.

Index

About the Author

❧

Physics, biophysics, philosophy, Aikido, Zen and a career managing people and projects through change make up the wealth of experience Dr. Ginny Whitelaw brings to *BodyLearning*. "The common thread is energy," Dr. Whitelaw explains. "Every discipline has taught me something valuable about our connection to energy: how to tap it, focus it and put it to good use in the world."

Beginning her formal study of energy in college, Dr. Whitelaw worked for several years in a high-energy physics laboratory. In 1977, she graduated from Michigan State University with degrees in physics and philosophy. Wanting to learn more about energy in living systems, she studied biophysics in graduate school. She developed computer models of the nervous system and tested their predictions in the laboratory, publishing several articles on the way the nervous system develops. In 1982, she received her doctorate in biophysics from the University of Chicago.

Dr. Whitelaw was a scientist and then a manager at Bell Laboratories. In 1985, she joined the National Aeronautics and Space Administration (NASA). As she moved up through the management ranks at NASA, she worked to focus and integrate the many organizations working on the Space Station Program. In 1993, NASA asked her to lead the management redesign for the Space Station and the transition to a new model of government-industry teams. Through her efforts to guide organizations through massive change and improve their effectiveness, she learned the importance of alignment in reaching one's goals, both individually and organizationally. Helping people and organizations successfully manage change and align toward important goals became a new focus for her work, and one of the catalysts for developing BodyLearning. In 1994, she left NASA to devote full time to management consulting, writing and teaching.

Alongside her career in science and management, Dr. Whitelaw has been active in martial arts for more than twenty years. She is a Zen Priest in the Rinzai tradition (ordained as Reverend Jiko Myoki), as well as a fourth-degree black belt and certified instructor of Aikido. As a member of the Aikido Association of America's National Teaching Committee, she has taught Aikido classes and seminars throughout the United States. She has also integrated Aikido and Zen into her management consulting, developing programs in conflict resolution, leadership development and stress management. Since 1987, she has been the chief instructor of an Aikido and Zen training center, first in Houston and now in Atlanta.

"I'm now in my third life, professionally speaking," Dr. Whitelaw says. "And it combines the best of the first two—all that I learned as a scientist and as a manager—with all that has come through twenty-some years of my own BodyLearning." As a management consultant, she now works with organizations and their leaders on ways to improve their effectiveness, reach strategic goals, and manage change. She also leads personal development seminars in BodyLearning, through which the methods and exercises of this book have been tested and refined.